Praise for *The Trail*

"Hocker writes from the heart. *The Trail to Tincup* pulsates with tenderness in traversing peaks and hollows of her family's life . . . [a] soulful memoir."

—Ira Byock, MD, author of *Dying Well* and
The Four Things That Matter Most

"A rare and honest glimpse into the soul and spirit of grief and sadness. Hocker emerges from the valley of suffering with a glow of love, insight, self-understanding, and wisdom. *The Trail to Tincup* is more than a memoir; it is an inquiry on meaning making, on what it means to be present to oneself—a generous gift to the life force."

—Arthur P. Bochner, Professor, Department of
Communication, University of South Florida,
and author of *Coming to Narrative: A Personal History
of Paradigm Change in the Human Sciences*

"Joyce Hocker's inspirational story of her journey through profound grief reminds us all that deep loss stems from even deeper love. This book offers both understanding and hope to anyone who has faced, or is facing, the darkness of grieving."

—Melanie P. Merriman, PhD, former hospice consultant
and award-winning author of *Holding the Net: Caring for
My Mother on the Tightrope of Aging*

"For anyone struggling with loss and the love that binds us to those we cherished, *The Trail to Tincup* places signposts along the path, shows how to bear both the beams of love and loss, and suggests ways that the distinction between life and death may be less absolute than we think. This is a well-crafted book written by a fine writer who has plumbed the depths of her own story."

—Thomas Frentz, Professor, University of Arkansas,
and author of *Trickster in Tweed*

The Trail to TINCUP

The Trail to
TINCUP

LOVE STORIES
AT LIFE'S END

a memoir

Joyce Lynnette Hocker

SHE WRITES PRESS

Published May 15, 2018
Printed in the United States of America
Print ISBN: 978-1-63152-341-0
E-ISBN: 978-1-63152-342-7
Library of Congress Control Number: 2017962317

For information, address:
She Writes Press
1563 Solano Ave #546
Berkeley, CA 94707

Interior design by Tabitha Lahr

She Writes Press is a division of SparkPoint Studio, LLC.

To my brother, Edward Lamar Hocker, and my husband, Gary Hawk, with deep thanks for your presence and love.

CONTENTS

preface

I Will Need to Know This

"Let everything happen to you: beauty and terror . . ."
—Rainer Maria Rilke

April, 1976: Boulder, Colorado

I am weeping in the waiting room of the University of Colorado's counseling center. I'm not crying softly, as might be appropriate for a thirty-one-year-old assistant professor, but sobbing loudly. What brought me to this collapse?

The powers that be in the Department of Communication have denied me a second contract after three years on the faculty, a blindsiding shock. In hindsight, I realize that the signs had started to pop up a few months earlier. For two years as the only tenure-track woman on a faculty of seventeen, I attempted to parse the rules of faculty life. I'm exhausted, and I've failed. I must seek another position if I want to continue my career in academia.

My ten-year marriage is unraveling fast; my husband moved out of our ranch-style home in South Boulder last month and into the newly available parsonage of the small church he serves. Rick and I married when I was barely twenty-one. We met at the university where I was a sophomore, and he was a new student at the same seminary that my parents attended in the 1930s and '40s. He took the beginning pastoral counseling class taught by the professor I worked for. Handing out psychological tests, I could not miss the tall, handsome student from Florida, who looked rather casual and even devil-may-care beside the stodgier seminarians from Texas. He won my heart with charm, wit, and courage when he informed me that, if I were not free to date him (I'd said I'd be free in a few weeks), he would move on. He underscored this declaration with an illicit motorcycle ride on the sidewalk in front of my dorm, sporting the cutest girl on the third floor behind him. We married just before my junior year. We have enjoyed adventures and friendship, idealistic goals and partnership, camping and travel, but we are not skillfully navigating the feminist movement or our indecision about whether or when to have children.

While Rick agreeably relocated to Boulder for my job, we are traveling different paths now. I experience a tearing sorrow as our dreams diverge. Rick and I taught school in a small town in South Dakota before we finished college and seminary. We led teenagers on backpacking trips to Colorado when we lived in Texas, and began a house church in Austin together. When my job offer arrived, allowing us to move from Texas to our dream town, Boulder, Colorado, we planned to stay for a long time. My whole family loves Rick; they are heartbroken that we are splitting up. Rick's move leaves half-empty rooms and awkward unfilled spaces in the sprawling house we bought from one of my colleagues less than a year ago. I haven't figured out the sprinkler system yet; the grass, brown and crunchy, announces neglect to my neighbors.

The ivory sectional couch sits marooned in the living room, brightened only by a Marimekko fabric panel of yellow, red, and black abstract daisies. I chose heavy, red, pressed-glass everyday goblets when we married, to complement the bright sixties-style pattern. My younger sister Janice loved them so much that she chose the same pattern, announcing haughtily to anyone who asked, "Just because Joyce and I like the same things does *not* mean I am copying Joyce." One ugly brown Naugahyde recliner remains, where I sit, wrapped in a green, red, and black afghan, as I prepare classes and grade papers. I wake up too early most mornings, sneezing with allergies that send me to the teapot for Constant Comment, lemon, honey, and temporary relief. I contract pneumonia, necessitating that I drag my tired body to teach interpersonal communication classes in the white Victorian building on Broadway Street. I hold on to the stair rail as I climb to my third-floor office. Taking the bus back home, I collapse into sleep that does not heal.

Almost too weak to walk the three blocks from my office to the counseling center, I don't know how to go on without help; I need a therapist. The receptionist tells me that the counseling services are only available for students, not faculty. Appalled by my noisy crying, I still can't stop.

The receptionist recognizes my collapse, reassuring me that she will ask if the on-call therapist will see me, at least for a referral. Her kindness helps me gulp and swallow my sobs. She hands me a tissue. After a while, I walk down the concrete block hall to an office. On the threshold I look into a spacious room, decorated with fairy tale posters and prints of Sulamith Wülfing's art featuring incandescent angels, children, and robed women. A poster of the mythic High Priestess in profile, robed in dark blue, hangs on one wall. On another is the Queen of Faery looking down at an ugly little gnome. On the desk sits a statue of an Egyptian cat goddess and one of a god with a snake wrapped around his staff. I recognize the snake and staff as a medical symbol, but I don't know the name of the god of healing yet.

A woman takes my hand at the door, showing me where to sit. I appreciate her warmth, her intelligent, clear, blue eyes and curly blonde hair. Tall and beautiful, she is dressed in high brown boots, brown leggings, and a short red skirt and matching vest. She introduces herself, Anne, in the midst of completing her credentials to become a certified Jungian analyst, works only a few hours at the counseling center. She's already finished her doctorate. She hears my story, and I recognize a sister spirit.

Anne's orientation connects me to my dad, a progressive minister then serving a church in Austin. He introduced me to Jung when I was a teenager. I think back to his study in Texas when he said, "I think you will like these, Joyce." I liked to read theology and psychology that my Dad pointed out to me. Dad was right; Jung's in-depth psychology opened up a welcome parallel universe that helped me make sense of my teenage years. I began to understand that a river of symbols and universal archetypes flowed under and through my everyday life. When our family moved twice during my high school years, because of our dad's outspoken and unpopular social justice sermons in the Texas churches he served, I took refuge in a deeper meaning of life than my own misery. My own search for understanding helped comfort me while enduring my new-girl status as an introvert who masked my need for solitude with leadership roles in student council and clubs and a lot of dating.

I feel at home in this office, with this woman. Anne specializes in depression, and I certainly fit that clinical category.

At the end of the session, I am distressed to hear Anne say, "I can't work with you here since you are faculty, and the counseling center serves women students only." She appears sorry to have to tell me this. We have talked easily, and she has listened respectfully to my interest in dreams and journaling. To my great relief, she offers to see me as a private client in her home office. She seems to sense a connection with me, as she smiles and treats me with personal understanding. Already, Anne is my ally. We set an appointment.

Along with exquisite attention by Anne to my emotional state and practical challenges, our sessions advance in earnest my earlier brief initiation into Jungian studies. We meet briefly in couples counseling with Rick, but it is clear that our earlier, companionable sense of being good married partners has shattered. I still love him, and I grieve the loss of the marriage, my job, my health, and my good friends in Boulder when I find another job. A chance or synchronistic meeting with my analyst changed my life. Since 1976, Anne has served as my trusted guide into the unconscious, analyzing dreams, helping me make sense of themes in my life, and eventually also working with my sister, Janice.

May, 1976: Liminal Space

While I've already accepted a job in Missoula, I plan to stay in Colorado for the summer. Rick and I sell our house; I will apartment-sit for a colleague and spend time in Aspen working on a grant.

My parents invite me to fill a last-minute cancellation on a trip they are sponsoring, part of a larger group from Texas. The ship will cruise for two weeks, stopping at ancient sites around the Mediterranean. My fledgling retirement fund provides the cash as I eagerly sign up. I want to take this trip with my parents and their friends, as well as professors from my college who will lecture on board the ship before we explore the archeological sites.

"I'm going to Egypt, Greece, and Israel!" I excitedly tell Anne at our next session.

"How wonderful! This is great timing for you. You will learn so much." Anne pulls books from her shelves to loan to me. I have only a few weeks before the trip, during which I must organize a move, but I stack her heavy books in my arms and take them to the home in South Boulder that I am already packing up.

Before I fly to Greece in mid-June, friends help pack my belongings. As we are loading everything into boxes and then into the back of the U-Haul, the phone rings.

"Hello, Dr. Frost?" That was my name then. "This is Chancellor Lawrence." I am puzzled about this call since I have only met the chancellor in passing as I completed some consulting work in the administration building. "I only just now found out about your firing. I would like very much for you to stay here at CU, if you would like. Have you signed a contract in Montana?" he inquires.

The Chancellor's offer startles me. I thought I had exhausted all the avenues of appeal, working with Affirmative Action and even hiring a private attorney. "Yes, I have. But thank you so much for calling." I watch friends carry boxes out of the empty dining room.

Only the plants remain: bright pink and purple coleus, asparagus ferns, spider plants, and trailing ivy in macramé hangers. I will give the plants to friends and start over in Montana.

The chancellor continues, "Do you want me to call the president at Montana and ask him to release you from your contract? I know him slightly." I am having difficulty processing this offer. What do I want? One of my male friends asks what to do with a wide, flat box.

"Will you excuse me for just a moment?" I am embarrassed to ask the chancellor to wait.

"That's my wedding dress!" I hiss to my friend Robert.

"What do you want me to do with it?" he whispers.

"Just put it in the truck," I whisper back, returning to my phone call. The interruption gives me just enough time to gather my response.

"No, I will keep to my plan to go to Montana. The job there suits me very well, and I think the department there is a better fit for me," I continue, wondering frantically whether I want to accept his late offer. Could my marriage heal? I can't think about the already-sold house. I love Boulder and my friends here, but I don't love my department, where I never fit in and where I worked like an indentured servant, mentor-less and clueless about how to manage the demands of teaching, publishing, and community service. Two life paths diverge. I veer on to the new trail, saying, "Thank you very much for calling. This means a lot, but I have decided to go to Montana."

"If you change your mind in the near future, let me know," the chancellor offers.

I don't change my mind. I drive my tinny red 1972 Plymouth Cricket, with barely enough engine power to crawl over Chief Joseph Pass, into the Bitterroot Valley. I follow Bill, who is driving the U-Haul. Bill is a colleague at Montana with whom I am writing a book. I don't know at this point that we will marry the following year. I gasp at the beauty as I drive through Stevensville at sunset for the first time. We arrive in Missoula and unload all my belongings into the garage of the apartment that will be available in August. As Bill drops me off at a local motel, I cry, "I want to go home!" like a forlorn child, although I am so disoriented I don't know where home is right now. The next day, I drive east on I-90, then south on I-25, back to Boulder where I stay with friends for a few days before leaving on my Mediterranean trip.

June, 1976: The Coast of Turkey

Sick and faint, I sink onto a warm granite stone outside the ruins of Pergamon, an ancient Greek city, now on the coast of Turkey. Our guide prepares to take us through the remains of the Asclepion, a healing center outside the ruined city. I've never heard of Asclepius until the lecture Dr. Stewart, an Old Testament professor from Texas Christian University, delivered in his signature florid Georgia style before we left the ship this morning. I remember Dr. Stewart as a vivid figure at the seminary where I worked as a secretary when I was an undergraduate. While I glimpsed a photo of a statue of Asclepius on one of the books Anne loaned me, I never got around to reading it before this trip. A statue of Asclepius sat on her desk as well. I learn from Dr. Stewart that over two hundred Greek medical centers existed in antiquity, serving as the primary medical system in the ancient Greek world. Our modern symbol of the medical world shows a snake twined around the staff of the god of healing.

Anchored to my rock, felled by Pharaoh's revenge, I am not going anywhere. I decide to wait out the tour, barely conscious. While the pneumonia, lingering from earlier in the spring, was slowly healing, I picked up a stomach bug in Egypt. Our solicitous bus driver, Isaac, brings me a warm Coke, which I sip gratefully. After an interminable length of time, some of the group filters back toward the bus.

"What did you see?" I inquire listlessly.

"Oh, just a bunch of rocks. Some kind of medical center where they thought dreams healed people," a Texas lady reports. Her blonde, teased hairstyle and her makeup wilt and melt in the heat. Her purple TCU T-shirt sticks to her back. She looks as though she's done with historical archeology; she's hot and wants to get back to the air-conditioned bus.

I want to cool off, too, but I begin to see pictures in my mind, imagining what happened here long ago: sleeping people in a bee-hive-shaped room—people crawling through a tunnel into a pool of water. Disoriented by a sense of being out of place and time, I perceive a line of priests and priestesses who interact with the seekers in some way. They speak through holes above the tunnel. I wonder if I am hallucinating from my illness. What is happening? I have never experienced a trance state like this before or since. From this waking dream onward, my life trajectory begans to tilt toward psychological healing.

After the tour, I return to Boulder to live in liminal space until the fall semester begins in Montana. Anne directs me to resources in the university library and on her shelves about Asclepion healing centers. Dreams served as primary healing experiences as long ago as 2000 BCE, probably earlier. What I experienced on a hot Turkish afternoon was my first initiation into the mystery school which taught its students to deal with death and transformation of Self.

1978: Memory and Forgetting in Greece

I have returned to Greece with Bill, whom I married in 1977, to travel from Athens to Delphi. In my spare time in Missoula, I've been a serious student of Jungian studies and mythology following my visionary experience in Turkey in 1976. Reading confirmed that somehow I had gained a glimpse into the past on that trip. I can explain this, by invoking intuition, my love for reading history and myth, but the cause does not matter. The proof of transformative experiences is in what happens next. I taught a course on dreams and healing at our church and have added to my library of Jungian studies. I write my dreams every day, working with Anne by phone. My sister Janice and I share this passion. We give each other and our dad books on Jung—Jung and Christianity, Jung and death, Jung and everything—for special birthdays and Christmas.

Academic life continues to challenge me. In 1977, the University of Montana went through a reduction in force, with many faculty members losing their jobs. I received a literal pink slip in December of that year, soon after marrying Bill *and* being promoted to associate professor. I appealed the termination and regained my faculty position. Only first-year professors should have been terminated, but my promotion placed me in a four-year category, so my appeal was successful. During the time when I thought I might be losing another academic job, I applied for and was accepted into a postdoctoral position in clinical psychology. A few months later, my faculty position reinstated, I decided to keep studying psychology while staying on the communication faculty as well. I continue to overwork, finding comfort in the thread that weaves through my life from my father's encouragement to read Jung and theology, to my secretarial work in college for Dr. Kemp (a minister and clinical psychologist), to classes in psychology when I studied for my communication doctorate, to now when I am finally engaged in my own study of psychology. I decide to continue toward a PhD in psychology and eventual licensing.

On this trip to Greece, I want to visit the temple of Gaia, which gradually transformed over time into the temple of Apollo where the oracle, as early as 400 BCE, prophesied. The priestess, especially chosen to forecast signs propitious to war, sacrifice, or love, answered questions put to her by supplicants. I'm with a day-trip of tourists from Athens. The van stops at an outpost by a quiet, small lake on the left.

"What is this?" I ask our guide, Marina, the pretty Greek woman who accompanies our small group. She is petite, intense, and well-informed about ancient Greece. She speaks with passion about the ancient site we visit.

"This is the Castalian Lake, flowing from the spring of memory and forgetting," Marina explains. She climbs easily up the rocky path, and I scramble to follow her, not wanting to miss anything. "The ancient Greeks made pilgrimages here when they wanted to be certain to always remember something precious or to forget something painful," Marina tells us.

"See, one spring over there, that is for memory; the other one is for when you want to forget." She motions to two streams flowing down the rocky wall. I am barely balancing as I keep up with her. She holds out a dipper, dripping from a bucket under the left-hand spring. "Which one will you drink from?" Marina inquires, with a searching expression.

I think of several scenes in my life that I would like to forget, such as the winter day in Boulder when my young husband and I decided to part. I'd like to forget the shock of our dad getting fired by several church boards when I was younger. I'm too young to give much energy to what I might want to remember.

My energy for remembering and forgetting meld together. The black swans and white swans swim in the pool where the springs of memory and forgetting splash together into one lake. I wonder if they are as confused as I am. Hedging my options, I lower the tin dipper, attached to a rock by the lake, into both springs as they emerge from the hillside, and drink deeply of the cold, refreshing water, thinking of all the pilgrims through the centuries who have done this. Lemosyne is the goddess who helps one forget, while Mnemosyne is the goddess who helps one remember.

I will need the ministrations of both goddesses in the coming months and years.

October, 2000: Gripped by Grief Stories

I'm forty-five now, attending a conference for Jungian psychotherapists at a North Carolina retreat center I have wanted to visit for a long time, sponsored by a nonprofit called Journey Toward Wholeness. I have earned a PhD in clinical psychology and have left university teaching to work in my private practice. Bill and I parted, painfully, in 1992. Gary, a former Congregational church minister, and I married; we live in our home in the University area of Missoula, where I can walk to work downtown as I once walked to my job in the Department of Communication Studies. My parents have somehow accepted my marital misfortunes. I know that what our dad told us three kids every night before bedtime is true—"Nothing can ever make us stop loving you." Something powerful pulls me toward the retreat center—the title of the nonprofit, the founding presence of Robert Johnson, and the opportunity to mingle for several days with other Jungian psychotherapists from around the country. I've not visited North Carolina since our family of four left in 1949, after a three-year stay. I associate the state with my younger sister and best friend, Janice, born in Charlotte. She's our Tar Heel.

A picture of a row of white rocking chairs facing a small lake adorns the retreat flyer. I want to sit in one of those chairs and look out, look in, reflecting on the surprising changes in my life. Wholeness, with its connotation of *completeness*, calls to me. Life moves fast, with my clinical practice, writing, consulting, and living in relationship. I want to slow down to reflect. Arriving alone after dark in a van from Asheville, I feel grateful for the plate of food, covered with foil and labeled with my name, that the kitchen staff left for me in the kitchen. Ah, Southern food. Hungry from my long day of travel, I enjoy the fried chicken, fresh green beans, mashed potatoes, dinner roll, and chocolate cake. Walking through the dark to the opening session, already in progress, I take some wrong turns on the unlighted path, stumble up a hill, and find the lights of the conference center. I feel quite alone, knowing no one. Since my family moved so often, I frequently feel outside of what I imagine to be the in-group. While I am not shy, I have learned to prepare myself before entering a situation with unknown people. I rely on my Southern social skills, a warm but formal persona, and my ability to ask questions of others as I enter new groups. I am used to traveling and rooming by myself.

Finding a seat in the back just as the speaker, Robert Romanyshyn, is introduced, I look around and settle in. As he begins to read from his next book, *The Soul in Grief: Love, Death and Transformation*, I begin to weep, trying to silence my surprising response. I feel a powerful connection to this man who tells stories of his transformation after the death of his wife. He reveals his feelings and how he found meaning in his loss in a raw and personal way. I don't know why I am weeping almost uncontrollably, but I have learned by this time to pay attention to unexpected tears. On the Myers-Briggs Type Inventory, I am an introverted feeling type; my emotions often arise before my insight about what I am feeling becomes clear.

Now I must meet all these new people with smudged mascara. I'm a mess. What is going on? After Robert's talk, I find a bathroom and repair my face.

While I had not yet experienced any of the losses that would send me on the same dark journey, I recognized a kindred spirit through Robert's honest stories and the sound of his voice. A persistent inner voice inside warned, *I am going to need to know this.*

After the reading, I slip out to find my cabin and roommates, feeling a resonance from all the weeks I spent in Texas summer church camps. The pine log cabin, fireplace, green painted Appalachian furniture, quilts on the beds in our separate bedrooms, and the smell of old fire and dust bring back nostalgic memories of church camp. I'm glad I have my own room. The two women sharing the cabin greet me, and we all head to bed. Exhausted, I ponder my weeping before I fall into sleep. *I am going to need to know this* echoes in my mind when I wake in the night.

chapter one

Family Camping

With someone like you,
A pal good and true,
I'd like to leave it all behind . . .
(popular song during World War One)

2015: At Home in Missoula

I study a crayon drawing, on crumbling Big Chief drawing paper, pinned to my bulletin board with sturdy red and yellow tacks. Last night, a dream of this drawing woke me. I went to bed asking for guidance from my dream psyche on how to continue my story. A color image of this old, partly forgotten drawing appeared in my dream, with no words or dialogue. I knew just where I'd stashed it. In the middle of the night, I made my way to my study closet, where I have stacked Janice's drawings, grade school writing, and special projects from her time at Hawkins Elementary School in Vernon, Texas. I took on the role of scrapbook archivist when I was in the second grade, and Mom and Dad gave me a photo album. Happy hours passed as I sat at the massive, secondhand, 1930s mahogany dining table in Dallas where I did my homework, pasting pictures from my Brownie Hawkeye camera on the pages with black stick-on corners. *This is important*, my seven-year-old self assured me. I knew I was doing something significant for our family, and it made sense because I was the big sister. Something solidified in my identity—family archivist—although I didn't know the word then. I knew I loved my family and wanted to keep track of all our doings. I haven't looked at this picture since 2004.

"She drew her perfect little world," reflects Gary, when I ask him to come to my study and see the picture. He leans over my desk as he looks carefully at Janice's drawing from her third-grade classroom. Gary made the bulletin board for me with a wide, solid oak frame; he knows I like to cut out notes and pictures to chronicle my days. "It's like Paradise before the fall."

"What do you see?" I ask Gary, an artist who takes the visual world seriously. Along with the details Janice drew, Gary points out the medieval construct of the idealized world contained in a single picture. Everything happens at the same time, and all the images are the size the child-artist thinks they ought to be—the baby brother as large as the father, the middle sister the same size as the mother.

I return to Janice's picture through the day, noticing details and filling in what I can't see on the page with my memories. Janice always kept our big box of crayons sharpened. By the time she drew our summer camping world for her beloved third-grade teacher, Mrs. Todd, I'd informally bequeathed them to her, since I was a seventh grader. Six decades later, I recognize her iconic images. Our family tents cluster in a Forest Service campground under aspens, pines, and spruce trees, one of the old-fashioned campsites with only two tables, one across the road from the other. She has drawn a slight hill for the pit garbage dump, and an outhouse tips on the rise above the tents. Grasshopper Park grounds our family summer after summer. The picture shows summer family camping life sometime in the early 1950s. My younger sister depicts our Texas family of five spending a day at home in camp, where we stay put for a month, escaping the Dallas heat and exploring new Colorado places. My mother would later write about this time as "spending those years when you all became Hockers."

Three tents define the colony. The seven-by-seven-foot umbrella tent belongs to Janice and me. We are old enough to set up our own tent, being careful to level the ground under the attached floor, zipping our dark green, flannel-lined Dacron sleeping bags together for warmth. Janice draws our tent with a bright-green crayon, although I remember the color as a dull olive. Our brother Eddie's pup tent sits right next door. Janice draws the pup tent larger in proportion than it was, possibly reflecting our shared big-sister worry that our little brother, by virtue of being the only boy, sleeps by himself. Mom and Dad sleep in the canvas, ten-by-twelve wall tent, which contains a wood-burning sheep-herder's stove. They sleep in double sleeping bags. We all blow up our air mattresses by mouth, although Janice and I help Eddie.

Mom and Dad place a tippy old aluminum table in the big tent, along with four folding chairs and one canvas fold-up stool. The table pinches your hand when you put it up, if you aren't careful. A clean bath mat lies in front of the stove for when we take our baths, using the plastic dishpans that are reserved for baths and not for dishes. We are not supposed to track dirt on the mat. My sister colors in the black stovepipe that emerges from the side of the five-foot-tall wall tent. We are able to take baths inside the tent, cook soup on the stove when it rains, and keep warm when the wind blows. The wall tent is also our living room. We play Scrabble, read our library books, play Go Fish and Monopoly, and bring a lantern in at night when it's too cold to build a fire. Daddy won't play board games. He says, "I'll leave that to you gals." The orange canvas smells a certain way when the sun shines and it heats up—something like wax, old cloth, and sunshine. We kids can come and go inside the wall tent except when Dad takes a nap.

We are on Spring Creek, which runs into the Taylor River, which joins the East River to make the big Gunnison River. We have heard that the Gunnison River joins with some other river to make the Colorado River, but we haven't been there yet. All these waterways are located in the Gunnison National Forest, in Western Colorado, which I can find on a map. Grasshopper Park, the name of the campground, really belongs to our family, since the Forest Service camp became our favorite place to camp once we discovered it. A next-door camper told Daddy about Spring Creek when we were camped on the Taylor River, which was much more crowded. We explored Spring Creek the last day before we had to go home, and decided all together that we definitely would come back here the following year. The Forest Service men who built the campground back in the 1930s must have seen a lot of grasshoppers, though we find none.

This camp must be the most beautiful place in Colorado. A wooden bridge crosses the creek just downstream. I can walk out at night by myself, since it is safe here and no one is around, to watch the moonrise and look up at the brilliant stars. There is no light pollution. The stream curves around to give us views of the water up and downstream. Almost nobody drives by, since we are close to the end of the road unless you have four-wheel drive, which we don't. Isolation appeals greatly to our minister father. His parishioners can't find him here. He refuses to go to town more than once each vacation, fearing that when he checks in with the church secretary, calling from a pay phone on Gunnison's main street, she might tell him someone has died and he needs to come home to perform a funeral. The weather surprises us each summer, since it never gets hot during the day like it does in Dallas. We can hardly believe that we need to wear coats at night. Memories of running through the water sprinkler in our Dallas yard fade fast. Colorado is the way summer weather should be.

Each year we take the family car, first a slope-backed, plum-colored, old Plymouth inherited from Dad's mother when she came to live with us, then the 1952 blue Pontiac, and later the 1956 two-tone-green Chevrolet Bel Air. Daddy packs the car starting at least a month ahead of time; we watch the garage fill up with camping gear, all neatly tagged. We also pull an early home-made version of the teardrop camper, this one made of plywood painted light blue, with what Mom calls a chuck box on the back for kitchen supplies, a space for luggage, and a big compartment for the rest of the equipment. When Eddie was younger, he slept in the trailer, but by the time of this picture, he's graduated to his own tent. Our dad treats the car like a jeep, steering it around rocks, and shifting it into first gear while roaring through washouts up Spring Creek Road. We peer eagerly ahead to see if our spot is available.

Janice carefully composes our idealized summer camping world. In the center of the picture, I see the back of our mother, sitting at the sturdy old Forest Service wooden camping table, anchored to the ground in concrete. On one end, Janice places the copper-colored cake cover. Mom makes Betty Crocker spice cakes and yellow cakes in the little sit-on-top oven on the Coleman stove. On the other end of the table sits one of our lanterns. Daddy takes a lot of time to tighten the tarp above the table; he's always making the tents and tarp nice and straight. "I need to secure the camp," he states, just as we are all in the car ready to go on an adventure. He tightens the center rope that holds the tarp over the table. He tightens the corner ropes with a wooden peg that slides up and down the rope. He checks to make sure the canvas tent doors are staked just right so the rain will run outside the tents. He zips all the windows closed, whether it looks like rain or not. Finally we can leave to go up Spring Creek, or to explore Crested Butte, or to drive all the way up the Taylor River to the meadows, past the reservoir.

At night, we hang one lantern on a wire made from a coat hanger. To the right in the picture, Daddy kneels to saw wood with the big, blue bow saw. He puts logs in three different piles, small, middle-sized, and large, sawn to the right length so we can cut off pieces to fit in the fire pit. When Janice and I want to cut big logs for the outdoor fire, one of us gets on each end of the blue saw; we guess how many strokes we will need to cut all the way through the log. We keep score of who wins, sometimes. Eddie, off to Mom's left, holds out an apple. Janice has drawn me with a bucket up at the spring, coloring in my dark brown hair. I seem to be shoring up one of the dams that make pools in the spring. The spring rises from somewhere way up the mountain, farther up than Janice and I have ever climbed. We haul our drinking water from the clear spring and our washing water from Spring Creek, using different buckets. I am proud of being old enough to carry a big galvanized steel bucket.

Janice and I play up at the spring, fascinated by the green, wet world of moss, granite, dark soil, and pine trees. We try to climb to the highest pool because we think the water is cleaner and colder there. No swimming in the spring. Although not in this picture, in my memory I see small, blond Janice stumbling back to camp with her chipped, white enamel bucket, sloshing water on her red tennis shoes. In this particular picture, Janice is sawing a big log, laid across another log for clearance, with our small red saw. We don't mind the chores. This is one of our jobs, although Daddy helps. The family depends on us to haul water, so Janice and I do it by ourselves.

Janice draws aspen trees with white trunks and small green leaves, triangular-shaped pine trees, and big spruce trees around the campsite. She places all these on a hill, whose peak is right at the top of the picture. Purple and red flowers grow evenly around the site. A chipmunk, about the same size as the people, perches on a rock. On the side of the hill sits the outhouse. Janice and I hold flashlights for each other when we have to go in the middle of the night. We don't make each other go alone because it's pretty scary in the dark.

After calling Dad to come back for a meal when he's fishing, we kids stop and bring lettuce from the two-foot-tall, cylindrical Morton's Potato Chip can that we use for produce. Meat goes in another can, placed in the side of the creek, weighed down with rocks, and covered with pine boughs to keep the sun off it. This spot serves as a refrigerator. Mom tries to keep butter, milk, and eggs cool in the battered, old, light green Coleman ice chest which sits under the picnic table and only holds ice a few days after each trip to town.

Later, when I'm a teenager, I will pack one of these potato chip cans full of tightly wound petticoats, defying Daddy's edict about not bringing anything unnecessary. Petticoats were necessary in 1957 for the occasional trip to church or a restaurant. Somewhere I have a picture of all the petticoats hanging from the tent Janice and

I still shared. Gleefully rolling up the pink, yellow, blue, and green starched net petticoats into a tight cylinder, I sequestered my stash in one of the potato chip cans. When we arrived at Grasshopper Park, Janice and I set up our umbrella tent. Wooden clothespins, which I found neatly secured with a rubber band in the miscellaneous bag, were perfect for hanging up each separate petticoat. Janice seemed nervously gleeful as we expressed girl power against Daddy, who thought these frills didn't belong in camp. He struggled, but finally broke down and laughed.

A small blue stream flows by our camp in this picture. We met the Carters the day we diverted the spring. The two adult brothers, Tom and Bob, walked into our camp the first year we were there to find out what had happened to their water, which *they* had diverted from farther up to their cabin over the hill. The Carter clan, with their wives and kids, camp in their primitive, sturdy log cabin that the two Quaker brothers built in the 1930s. They floated logs down Spring Creek and hauled them up a hill to build a wonderful, hidden cabin on a Forest Service lease. They call it "Thee Cabin." I watched the men negotiate the water diversion problem. Daddy said that since the Carters had been here first and spent most of the summer in Colorado, they had a prior claim to the little stream. We could haul the water from the spring. This early lesson in peaceful conflict resolution satisfied Janice and me. An agreeable water decision resulted in all of us being friends. The Carters take us on jeep trips, and we invite them over for campfire meals.

One day, fourteen years later, Janice will marry her first husband, Don, by the Carters' part of the spring. After the ceremony in 1972, she will swing across the small stream in her navy-blue-and-white, eyelet hippie dress made by Mama, yellow wildflowers in her hair. A friend made an oil painting of this scene, Janice with her long, blonde, California-girl hair, and her tall, thin, young Air Force Academy graduate husband catching her on the other side. I wear a lavender-and-white gingham dress with purple asters in my hair, and my first husband, Rick, and our dad officiate at the ceremony.

During the summer of Janice's picture, we kids all swing on the rope swing in jeans and striped T-shirts. The place already holds for us time past and time future. The pristine, hidden spot feels holy. Janice's picture frames events in her memory, and in mine. Sometimes the Carters come over to our campsite for supper and s'mores, roasting hot dogs around our campfire. Or Mama might make a fancier dinner of foil packets with bacon, hamburger, onions, carrots, and potatoes cooked right on the coals. Janice and I learn to slice the vegetables thinly enough that they will cook but not burn. Sometimes, we go to the Carters' cabin, hauling up meat and produce from a deep cellar with a trap door right into the kitchen. The campfire pit in Janice's drawing shows up as a large, perfectly round structure with nine round stones and neatly stacked wood, awaiting our campfire singing and storytelling after supper. This ritual continued right up to 1980, when Mom and Dad built a retirement cabin on Willow Creek—but we don't know about that cabin yet.

Janice drew a log in Spring Creek. The summer of the picture, spring rains washed a huge spruce log downstream across from Grasshopper Park. Janice's picture suggests hours of play, which I fill in with my memory. We pretended the log was an ocean liner, which carried us to imaginary foreign lands. Janice drew fluffy white clouds in a blue sky. Certainly it rained, especially in August, but this is what she remembers. We talked about our camping trips all through the year. We couldn't see some of the important details in this picture, but I supplied them with my memory and augmented the stories by talking with our brother Ed this past winter when he visited Montana for Christmas. Ed and I tried to remember who had which colors. We each were issued an army surplus duffel bag for our clothes, a small kit for our toiletries, and the family shared a large duffel bag for our jackets and coats. To make unpacking easier, each of us—Lamar (our dad), Jean (our mom), and we three kids—marked our gear with colors from the box of crayons which we ground into the seams of the army bags. Janice was yellow, Mama blue, Dad forest green, and I thought I was red. But Ed corrected me recently in no uncertain terms, as we talked last Christmas in my living room.

"I am *red*," Ed informs me. We are sitting in front of a fire in our stone fireplace in Missoula, looking at Janice's drawing. He is balding now, with gray in his short beard, still trim and athletic in his sixties.

"I thought *I* was red," I reply. "So what color was I?"

"I don't know, but I am red." Apparently he still is. I must have been pink. Occasionally we find a duffel bag at the cabin that still bears those early marks of identity.

When I show Ed Janice's picture, he studies it very carefully. Ed is a quiet, thoughtful man.

"She put in everything you could see from the outside," he observes. "This could have been any year."

"Remember all our negotiation about library books?" I say.

"No, I guess I was too little. I remember that sometimes you and Janice would read to me, though."

Looking at the picture, I remember books. Books are a big deal at camp. Daddy proves himself a hero to me one year when he talks the children's librarian at the downtown main library in Dallas into letting Janice and me each check out twenty-eight books, fourteen fiction and fourteen non-fiction, instead of half that number. The check-out period is only two weeks and we are going to be gone for four. When he finds me crying in the children's section after I discover this unfair regulation, he takes action. Bereft at the prospect of borrowing so few books, I listen to Dad explain to the librarian the reading habits of his two daughters. She graciously relents. The books have to be packed in cardboard boxes.

In the tent Janice and I share, we make a bag-side table from an apple crate. I'm older so I get the top shelf; Janice has the lower one. We put the books we are currently reading on our shelf, propped up with rocks as bookends; also Kleenex, a cup of water (this is before water bottles), and our flashlights. Late in the vacation, I have to stretch out the twenty-eight books from the Dallas Public Library, warily watching the mother lode, stored in the trailer away from the mice, diminish. Janice is in the middle of the *Little House* books. I might be rereading our grandfather Roy Lightfoot's novel, *North of the Rio Grande*. I have read his novel lots of times, but I read it again when I'm afraid the main supply will run out.

I am the oldest of three children. Our dad, a progressive Protestant minister from Central Texas, relishes camping and showing us, along with our practical, innovative mother, how to live well outdoors. He recreates with us the tradition established during the years when his banker father, Ed, took him and his friend Royal Williams camping on the Colorado River, close to Lampasas, in Central Texas, for a two-week vacation every summer. Back then, the women drove out to camp only for Sunday picnics; we can see pictures of them dressed up as they came from church. We've seen pictures of Dad and Royal holding up bass and catfish they caught in the Colorado. Dad's mother played the organ and piano in their church for fifty-nine years. Maybe that's why she didn't come camping, but I think camping was considered something the men did.

Our mother grew up in San Antonio. She studied hard to earn her spot as valedictorian of a large high school class. Her father sold various items to make money during the Great Depression, goods ranging from picture frames he assembled in his garage, to a sticky substance he invented that was supposed to keep rain from leaking through on the cloth tops of Model As.

"That stuff stank to high heavens," my Uncle Fred, Mom's brother, told me. "He used pitch, rubber, kerosene, and maybe some other substances. I always tried to be somewhere else when Dad was stirring that stuff up. He would want me to stir the mixture, which made me want to throw up. But still, he was inventive."

During the Depression, Mom's dad wrote an unpublished novel about being on the road, *The Little Drummer Boy*. Salesmen were called "drummers," as in "drumming up business." Mom tells of running to the mailbox, hoping for a letter with a dollar in it. Her dad sent home money when he could. Sometimes there was nothing, she told us. She still looks sad and disappointed when she recounts the story of her father's inability to provide for his family. That dollar meant a lot to the family back in San Antonio. Her mother, Dr. Freddie Lightfoot, supported the family with her work as a chiropractor. Even though chiropractors were considered just above quackery in the 1920s and '30s, Dr. Freddie maintained a regular clientele in the small towns around San Antonio—Bastrop, New Braunfels, Seguin, and San Marcos. She was the first licensed female chiropractor in Texas. During the 1930s, sometimes her patients paid her with produce and chickens. She became successful enough to set up an office in the Majestic Theater building in downtown San Antonio. Not much time for camping in that family, I suppose.

Our parents met when Mom received a college scholarship, enabling her to leave a local college in San Antonio to spend her senior year at Texas Christian University. Dad studied in seminary after college to become a minister. Mom enrolled in one year of seminary after college, worked at a church as a religious education director, and then married. Women married to ministers in the 1940s did not follow their own careers.

I was born during Dad's first full-time pastorate in Atlanta, Georgia, Janice in North Carolina, and now we have returned to Texas, where, as Janice says, "we got Eddie at Parkland Hospital." During the time of Janice's drawing, Eddie is three, Janice is seven, and I am almost eleven, although the archetypal elements in this drawing could illuminate almost any time from 1952 through 1963.

"I'll read you some more of Granddad's book if you'll loan me some of your *Little House* books," I offer Janice. I'm desperate. I haven't read the *Little House* books for a few years; they will have to suffice.

"OK, but you can't cheat," Janice admonishes.

She's got me there. Janice sometimes sits and watches me read my book when I've promised to read to her "later." She counts the negotiated-upon number of pages until I read aloud to her, because sometimes I read more in my book than I've promised. Reading aloud slows me down, and reading Janice's books extends my supply.

One day, perhaps the summer of the picture, the family explores Willow Creek, which empties into the Taylor River, which joins with the East River to form the Gunnison at Almont.

As usual, Dad fishes until dark. We all fish, but our child-sized fly-and-bubble arrangements don't work well in very small streams. Janice and I watch our parents fishing in the meanders, using dry flies and lightweight fly rods. Napoleon Peak and Fitzpatrick Peak catch the last light in the distance. For dry-fly casting, Dad likes Grey Hackle Yellow, Parachute Adams, and Royal Coachman flies. One of our games is learning the names of all of the dry flies, being sure to put them back into the right tray in the fishing tackle box.

Janice and I are bored, so we explore. Climbing up a hill, we are delighted to find a cemetery outside the ghost town of Tincup, with graves from the mining days of the 1870s. We are certain we are the first human beings to rediscover this magical place, as we sisters explore around the cemetery, unafraid because we can see our parents, and we are together. We read old markers, most of them for men who died in their twenties and thirties. The cemetery is overgrown by brush, with graves scattered in haphazard plots. We see some markers with the same names, buried in the 1940s; we guess they are descendants of the miners, since no one lives in the town of Tincup now except in the summer. We go back to the hill at the edge of the cemetery, where we can barely see our parents in the distance, as twilight dims. Janice sits on the split rail fence in her blue-striped T-shirt and red cotton pedal pushers, and two messy blonde ponytails. She looks happy.

"When I die, I want to be buried here," she confidently proclaims. She sits with her legs splayed out, leaning against one of the split rails on the falling-down fence.

"OK," I say.

We both agree that this is the most beautiful place in the whole world.

"Let's see if we can get them to go back to camp," I suggest. We wade carefully in the dying light, through the sagebrush, trying to avoid the rivulets of Willow Creek. Since it's getting dark, we scramble down to where our parents are fishing, light reflecting off the beaver ponds. Eddie plays close by them.

"*Please*, can we go home now?" we whine to our parents. "We're cold and hungry."

"Just one more cast," Daddy replies.

Right, we think. We've heard this before. We decide to stay close and whine that we are cold, hungry, bored, tired. Eventually this works. We drive down the Taylor River and up Spring Creek. Now it's really dark.

Mom is practiced at making simple suppers by lantern light. She fixes trout rolled in cornmeal, minute rice, carrot sticks, and canned green beans.

"And Oreos for dessert?" I continue to negotiate.

"Yes, OK, Joycie, and please set the table and put out the water and bread." Our colors are on our cup handles. We put one lantern under the table to warm our legs and hang one overhead. I'm big enough to do these chores now.

"And *please, please, please* can we have our campfire?" I ask as self-designated sibling delegate.

"It's too late, Joycie," Dad replies. "We'll do it tomorrow night." He's in charge of campfires.

Whose fault is that? I think, but I don't say it out loud.

Janice and I find the Big Dipper before we take the small red lantern into our tent. In the morning, I drag her up from the bottom of the sleeping bag where she always burrows to keep warm. I'm afraid she will smother, and it will be my fault.

The next night we will sing camp songs our parents learned at Texas church camps in the 1930s and 1940s. We sing in the car to pass the time during the two-day drive to and from vacation. Our parents tell us stories of their childhoods and how they met.

"I saw this pretty, red-headed gal working at the cash register," Dad tells us again.

"And I was trying so hard to get all the kids' names right, but I called him Rollins Cherryholmes, one of his roommates," Mama recounts. We know Mr. Cherryholmes.

"She finally got my name right and let me take her for a Coke at the TCU drugstore," Dad recounts their love story yet again. They tell us all about their days at TCU, and we learn the names of their friends, ministers and families now scattered across Texas. We know their roommates' names, the classes they took, the student pastorates Daddy served in college, and we especially know about football. Janice and I compete to name the starting lineup of the 1938 TCU national championship team.

In the car or around the fire, Daddy says, "OK, who wants to try to get the whole lineup?"

"I do, I do," one of us volunteers. Janice and I like to show off our memory skills. "Ki Aldritch, Davy O'Brien, I.B. Hale, Connie Sparks. . . ." We've seen pictures of all these football players in the TCU annuals.

In the car, and at camp, we usually sing, "There's a long, long trail a-winding into the land of my dreams." We end the song with "Till the day when I'll be going down that long, long trail with you." These songs make up part of the memory DNA of our family. They will bring us together in years to come.

During at least fifteen years, our camping vacations made us Hockers. When I married at twenty-one, I converted my Florida husband to the camping life, and we continued camping in Colorado, sometimes with my family. We divorced ten years later, but he and his family still camp in Colorado.

Campfires Burn in Memory

My husband Gary and I married in 1993. Because Gary came from a fractured family, he used to call our family "intact," even after all the deaths. When I heard his word for our family, I used to feel angry with him, as if he had not taken the full measure of our losses. Now I believe he is right to call us "intact." The stones of Grasshopper Park, Cold Springs, One Mile, Lottis Creek, and other Colorado camping sites still form campfire circles, even though many of the tables have gone missing due to campsite consolidation. My brother and I stop at Cold Spring Campground on the Taylor River as we drive to the family cabin that our parents built by Willow Creek when they retired. Driving up the Taylor River Road from Gunnison, we fill our water bottles, saying each time, "This is the best water in the world." The log boat on Spring Creek where we three played and made up stories that took us traveling all over the world has long since deteriorated. But a small piece of wood from the boat sits on a windowsill in the family cabin. And at night, the Big Dipper and Orion wheel over the starlit sky, and somewhere, songs and stories echo around the campfires of long ago.

chapter two

Three Weddings and a Funeral

October 6, 2002: Anniversary on the Big Hole River

The Montana wind blows unseasonably cold, skittering snow and sleet along the parking lot of the Sportsman Motel in Melrose, a small former railroad town on the Big Hole River. Gary and I enjoy coming here for our anniversary. Before I can concentrate on dinner, I want to call my brother, Ed. Dianne, Ed's wife of less than a month, received a diagnosis of lung cancer six weeks ago. She is in the hospital in Colorado Springs. Securing the fake, black fur around the hood of my corduroy parka to keep out some of the cold wind, I shove change in my pocket, then pull on my gloves to make my way to the pay phone outside the office, across the parking lot. I recall a lot of pay phones in my life on the back roads of the Rocky Mountains. Once I called my answering service from this phone a few years ago, almost running out of quarters as I scribbled the messages while standing in the snow.

Pulling off my right glove, I dig for coins in my pocket as my hands fumble in the cold. The darkening twilight makes it hard to find the coin slots. Ed answers; he's at home for a brief respite before he goes back to the hospital.

"How is Dianne?" I inquire, knowing the news will be discouraging. I already feel sad. Dianne has been in and out of the hospital for more than a month.

Ed pauses for so long that I wonder if he can hear me. When he speaks, his voice shakes. I can hear him swallowing, and I think he's working to get the words out.

"Not good. She's unconscious some of the time. She doesn't want hospice care—she still says she will beat this, but I don't think she has long."

"But hospice could help so much," I unhelpfully comment.

"I know. She got mad at me, really angry, when I brought it up. So that's a no." He sighs.

"Oh, Ed." I wait through another loud blast of wind, sheltering the phone. Dianne received this unexpected diagnosis only in August. I wonder how her death can be happening so quickly.

"Do you think I should come now?" I ask. I'm almost shouting over the wind. I hope Ed will tell me what I should do. I love him and want to support him. I also feel overwhelmed by the thought of cancelling and rescheduling all my clients in Missoula to make a trip. For much of my adult life, I have longed for Ed to find a true partner of his heart. His first marriage didn't work out; Ed raised his daughter, Katie, from the time she was six years old until late in high school, when she left Colorado Springs to live with her mother, trying out their relationship. As the oldest sibling, I often feel a lot of responsibility for my brother and sister, who don't require this kind of emotional caretaking. At this moment, I can't find within me what I want to do. Should I be with my brother and Dianne right now, or wait a while, see my clients, and go later? I would need to return to Missoula in the morning, book a trip, and leave for an indefinite period of time. Along with my love and concern, I recognize more than a touch of selfishness. I don't like my interior discovery, and I feel blindsided by Dianne's illness.

"That has to be up to you." Ed sounds exhausted. "She doesn't have much time." Later may not be an option.

"You sound so tired," I say.

"I am. I offered the guest room to April, Dianne's older daughter, and she is here with her husband and three kids. It's very chaotic. I still have my room, but I'm not sleeping well at all," he tells me. Dianne's younger daughter is coming tomorrow.

"How are you feeling, Ed?" I don't know what to ask. This question requires too much of a grieving person. An implicit reply of "Oh, I'm OK," seems embedded in the question. I don't yet know to say, *I am devastated that you and Dianne must endure this. I want to be with you.*

"We're making it through," he replies. Ed seldom speaks dramatically. He sounds just like our dad when he says this.

"OK, we'll stay in touch. I'll call you when we get back tomorrow." I hang up the phone and run back to the warmth of the cabin, sleet plastering my face as I make the dash. I tell Gary how dire the situation is. He's been predicting that Dianne would decline very quickly.

Gary and I come to this humble log cabin lodge for late-season brown trout fishing, and hikes through cottonwoods turning yellow and along paths lined with red osier dogwoods near the river. In the past, I've enjoyed speculating about the plain, humble houses and the people in them, the residences lined up along the railroad track where the train doesn't stop these days. I once explored up the back outside staircase of the old hotel, thinking it was deserted, only to find to my chagrin a couple of rooms on the second floor where old men were living. I have loved walking along the Big Hole, sometimes fishing, but mostly hiking out into the great wide-open prairie west of the river. I covet a small log cabin with blue shutters, placed just right under old cottonwoods and blue spruce trees, by a small channel of the main river. I fantasize about writing there, in a private retreat space, unplugged from my busy world.

We are celebrating our ninth anniversary. I've brought home-made pasta sauce and a special treat of bison tenderloin for our two nights here. We stopped by Bernice's Bakery for our favorite chocolate-buttercream-frosted cake with raspberry filling. I like to make do in the simple kitchen, turn up the gas heater, play Bach and vocal jazz CDs, light a beeswax candle, to make a homey getaway for us. We bring an extra comforter to toss on the red-and-green-plaid bedspread in the cold back bedroom. A mounted brown trout hangs on the dark paneled wall above the bed. Dry flies have been hooked into a lampshade; I don't know whether in celebration or disgust.

We hang our clothes on hooks, since the cabin serves primarily hunters and fishers, who apparently do not need to hang their gear. Once I awakened to the sight of a brown-and-white horse nudging the back window. The owner pastures a few horses out front; this one must have wandered away for a while. I like the Montana character of this small town on the Big Hole River.

Gary usually fishes while I hike, but this year's early storm sent us inside to read our anniversary gifts sheltered in the cozy cabin. As the wind shakes the windows of our hideaway, we prop our feet up on the maroon ice chest. Gary savors each poem in Mary Oliver's new book, *What Do We Know*, while I slowly enjoy Joanna Macy's *Widening Circles*. I relish our warmth and peace, knowing at the same time that Ed has no such refuge.

I return to my practice on Monday and don't make plans to go to Colorado Springs yet. I speculate that I have time to plan a visit. I call my sister Janice, who is teaching communication studies at the University of Arkansas, and we try to decide together what to do. Janice and I both feel gripped by cycles of overwork—she is determined to finish her book on the relationships between men and women in academia by next summer. She has suffered from middle-back pain and insomnia for several years, making it hard for her to make the progress she wants. When she and Tom visited Missoula in August, she consulted with my doctor, an expert on women's health; she also tried different yoga postures to relieve her pain. She'd do legs-up-the-wall pose every afternoon. She slept a little better on vacation in Missoula but now sleeps poorly, and as she is so small (barely five feet tall), she's having trouble getting medication that helps her sleep without knocking her out all day. We agree that we will wait a few days to decide whether to travel to Colorado at the same time.

I have taken on a time-consuming consulting project for the Indian Health Service in addition to my full clinical practice. Janice and I often write and talk about how we must learn to cut back. Last spring, the four of us decided not to travel to France because she had no energy for planning.

Ed and Dianne's short relationship plays out in my memory.

Our whole family—Mom and Dad, Janice and Tom, and Gary and I—welcome the new relationship Ed and Dianne have developed over the past months. Friends introduced them; after a few shy starts, they began to date and explore Colorado together. Ed's daughter Katie drove back to Colorado the day after she graduated from high school in Oregon, magenta hair in spikes, and a valedictorian speech just behind her. She's met Dianne and likes her a lot. That's high praise. Ed, eight years younger than I, works as a transportation planner, having gone back to school after his hippie dropout years when he worked as a stonemason. His wide shoulders and sinewy frame embody a man who hauled rocks up and down ladders in his twenties and thirties, holding them aloft while he found just the right place to set them in a chimney or wall. His long-haired seventies look past, now he has a neatly clipped haircut and wears sports coats to work.

I pass the iconic picture in our hallway of Ed and his best friend Clyde, from the time they took over an abandoned miner's cabin in the Gunnison National Forest in Colorado. Clyde sports a taped-up broken nose from wood-splitting gone awry. Ed wears rimless glasses; behind them they've burned words into the doorframe of their cabin named "The Wooden Ship," from a Crosby, Stills and Nash song. I remember sending giant jars of peanut butter, homemade cookies, and used books to Ed that summer and fall of 1973, when I was still in graduate school in Austin. Sometimes, when they couldn't catch a ride, Ed and Clyde hiked the ten miles to the Taylor Park Trading Post and back to their cabin, to pick up mail and supplies. We all loved the Gunnison National Forest where we camped earlier as a family. We still go to Taylor River country when we can. Ed dropped out of college when his draft number was too high for his conscientious objector papers to be processed by the draft board. He didn't go to Vietnam or Canada, but he needed to get away from mainstream American culture for a while.

Ed brought Dianne to Shalom, our parents' retirement cabin in the Gunnison National Forest, so they could all meet. I know Dianne only through pictures so far. One shows our folks and the new couple beaming, seated on the couch at the cabin close to Tincup. Janice and I each display a framed picture in our homes of Dianne at the bottom of the Grand Canyon of the Gunnison, reading a book, with her toes in the water, a red bandana around her head. We want to know this person who will most likely become our sister-in-law. Dianne looks lovely, with a strong runner's body, brown hair, and lively brown eyes. Ed tells us on the phone that Dianne has contracted a bad case of bronchitis, exacerbated by the many forest fires this summer. Breathing with difficulty, she almost could not climb out of the Black Canyon. This was shocking to her, a competitive runner who has climbed several of the fourteener mountains in Western Colorado. She is on antibiotics, hoping to heal from several rounds of the illness.

We plan to meet her at our parents' sixtieth anniversary celebration in late July. In the spring and summer, Ed and Dianne are in the first heady phases of falling in love. They share a passion for the outdoors and progressive social values. Dianne is a social worker who comes from a scattered family. Her father was Choctaw and her mother is white. Dianne tracked down her father's family shortly after he died, connecting with his relatives in Western Oklahoma. Her Native heritage becomes more important to her as she relates to her father's family.

Ed tells me on the phone that Dianne has wandered around a lot in her life and only now has decided to stay put in Colorado Springs. She has just finished her social work degree, planning to accrue her licensing hours, beginning with her job at a women's shelter. Because of her peripatetic lifestyle up until now, she has allowed her daughter to live in one place with her father, Dianne's former husband. Dianne is looking for a home, Ed tells me, and she seems thrilled to have found both Ed, whom she loves, and our family. On the phone in early summer, I remember Ed telling me, "I know she loves me for myself, but I have to say, what she already knows about our family isn't hurting my case."

"What do you mean?" I ask.

"She has always wanted to belong to a family like ours. She asks me a lot of questions about you and Janice and already seems to love Mom and Dad. She told me she has never been happier," Ed continues.

"I can't wait to meet her," I say. I'm eager for our parents' anniversary celebration so we can be together.

"I really want her to meet all of you." Ed sounds excited and happy.

Janice and I don't want Ed to be lonely any longer. We are ready to love Dianne.

July, 2002: Jean and Lamar's Sixtieth Anniversary

In early July, I copy Mom and Dad's wedding announcement from their 1942 marriage in Corpus Christi, Texas. Their wedding was held in the church where Mom worked as a director of religious education after completing her college degree and one year of seminary. Mom didn't finish seminary; in fact, she was unusual in her day for having attended at all. Janice and I have inquired both seriously and playfully through the years, "Do you sometimes wish you'd followed your own career? You are so smart and could have done so many things." This comment was issued by two daughters who did not bear children and who are definitely following their own careers, with consequences for past marriages.

"No. I chose my life. I did exactly what I wanted to do," Mom always replies. Janice and I agree that somewhere, somehow, she must have felt doubts. Daughters often live out the unconscious, unlived lives of their mothers. Janice and I have three PhDs between us. We don't know what Mom might have wanted for a career because she always sticks with her story about choosing her life, and she is a rigorously honest person. We have to believe her.

Mom and her best friend, Mollie, across the road from each other in their summer homes, have already begun cooking and freezing treats for the celebration. Dad and Morris go for walks to get out of the way of the ladies' talk about the party and to enjoy their thirty-year friendship. They built their cabins at the same time.

Shalom reflects our years gathering around the campfire, singing camp songs, and telling stories. Dad completed thirteen interim ministries after he retired in order to make enough money to pay for the cabin's construction. On the wall of the main bedroom hangs a framed poster from the trip I took with our alumni group to Israel, with a quote from Isaiah: "They shall beat their swords into plough-shares and their swords into pruning hooks." *Shalom* is Hebrew for peace. While Mom and Dad backpacked the Timberline Trail after they retired, now they mostly stay close to the cabin. They feel peaceful here. Janice says it's the place she herself feels most off duty. As we gather for the anniversary celebration, I look around, in the company of all my family. We seem to be living out a family dream of a retreat, a place to call home, and life in the unspoiled forest of Western Colorado. As we plan what to do at the celebration the next night, we agree that of course we'll sing "There's a Long, Long, Trail A-Winding," and "With Someone Like You." It wouldn't be a Hocker celebration without these favorite songs.

Janice and I looked through our parents' TCU yearbooks as children, asked about what they did at school, and learned the TCU school anthem in our earliest years. We both went to TCU, following our parents. I can still chant the "Riff, Ram, Bah, Zoo . . ." cheer, should anyone request it. I roomed with the daughter of Dad's college roommate.

With Dianne coming tomorrow, we are gathering again to remember, celebrate, tell stories, sing, and welcome a new family member to love. Gary and I have driven to Shalom from Missoula as Janice and Tom make the two-day drive from Fayetteville. We towed a small U-Haul behind Gary's truck, with the anniversary surprise we all planned, a new oak table to replace the French provincial one from the fifties. Mom antiqued the old table in a weathered yellow color after too many marks and glue stains marred the surface during our homework years. We eagerly antic-ipate surprising them with our gift. As I later read at the party, "We knew we had the artist, Gary, to build the new table, but we did design it by committee. We gave Gary the final say on the design." Gary has built the table with a clever mechanism that eliminates the need for wrenching the table apart when additional leaves need to be placed in the table.

Gary and I wait for Tom and Janice to arrive from Arkansas before we unveil, or un-tarp, the table. Ed's here, looking forward to going to Colorado Springs to bring Dianne to join the festivities. Gary and I briefly settle in one of the downstairs rooms. Mom made a Cherokee-style patchwork crazy quilt with scraps from fancy dresses she made for Janice and me growing up. The quilt brightens the lower-floor walls. Her great-grandmother walked the Trail of Tears in the 1830s, settling near Tahlequa, Indian Territory. Earlier in her life, Mom studied the designs that Indian women used for their quilts during the Great Depression, selling them along the side of highways as a source of cash during lean times. The green velvet, red-and-gold taffeta, and turquoise velveteen complement the forest green carpet. We unpack quickly, and I make my favorite walk up Willow Creek to where the covered spring provides water for the cabins. Turning back downstream toward the Sawatch Mountain view, I see Janice and Tom walking up the stream to greet me. I am so happy as I hug my petite younger sister, who seems quite thin, even for her small frame.

Janice and I don't look alike; she has long blonde hair, and I am a taller brunette. People often look at us, cock their heads, and say, "I can see a resemblance in your eyes, maybe." We just laugh. We are sisters of the heart and blood, but we look nothing alike. Janice resembles our red-haired, petite mother, and I take after my father, with his used-to-be-dark hair. Tom is older than Janice, who is fifty-three. Because of his full head of brown hair, we tease him about his youthful looks. Janice and I somehow never thought we would live so far apart, and our first moment of reconnection always brings joy. I feel the same way when they get off the plane in Missoula. We fantasize about living together when we all retire. When they visit Missoula, we walk around the University area where we lived until recently, pointing out houses that are big enough for us to share.

"There's one," Tom says as he sees a huge neo-Tudor house on Gerald. "Let's go ask them how much they want," he teases. With Tom, we can never be sure whether he will act on some crazy notion.

"Why not?" We plot. We talk about living in Arkansas in the winter and Montana in the summer.

Ed arrives, and we proudly surprise our parents with the new oak table. They express gratitude and astonishment that we pulled this off. We have our first meal together around the anniversary gift; Ed's daughter, Katie, with her magenta hair, Dad and Mom at each end, everyone looking happy. Ed leaves to pick up Dianne in Colorado Springs.

As we gather around the woodstove in the cabin after our supper together, I look around with great appreciation for what Mom, Dad, and Ed have created. The hexagonal shape of the cabin makes me think of the way we laid out our three summer camping tents. The stone fireplace Ed built reminds me of our many camp-fires. He's set a stone shaped like Texas in the middle. On the left is a Native grinding stone from Central Texas that served as a doorstop in Dad's home in Lampasas. In their bedroom, Mom maintains a neat sewing corner where she quilts and still makes clothes for herself and sometimes for Janice. Unlike me, Janice sends patterns and snippets of material, with sketches of what she might like. She and Mom function well as a team, even from a distance.

When I suggested Mom take over the main floor guest room for her sewing, she replied, "Oh no. I want to leave it set up for guests. Some of our visitors need to be upstairs instead of taking the stairs to the basement." Mom loves visitors. As the only extra-vert in the family, she's learned it's up to her to maintain their social life. She created a hand-stitched tan, rust, ivory, and turquoise story quilt for Ed and his first wife, with each block representing a time in their lives. She confided to me that she doesn't think she'll do such a big project entirely by hand again. The four-bedroom log cabin provides a permanent home for family antiques. In their bedroom, they've hung pictures of all the family, including one of them paddling a canoe on their honeymoon in Kerrville, Texas.

Our family moved often because Dad and Mom supported social justice issues of the day, starting with race relationships in the late 1940s, through integration and school desegregation in the 1950s and '60s, the anti-war movement, capital punishment, gay rights, and environmental issues. Often Dad's sermons and teaching pushed his congregation further and faster than they wanted to change, so the board of elders fired him. We grew up knowing he was right in his views but wishing we didn't have to move so often. Janice and I often joke that it's no mystery that both his daughters went into the field of communication—we thought people ought to learn to work out their conflicts instead of firing their adversaries.

A Harbinger

While the new table provides plenty of room, and the family circle easily expands to include new additions, we now face an unwelcome development. Ed left early the morning of the party to collect Dianne and bring her back in time for the celebration. He called later that morning to say that she had to go to the hospital for tests for chronic bronchitis and edema, and he needed to stay with her. We can hardly take this in. Dianne has been fiercely determined to get to the anniversary celebration, but she can't. Her medical needs have quickly overtaken her desires. She sounds very upset as she talks to us on the phone. Ed is clear that he needs to be with Dianne, and we all agree. We won't all be present. I don't know why Dianne needs to be in the hospital for bronchitis.

Neighbors in the summer home group where Shalom is located gather for the party. Mom's sewing friends have crafted a blue-and-tan quilted depiction of the hexagonal cabin, embroidered with all the names of the women in Mom's sewing circle. Janice and I confer at the dresser upstairs, the same one we shared as girls in San Antonio, about what to wear. This furniture replaced the small painted plywood chest of drawers that Janice used to crawl inside, after removing the drawers, to read as she created her undisturbed imaginary world as a young girl. Janice and I love preparing for events together, sharing jewelry, deciding what to wear, and simply being sisters together. We have always gotten along very well; we're best friends.

Mom is in her element, preparing the new table, getting out her wedding china and dozens of punch cups that, as a minister's wife, she has collected. She sets out the silver tray I gave her for their twenty-fifth anniversary, borrowing a silver tea service from Evelyn, downstream. She loves to place these table decorations just right. We've ordered a sheet cake from the bakery in Gunnison. Mom enjoys bits of elegance in the rustic setting. The main room is still carpeted in her original orange shag patterned carpet; yellow Formica tops the kitchen counters.

Gary speaks first, using the metaphor he took from a honeymoon picture of Mom and Dad paddling a canoe: "Courageously, they paddled across the stormy water raised by social injustice, racial prejudice, and war. When one could not paddle, the other pulled harder. When they grew uncertain about their bearings, they conferred and found a new way. At times, they could not paddle at all because they were laughing too hard." Gary honed his eloquence during his years as a minister in the United Church of Christ before he came to Missoula to marry me and take up teaching at the University of Montana's Honors College.

In my tribute, I continue, "We three siblings grew up around a dinner table where our parents inquired every day about our lives and listened to our answers. Along with spaghetti, fish sticks, pot roast, ginger spice cake, hot dogs, and pork chops, as Mama stretched a tight budget to feed five people well, we drank in laughter and dished up opinions." I referred to our family camping trips from Texas to Colorado, beginning in 1952, where the picnic table was the center of camp. Many nights we returned to a dark camp soon made cheerful by lantern light and sat around the Forest Service table to devour the trout Lamar had caught with his famous one last cast.

Then Janice passed out the words and led us all in "There's a Long, Long Trail" and "With Someone Like You," ending, "We'll build a sweet little nest, somewhere out in the West, and let the rest of the world go by." These songs came to define our parents to us kids. We miss Ed and Dianne, but it's a good celebration. Later I look at pictures of Janice, Tom, and me in the kitchen, pretending to be exhausted with dishwashing in our non-dish-washer kitchen. We look tired and happy. Dad relaxes at the end of the cleared table.

Hard Conversation

Ed comes back to the cabin to see us before we leave.

"It's lung cancer," he tells us. He wanted to tell us in person. He looks unutterably sad as we sit around the table in silence.

Gary and Ed walk up Willow Creek.

"I don't know how to do this," Ed says to Gary. "I've never done this before."

"You will find your way," Gary replies, knowing Ed's character. They walk the creek they have fished together many times. I don't know what else they talk about, but I do know Gary is a calm, realistic presence in the face of devastating news.

Gary and I drive to Montana; Janice and Tom will travel north to us in Missoula after more time at the cabin. Janice and Tom visit Ed and Dianne in Colorado Springs. Ed brings Dianne over to his house to meet them, hauling her portable oxygen.

"I don't remember what we talked about," Tom tells me when I asked him to describe that meeting. "We were just getting to know each other. And that's when I took that unbearably sad picture of Ed and Dianne on the porch." In the picture, Ed's eyes look deep and knowing. Dianne is smiling. Chemotherapy is scheduled very soon.

One night, Ed and I talk for a long time on the phone while Janice, Tom and Gary sit on the deck, watching the summer twilight fall as the first stars come out. They are quietly discussing the news about Dianne, deciding who will visit, and when. After giving me more medical bad news, Ed confesses, "I wanted to marry her." A silence ensues. "I know for sure that I want to move her into my house and take care of her."

"I'll come help you," I volunteer. Time is running out for me to be with Dianne.

"That would help, thanks. I'm trying to think about the impact on my life and hers if we go ahead and marry," Ed continues.

"You know you can count on the support of all of us." I state what for me is obvious, but I wonder if Ed has concerns. Does he think that his family would not support a marriage in these circumstances?

We mull this decision over for a while: what if they go ahead and marry, what if he doesn't bring it up, what if they decide to wait? I know to not give advice, only support. At the end of the conversation, we make plans for me to come to Colorado Springs just after Labor Day. Ed ends our conversation, "I'm going to go buy a ring."

In Colorado Springs in late August, friends gather; we move Dianne and her furniture and personal things to Ed's two-story Victorian house. Dianne wears the ring, other intimate objects, and an arrowhead Gary gave her, in a medicine pouch around her neck. Her hand is too swollen for the ring. Gary wrote to Dianne that the arrowhead, which he found on a trail outside of Helena, where he was living at the time, had survived the Casey Meadows fire of 1988. Intense fires burned all the humus out of the soil. He hoped the invulnerability of the arrowhead would help her as she endured chemotherapy. Ed clears a shelf for her Southwestern bowls. He moves black-and-white Zuni pots and others from her collection into his living room. Dianne brings a grand supply of luxurious towels and linens in rich jewel tones, the likes of which have not been seen in Ed's bachelor house for many years. We worry about whether Dianne will be able to climb the narrow, winding stairs.

Dianne and I begin a series of interrupted conversations about big questions. We talk as she lies on the couch in the living room. I am arranging the kitchen and her clothes. I don't know whether to stop the practical moving-in tasks and just talk, or whether to try to do both. Dianne wants to know whether I think they will make a good couple. She wonders about how to fit in with Mom and Dad, and she wonders why Dad doesn't tease her very much anymore. She'd liked his teasing at the cabin. I can easily imagine that my dad's heart is breaking, and he doesn't have teasing in him now, but Dianne thinks it means he doesn't like her as much. I realize, as I explain what I imagine is going on with Dad, that Dianne does not acknowledge that she may not have a future. She asks what I like to do so we can make plans to do things together. I stumble as I try to think of things I like. I think, but don't say, *I want you and Ed to have a future. I want my brother to be happy. I want you to live.* I can't think of a single recreational activity that makes any sense to me right now. Clearly, Dianne envisions a long-shared life in our family. She sees herself as a warrior, a strong and resilient woman.

I'm careful to ask Dianne where she wants her personal items. One night she decides to sleep on the couch. Ed and I make up a bed for her; I know intuitively that Dianne will not be climbing the stairs for long. I take a picture of Dianne and me on the porch; she is smiling, and I look pensive. Dianne has to go to the hospital for more tests and a chemotherapy treatment. Together we find the one dress, a long purple one, which will fit her body now swollen with edema. This bothers her terribly; she is used to being lean and fit. In a photo of Ed and Dianne taken the same day, the depths of sadness in Ed's eyes are not mirrored by the joy in Dianne's. She has found a home and a family at last. She feels fortunate to be joining our clan. Ed and I look devastated. Our parents plan to come to Colorado Springs to help out. Will they, now in their eighties, manage climbing up and down the steep stairs? Ed installs a grab bar on the stairwell, for everyone. We draw the circle as tightly as we can, feeling time and possibility slipping through our hands.

"I'd really like it if you would stay longer," Dianne quietly entreats. After the picture-taking, I prepare to go to the airport to return home.

I flip through my obligations in my mind. "I really need to get back to my practice. I'm so sorry." She shows her disappointment. "I'll be back, and we'll talk on the phone." After I return home she feels frustrated when I'm not available on the phone; Ed tells me, "She may not have the time to wait until you are less busy." He's not guilt-tripping me; he's trying to get my attention.

I confide in Janice via email that I am failing Dianne when we talk or if I can't respond on the phone. She wants to talk about whether to go ahead and plan the wedding or wait, her plans for healing, her spiritual life, what to do about despair and how to keep her spirits up, and how she and Ed might be heading onto divergent spiritual paths and what to do about that. She asks for spiritual help; Gary and I read poems and prayers, and some scripture, into a tape recorder. Later, Ed tells me that Dianne greatly appreciated that we made this tape, but she never listened to it. She needed close personal conversation, not a tape of our voices. Dianne sees in me an older sister figure and she wants to talk every day when I am at work or immediately when I come home. I write to Janice that I feel "scared, compassionate, and swamped . . . I simply can't do this."

As always, Janice understands my dilemma without making Dianne wrong in any way. She writes, "Oh, the situation with Dianne is so heart-wrenching—for all involved, including you. That's what you get from walking in with a sign on your T-shirt: 'I'm a loving sister and oh, by the way, a really, REALLY good therapist.' Read your note to me, 'I simply can't do this'." Janice and I reinforce each other as shared Myers-Briggs feeling types and as people who struggle with the limits of our ability to respond to genuine human need—Janice with friends and students, and I with clients and, in this case, family.

Janice writes a lot for her academic work, often by invitation of people in her field. She signs off this email saying, "OK, got to work on this 'mythic criticism' chapter to which I committed us in a moment of insanity. Love you lots, Jannie."

As September progresses, I face another dilemma. Ed and Dianne have set their wedding date for September 21. So have Andy and Heather, Gary's older son and fiancée. Andy proposed to Heather at our house last year. Their wedding will be in Southern California. For days I cannot decide what to do. I finally decide to accompany Gary to California to be with his extended family, in the service of life and hope. When we arrive and check into our Palos Verdes motel, I dissolve in tears, knowing in my heart that I have made the wrong decision for me. I even consider flying immediately to Colorado, but I don't want to face the disapproval of all the California family and, I fear, Gary as well. I stay, but I am not truly present. While we are in California, I receive an email and pictures from Ed, entitled, "Happy Day!"

Ed and Dianne marry in her hospital room at Penrose. Our parents attend, along with Clyde, Ed's friend who is like a brother to him. He used to live next door to the family after I was in college, when Dad had a church in Colorado Springs. Clyde is as solid as the rock with which he and Ed used to build. He's the friend who squatted with Ed in the old miner's cabin on Pine Creek. Ed's minister and the two friends who introduced Ed and Dianne attend. Janice, Tom, Gary, and I send readings and poems. Dianne's younger daughter is back at home with her father, and her older daughter, April, is back in South Dakota with her family. We see a picture of Dianne in a white blouse, propped up in her hospital bed, with a white scarf around her head, Ed seated on the side of her bed. They are scattering red rose petals over the white hospital blanket. Dianne looks happy, Ed and Dad look haunted, and Mom smiles tensely. She always makes the best of everything. Mom and Dad immediately accepted Ed and Dianne's decision to marry, never voicing any questions. That's the way they are. Dad helped officiate, ending with a prayer that subtly acknowledged "the tangled trails of our human lives," as he prayed for love to strengthen their union. He asked for a "measure of the joy and happiness they so richly deserve." He knew the probable course of her lung cancer.

When we talk on the phone, Dad tells me, "It's bad. But of course we want to support them any way we can. My heart breaks for them." His voice cracks as he tells me this. Dad has spent a lot of time in hospital rooms; I doubt if he ever officiated at a wedding in one before, but I don't know that for certain. I remember him dropping me off at branch libraries in Dallas while he called on people in the hospital; I remember the quiet afternoons waiting for him in hospital lobbies with my new library books. Dad did me the favor of bringing me along in his life. I got a good look at his work.

In Southern California I am not grounded. I dance with Gary at Andy and Heather's reception, but my heart leans toward

Colorado, and I find the tense dynamics of Gary's family difficult. His mother attends, as do his father with his second wife. Seating arrangements present difficulties, as do pictures. I soak up the tension in the extended family, feeling little of the buffer I need to protect my raw feelings. Gary's first wife, the mother of their sons, helps host the wedding. She is gracious to me; nevertheless, I feel conflicted and uncomfortable.

I write to Dianne when I return home, welcoming her as the new sister of my heart, assuring her that "Janice and I widen our circle of loving siblinghood to include you." I marvel at the widening circles of love, and how love seems to expand, a great mystery to me. Dianne is not able to talk much on the phone now. She goes in and out of the hospital, sometimes with emergency admissions. Ed contacts Dianne's two daughters, who make plans to come back to Colorado Springs. I don't know how Ed will handle all the pressure and company.

Another Harbinger

On the phone at home, Janice and I breathe a big sigh of relief when she gets the news, after her breast biopsy, that there is no cancer. Our mother survived breast cancer. In an email on October 7, Janice explains that celebration was a bit premature; with severe hyperplasia, she will likely have to continue getting biopsies. Her doctor called it a harbinger of the future. She writes that her risk factors seem alarmingly high, with family history and not having borne children. She continues, "I'm realizing that after fifty, you really do need to learn to live each day as a gift. I'm so future-oriented, I'm not very good at that, but I'm trying. Other than all this cancer stuff, life is good. Love, Jannie."

Dianne refuses hospice, denying that her lung cancer is ending her life; she fiercely wants to live. Ed ultimately makes plans to move her to the hospice wing anyway, which will give her a more peaceful end. The move does not happen quickly enough. Her older daughter, son-in-law, and three grandchildren are at Ed's house. On October 22, soon after our call when

I was on the Big Hole for our anniversary, Dianne dies in Ed's arms at the hospital. He calls Gary and me. "She's gone." We are all weeping.

"I love you, Ed," I choke out.

"I know. That means a lot."

We all make plans to return to Colorado Springs—Mom and Dad from their winter condominium home in Grand Junction, Janice from Arkansas, Gary and I from Montana. Tom stays in Arkansas to teach Janice's classes along with his own. We check into the historic Antlers Hotel downtown, close to Ed's house. The service for Dianne takes place at Ed's Unitarian Church. Ed assembles a table of objects in the foyer—a black-and-white Zuni double-spouted wedding pot, a poster of the Black Canyon of the Gunnison—where Ed and Dianne camped so happily, looking at the Pleiades, but which resulted in Dianne's ordeal of trying to climb back up—Dianne's backpack, a framed picture of Ed and Dianne on his porch, Dianne wearing the purple dress, and a rotating slide show of too few pictures. Glad to see some pictures of Dianne from earlier years, I see that she was always radiantly beautiful.

My photo album skips disconcertingly from the pictures of the brave wedding in the hospital to the pictures of the memorial service. I see a photo of our father and Gary, wearing ties and suits, going over the plans for the service. Janice, Gary, Dianne's daughter Katie, and Dad sit outside the sanctuary in a row on a church pew. In one picture, Ed rests his arm on my shoulder and we look as somber as we feel. We all put together a meaningful service. Ed, Janice, Gary, and I speak, along with Dianne's daughter April. Gary stands by Ed as Ed reads his tribute to Dianne, referring to the fires of passion and the wildfires of the summer. Ed wonders whether he will get through the reading, so Gary stands ready to help if needed. Ed does just fine.

Later, Janice remarked to me, "Well, we *do* know how to do services." She's telling the wry truth. We have spoken at each other's weddings, our aunt's memorial service, countless youth Sunday services, sometimes preaching, all three of us, or taking part in various camp services in Texas and Colorado. Janice and I served on the board of a large student congregation at college. We taught public speaking. We've been in front of various audiences, secular and sacred, for most of our lives, as have Mom and Dad, of course, and Gary. This is home territory for us.

A lifetime of being "PKs"—preacher's kids—prepared us siblings to speak when needed. Janice, always searching for cultural and mythic meanings not apparent on the surface, wrote a convention paper a few months later called, "It Should Have Been a Wedding." She wrote about how our family rose to this occasion, helping to provide a meaningful service, and welcoming Dianne with our presence into our family, even after her death. She also speculated with honest discomfort that we edged out Dianne's daughters and the remnants of her splintered family. Janice looks beneath the surface to find that we left few gaps for others. She exposes our privileged position and our unconscious expectation that we would take charge. Dianne's older daughter refused to let Gary look at eagle feathers Dianne had collected. Gary sees himself as respectful and reverent of all spiritual traditions and felt hurt. But this may have been a way for April to claim some sense of "this is ours, not yours."

Ed invited all the out-of-town guests to a dinner at an Italian restaurant, where he presided, reading with tears and pride Dianne's list of what she looked for in a man, a list she gave him after they fell in love. He reported that she said he failed only in "wears glasses, which shows intelligence," since Ed recently had his vision corrected with surgery. He guessed that twenty-seven out of thirty qualities was a passing grade. He smiled through his tears as he read "knowledge of survival, camping, and the outdoors; nonviolent and even-tempered; intelligent but not arrogant; not a complainer; and industrious, fixes things at home." While Dianne wrote the list before she met Ed, the list describes him perfectly. Ed and I will talk about how they never had to go through disillusionment. We both speculate they would have made it through. Ed spoke of the fires of that summer, and the fire that will always burn in his heart. He called them soul mates.

The afternoon after the service, Ed joined the family at the Antlers Hotel, fleeing the crowded chaos at his house. Gary commented, upon watching Janice and me massaging his back as the rest of the family sat quietly in Mom and Dad's room, that we seemed like a pod of whales holding up its weakest member. Gary wrote to Janice about the odd juxtapositions of the event—the hostility of some of Dianne's family, playing with kids one minute and helping Ed divide the ashes the next. He continued, "I'm not able to make sense of it at this point, but would love to read anything you write about it." Gary knew that Janice would be reflecting deeply. When Tom and Janice visit in the summers, we always have a reading night. Tom and I joke about trying to go before Janice and Gary, whose prose and poetry stop us in our tracks.

As I leave, I want to help in some tangible way. "Would you like me to write the thank you notes?" I inquire of Ed.

I can tell he's thinking, *What thank you notes?*

"You know, for all the flowers and food." Even as I say this, I realize this gesture is pathetic. Southern hospitality really won't help now. I gather up all the notes and tags, though, and as I write each note at home, I realize that writing helps me begin to deal with this loss. I don't know what else to do.

As Ed and I talked recently about these events, he said to me, "We hadn't had any tragedies as a family then."

"You mean, not counting all the church firings, having to move, having hardly any money, divorces, and academic job losses?" I tease him back.

"Right. They don't count. We didn't know what we didn't know," Ed summarizes.

Closing the Circle of Life and Death

The following summer, Ed and Gary climb Mt. Harvard in the Collegiate Range close to Buena Vista, Colorado, ascending from the north. Dianne had climbed this fourteener when she was eighteen; Ed and Dianne had planned to climb it together. Ed and Gary pitch their tent exactly where Dianne pitched hers, sleeping where she had slept. Ed must have ascertained this from Dianne before she died. As they reach the top, they watch mountain goats playing beneath them. They gather some of the goat hair, caught on the branches, to collect and keep. They sit in silence for a long while. Just in time to get off the mountain before dark, Ed and Gary release some of Dianne's ashes, which float down among the mountain goats and clouds. Ed keeps his promise, climbing the mountain with Dianne's spirit and physical remains. Later, he places a plaque tucked away in a high stone alcove on Pikes Peak, a mountain Dianne also climbed early in her adult years.

One of the circles of Dianne's life reaches completion. When they arrive back at the cabin, I can still see the awe of the heightened experience on their faces.

chapter three

The Divine Ensemble

Miami Beach, 2003

November finds me attending the National Communication Association meeting for the first time in years. Since I opened my psychology practice, leaving university life for good in 1988, I have not joined my previous colleagues at this conference, focusing instead on continuing education in psychology. Janice, a professor of communication at the University of Arkansas, encourages me to write for the ethnography division: "You can write for these people. Academic writing has changed dramatically since you left communication." Janice is a prolific writer, specializing in the Jungian analysis of popular films. This year she is also almost finished with her book which analyzes the relationships of women and men in the university; she uses Greek myths to delve into the relational intricacies of complicated mentoring arrangements. This will be her most personal academic writing so far. I have missed connecting with Janice and Tom at conventions. For my reentry into the professional world of communication studies, as I rejoin my colleagues from the seventies and eighties, I write a paper analyzing my interview with a Jungian analyst, David Hart, whom I'd met and come to know during his summers in Missoula. I explore convergences in analysis, psychotherapy, and communication theory.

Janice, Tom, and I enjoy an evening of fun and reconnection, eating shrimp scampi outside in Miami Beach, then shopping while modeling our matching black strappy sandals. The next night, Janice's student friend Stace tells me that Janice just cancelled an evening out with friends.

"What's wrong?" I ask Stace, hardly believing what he is telling me. Janice cherishes her far-flung professional friends, carefully setting up their social calendar for conferences to spend time with colleagues she and Tom know.

"She said she was too tired to go out. She's not feeling well, so she and Tom are in their room."

I go up quickly to their room, where I find Janice lying on the bed, eating trail mix. She wears jeans; her face looks pale. Tom stares at ESPN; I can see the worry on his face as he greets me. I sit by her on the bed. "I just couldn't go," she says. "I don't have the energy. I feel terrible about cancelling, but I just want to order room service, or not, and go to sleep." I hug her and promise to check on her the next morning. We talk on the phone before she leaves for the airport; "I'm so tired," Janice says in a small voice. "I want to get a good night's sleep, finish my book, and close out this semester."

"Take good care of yourself, Jannie," I reply. I'm her big sister, and I want to take care of her myself, but I can't. We all fly home, they to Arkansas, and I back to Missoula to my home, my husband, our cat, Lightfoot, and my psychotherapy practice.

December arrives. Janice and I collaborate on gifts for the family. We love getting our mother special gifts from Coldwater Creek or somewhere else fancier than she is used to. She sews most of her clothes; we delight in hearing her exclamations of surprise over the gifts we select. "You girls spoil me!" makes us smile when Mom thanks us. We draw names now, to simplify gift-giving a little.

Janice calls me in mid-December to exhort, with uncharacteristic exhaustion and asperity, "Can we *stop* doing stocking gifts now? They just add so much more detail to an already packed time." I agree, feeling my "note to self: *anxiety*" kick in, since Janice always treasured these childhood holiday rituals. Janice does not want to continue this carryover from childhood. She sounds spent. She wrote me a week or so before, telling me about her storm of tears when a colleague would not take no for an answer when she declined to chair another out-of-department dissertation. I emailed her an all-purpose script to just say no to professional requests, which she put in her book that week after circulating it to women friends.

Christmas, 2003

Janice calls us on Christmas morning, not too early. We always call each other to talk about our gifts, share what we're planning for dinner—to connect from two thousand miles away. Since Janice and don't have children, long ago we claimed the luxury of sleeping in. We call Ed in Colorado later, after he's recovered from an earlier rising with his daughter. Somewhere we are still the sisters and younger brother who rush out on Christmas morning to open our simple gifts, secure in our family circle. Any Christmas could be the one in Dallas, when Santa brought our first black-and-white TV, the kind on its own legs, with rabbit ears on top, far later than the other kids in the neighborhood. At Shalom, we display a framed black-and-white picture of the five of us with that new TV. In the picture Janice plays with a toy set of bells she could sound out on a keyboard, and Eddie (now a nonviolent man) holds his toy gun out to the photographer with a grin.

Christmas morning always evokes the time when Rick and I drove through the star-filled, quiet night from South Dakota, where we were teaching school and serving churches for a gap year in 1966, to the family's new home in Colorado Springs. Dad met me at the door holding a brown-and-white puppy with a red bow around its neck, as a joke, knowing I didn't like dogs. He wasn't prepared for me to fall in love with the puppy, but I immediately decided he'd be happy in our teacherage, the old school built in 1909, now housing two families of teachers. I cried when he had to return it to the neighbors, and my dad hugged me gently saying, "Joycie, I'm so sorry." Any Christmas could be the few precious times, in Fayetteville, Boulder, or Missoula, when Janice and I were together for the holidays.

Any Christmas could be the week in 1979 when Janice and Tom arrived to a solid week of below-zero temperatures in Missoula. During that long cold spell, Janice and I bundled up to walk to Freddy's, our friendly book and grocery store, in the University neighborhood. We enjoyed a cup of coffee and a treat, then set out through the deeply drifted snow back home. We walked mostly in silence for the five blocks as the snow leaked over our boots.

Wow, this is really cold, I thought. I didn't say anything, because I felt guilty about luring Janice out into the sub-zero, windy weather. She marched grimly home, uncomplaining. Images of Dr. Zhivago struggling to Lara's house came to mind as I fervently hoped Janice wasn't getting frostbite.

We trudged on. The wintry maples on University Drive formed a ghostly tunnel of black branches. I was thinking that we were a long way from Texas.

We opened the front door of the 1920s bungalow house, unwound our scarves and pulled off our down coats. Janice had borrowed one of mine, so she looked like the Michelin man. Her sexy black broad-brimmed felt hat, with a jaunty feather in the hat-band, was crusted with snow. Her long blonde hair crunched with ice as she pulled her hat off. She looked at me with about as much consternation as I had ever experienced from her and demanded, "Exactly how do you stand this?"

On this Christmas when we talk, I'm sitting in the dining room with my Aynsley china cup of coffee, brought out for the holidays. We've finished the gifts, the guys are cleaning up the paper, and I have a little time before starting dinner. Gary's son, Andy, and Andy's wife, Heather, are sharing the holiday with us.

Janice tells me, "I can't play the piano right. And last night, I couldn't get the songs from my brain to my hands, so the Christmas carols were terrible." I picture the spinet piano that our Grandmother Hocker gave us one Christmas in Vernon, Texas. Janice kept up her piano lessons, while I quickly dropped out. Janice relaxes after work by improvising on everything from

Willie Nelson's "Time of the Stranger" to Fannie J. Crosby's hymns, to Chopin études from her childhood book of simple tunes. "Bill and Heather came over," she continues, "and I didn't do my usual over-the-top Christmas Eve dinner where I try to make everything beautiful and delicious. We just pot-lucked it." This is not like Janice, I am thinking. "But I was having a good time, so I didn't care," she summarizes.

I envision Tom and Janice's gold-rimmed bone china inherited from Tom's Aunt Lillian, and the red Fostoria crystal just like mine, which she always uses during the holiday season. I imagine her missing notes, and not knowing what to make of her mistakes.

"But I'm worried," Janice continues, "and I'm sleeping all the time after not being able to sleep well for four years. Go figure. I must be more tired than I knew from writing the book and the end of the semester."

When they visited us for two weeks the previous summer, Janice was so sleep-deprived that I called one of my neurologist friends who saw her at the end of his day. He did a preliminary sleep analysis, recommending that she complete a full sleep study back in Fayetteville. She followed through back home, to inconclusive results. She called me in the fall to tell me how furious she was to be told that she was depressed and might consider Zoloft.

"I'm depressed because *I can't sleep*," Janice declared with exasperation. "I'm not *sad!* Of course I feel negative, helpless, and hopeless *because no one is taking me seriously!* Do *you* think I'm depressed?" I thought she sounded frustrated, baffled, and angry, not at all depressed. No one in my practice had ever spoken with this angry energy while depressed. People who are depressed usually sound flat, tired, and out of energy.

During our Christmas morning conversation, as Janice recounts her odd Christmas Eve, a conversation in Miami comes back to me in vivid detail.

"I lost track a few times in class," Janice recounted about her fall classes. "I just went away, and when I came back I couldn't tell whether the students knew I'd been gone or not. I think I'm losing my mind." We were sitting in the warm breeze in Miami Beach.

We pondered whether these times might have been some kind of wrinkle in time, or weird déjà-vu experience.

On the other end of the phone, I am not pondering. I am frightened. "You must promise me to see your neurologist, as soon as possible. Tell them it's an emergency."

"You don't mean *today*, do you?"

"No, but will you please call tomorrow and tell them you have to get in right away?" Janice promises to do this. I am concerned; I don't usually corner her like this.

I am more than concerned about what is happening in Janice's brain. My daughter-in-law and I walk later in the cold sunshine, and I share my fears with her that something is really wrong. I remain busy and distracted for the next few days until the kids return to Albuquerque. Janice reports that she has an appointment with her neurologist.

On January 3, 2004, Janice's fifty-fifth birthday, I send her May Sarton's poem "New Year's Resolve" which includes the lines, *"Let silence in like a cat / Who has sat at my door . . ."* Janice emails me about her spontaneous tears of recognition evoked by the poem. "I am going to adopt this as my theme for the year," she writes. Knowing that she is exhausted, she recognizes that letting in silence, which would sleep on her bed and ask little of her, seems just right. We both know she is also thinking of Mollie, her formerly orphaned cat, who showed up at Tom and Janice's door a few years back and would not be dissuaded from taking up residence in her chosen household. Although Mollie disturbs Janice's fragile sleep when she sleeps on her bed, she would deny Mollie nothing.

Janice has been dealing with back pain and insomnia for more than three years, so much so that I had urged her, in the fall, to request a medical leave. Janice took my suggestion about a leave seriously, but she wanted to finish her book first. Her spring semester was already planned, she looked forward to teaching a seminar on using myths in rhetorical criticism of films, the area of most of her academic writing. We often discucs Jungian books and ideas, Janice analyzing popular films while I analyze dreams and individual lives.

Another email from Janice arrives: "No, you didn't push too much about my seeing a doctor. I will be really glad to find out what's going on and why I want to sleep all the time." The doctors speculate before tests that maybe she has an inner ear infection, which would account for her nausea.

January 5, 2004

Listening to clients during the day presents a challenge, since I am worried and distracted; Janice is undergoing diagnostic tests today. Grabbing my coat and keys, I leave my case notes unwritten to hurry home to receive Tom's promised call. In the alley behind my downtown building, wind whips past the kids smoking out back and blasts me when I shortcut through Butterfly Herbs' back door, heading for my car. I am friendly with the people who work at this coffee shop close to my office, since I often take a detour through it on my way to and from work. I don't turn on NPR as I drive south toward home, feeling as frozen and bleak as the Missoula weather. Entering through the garage door, I dump my briefcase and heavy purple coat on the kitchen table, unwinding the knit scarf that did not keep me warm on the drive home. Gary looks grave and contained. "I'm so glad you're home, hon, we have to call Tom. I've been waiting for you to get here." Gary places the call and hands the phone to me.

Tom answers quickly. "Hi, Tom," I say, "What can you tell me?"

"Not good," Tom replies. "Multiple lesions of the frontal lobe, a mass on her lower spine, spots on her lungs." Tom goes into more detail, but my brain turns his speech into noise and he seems to be speaking from far away. I am trying to think what *lesions* are. Maybe not as bad as tumors, I frantically tell myself.

"Can Janice come to the phone?" I ask. I want to hear her voice, which reflects fear and fatigue when she takes the phone and weakly says, "I guess it's pretty bad." She can't keep talking for now. This makes sense; still I long to talk this through with Janice, the way we always do. Not this time. Gary takes the phone and gathers details from Tom. Suddenly I am flattened on the hardwood of the dining room floor, wailing, keening, with no memory of falling. Gary hangs up the phone, promising to call back the next day, and gets down on the floor with me, holding me, covering my body with his. He stays quiet as my downward descending cries of "Nooooooo!" fill the room. Lightfoot stretches out alongside us.

I stay on my hands and knees for a long while, head hanging down, before I stand up with Gary's help. I grab onto the kitchen counter where the phone is, still wailing, "No, no, no!!" as though my words can change the awful message. My eyes fall on the page on the daily tear-off calendar: January 5. That day displays a quote from Joanna Macy, which consoles, "The heart that breaks open can contain the whole universe." But all I want is to *shut out* the world, my present world. I have always known this dire news, if it ever came to me, would be my worst fear realized. Somewhere in my psyche, I have always dreaded that my beloved sister might be stricken ill, ever since the day Dad put my tiny blonde sister on a pillow on my lap in Charlotte, North Carolina. In the parsonage, he handed her over carefully. "Don't drop her, Joycie," he cautioned.

"I will *never* let anything happen to her," I vowed with three-year-old vehemence. I have always declared that I could handle anything in my life as long as Janice and I could be together. We have called each other countless times, beginning, "I really need to talk to you." Never like this. Through the evening, Gary and I obsessively rehearse every detail that brought this call.

"I thought we might escape this. I hoped it was an inner-ear infection," I plead with the universe.

"I know, hon," Gary confirms. "This is very bad."

I don't want to hear Gary say "This is very bad." I want him to offer some hope.

"When did Tom say they would go to the oncologist? Or will they—can you operate on lesions?" I am not able to take it all in. I hope for operation magic. We've been waiting for a diagnosis, but *not this one*.

My eyes focus on the Swarovski star, still hanging over the angel in the crèche. Each year I hang the crystal star above the manger scene. I love the way the rays of candlelight refract through it. The Christmas tree is down, but we keep the crèche in its lighted alcove until Epiphany. Today is Epiphany.

The next day, after almost no sleep, I keep my appointment with Gina, my young wise hairdresser. Talking with her, I fret about whether to go to Cape Cod as scheduled in a few days to celebrate Gary's father's eightieth birthday. I know Gary wants me to go; picturing the somewhat fragmented family scene, I want to be supportive. Yet my heart yearns toward Arkansas.

"I don't know why you are even still thinking about going to Cape Cod," Gina flatly states. She can be blunt.

"Well, Gary is close to his father. The grown children have put together a surprise visit, a scrapbook, and have it all planned for us to burst in before dinner. I don't much like his stepmother, but I think I should go, to be part of the family."

"I'd be on the plane to Fayetteville by now," says Gina, unimpressed. I recognize the truth of her words. I cancel my flight to Cape Cod, and make emergency flight arrangements to Arkansas on Delta, which still has a plan for medical emergencies.

At my psychology consultation group later that day, one of my colleagues, seeing my stricken face, asks, "What's wrong?"

"My sister has brain cancer," I choke out. I didn't want to cry, to take up too much time in the group. "And I don't know what to do. I just don't know what to do," I repeat, giving in to weeping. These are therapists, but still I don't want to presume on their time.

I have never before experienced knowing something is disastrously wrong, and I can't think of anything to make it more right. They sit with me in silence. A woman asks, "Do you call her Sissy?" Why am I enraged at her question? She is Southern and she is trying to be kind.

"No. Her name is Janice."

"But what's your pet name for her?"

"I don't have one." I'm not willing to say that I call her Jannie. My name for her seems private.

My colleague is attempting to soften a hard situation, but nothing can change my anxiety and sorrow at this point. I don't want my feelings to be soothed. Instead, surprising to me, I feel rage. I'm directing my rage at my colleague, but fortunately keep my feelings to myself. I don't want to make this disaster sentimental. I feel shaky, ungrounded, and desperate.

South to Arkansas

I walk the long moving sidewalks of the Minneapolis airport, feeling caught in the liminal space of nothing and nowhere that I want to be. The sidewalks carry me along anyway. I'm hungry but can't imagine eating, suspended, numb, and empty.

When I arrive in Fayetteville, Stace gives me a big hug as he picks me up at the airport. He will perform his compassionate transportation service many times for our family. He turned around from a road trip to Missouri when Tom called to ask if he could pick me up. I feel relieved to see Janice's teaching assistant, the man who told me she was sick in Miami. He takes me directly to the Northwest Arkansas Regional Hospital. Tom, haggard from spending the night there where Janice is undergoing tests, also hugs me, and Janice clings to me as I lean over her bed. After a while, I go back to their house alone since Tom wants to stay with Janice. I partially unpack in the main floor bedroom across from Janice's study. Somehow I don't want to go downstairs where I usually stay, where I would feel more alone. Mollie, Janice's cat, bounces in and settles in my suitcase on unpacked clothes. I am glad for her company as we both go to sleep.

The next morning, back at the hospital, we consult with Dr. Sarah, her compassionate general practitioner, who asks if there is anything she can do. No tests will take place over the weekend. I can only think of one thing: "Get Janice out of here."

"I'll work on it," Sarah says. Soon she comes back with the orders discharging Janice. "Is there anything else you can think of that I can do?" She's already set up a consultation with an oncologist on Monday. I can tell that Sarah wants to help. She looks hopeless.

Janice wants to go home. Tom, fraught with anxiety, will sleep better in the comfort of their home. When we realize that no tests or treatment will happen over the weekend, we decide to break free of the cold and uncomfortable hospital environment. Packing up Janice's few clothes and toiletries, we feel an odd kind of celebration, happy to be going home, as though this will make things better. I want to make something, anything, better for Janice. We settle Janice into her small writing study, making up a bed on her comfortable white down-filled couch, tucking a red, turquoise and gold fleece afghan over her. The bare trees filter the view to the west, over the hills of Fayetteville. Janice wants to face the hall, not the view, saying, "I'll feel less lonely that way." Privately, I vow not to let Janice feel lonely, even though I know I do not have that power. Mollie does, though. She sleeps on Janice's stomach or snuggled beside her on top of the fleece cover. I move in downstairs, so Tom can sleep across the hall from Janice when he needs to. The bedroom, living room and downstairs provide a view to the west. The sky shades from pink and lavender to indigo. Gary and I have stayed here many times before. Family pictures hang on the wall, and comfortable bedding and pillows cover the bed.

I begin notifying local friends who have offered to help with food or anything else Janice needs. Their friend Jean steps in to organize meals, transportation and shopping, telling me that more friends want to help than we have need for. I send an email to friends around the country, explaining that Janice has cancer of the brain, that we hope radiation will restore her brilliant mental clarity—for a while. Imagining these friends opening their email to this devastating news connects me to a network of people who love her. I ask them to write rather than call. Her friends and colleagues can barely comprehend that Janice cannot read their responses or take their calls. Many recently saw her in Miami at the conference. Tom and I read some of their letters to her. Friends write encouraging notes; former students catch her up on their lives, though we don't read all these letters to Janice because she can't make sense of what they write, and the effort exhausts her. Janice mentored dozens of students, and many of them want to tell her about their recent lives and adventures. She feels guilty that she cannot communicate by email to the many friends who write her. I save all the letters, in case she can.

Janice dictates a note to Gale, her closest friend, in California. Janice tells Gale through Tom, "I'm not doing too well. I'm pretty tired most of the time, and have all kinds of trouble remembering things—even the simplest of things. Knowing me, you can well imagine how incredibly frustrating that has been. Joyce has set up two systems, one for those who will drive me to radiation and another to bring food over so that Tom doesn't kill both of us trying to cook."

Mnemosyne and Lemosyne, Two Sisters I Need Now

We live in the realm of the mythic twin sisters of remembering and forgetting. Janice, Tom, and I, along with her doctors, join in the fight against forgetting. Janice cannot remember her appointments; worse, she knows she is forgetting. She wrinkles her forehead with the effort to remember.

I am worn out with answering Janice's questions. She keeps trying, but can't understand how to choose her clothes, what day it is, and the difference between vitamins and medication. Noticing that Janice wears workout clothes, T-shirts, and sweatpants, I move her professional clothing downstairs to the guest room where I now sleep, so she is less confused about what to put on. I like seeing and touching her beautiful clothes, hanging now at one end of the long closet. Her sandalwood smell lingers. We shared a closet during our childhood and adolescent years; these clothes bring some small comfort. I touch them and take them out to look at a jacket our mother made, or a short black skirt I have seen her wear many times.

I am afraid as I watch Janice struggle against losing words, forgetting routines, losing track of what is happening. This professor and incisive writer finished her book several days before Christmas. Her query letter file shows on her computer desktop; she placed sticky notes in a thick book of potential agents, and her manuscript sits by itself on a clean desk. Over her desk hangs a poster of a saucy blonde cowgirl standing on a trick pony, twirling a rope. Janice likes country music and identifies with spunky women of the American West. She despaired of the effort to teach me country swing dancing. She and Tom wrote a book on the myths of the American frontier as they reappeared in movies set in space. Over her bed hangs a calligraphy piece I gave her some years ago, "Happiness Makes Up in Height for What It Lacks in Length," the title of a favorite Frost poem.

For the second time in my life, I teach my little sister how to wash her face, choose her clothes, brush her teeth, and eat her fruits and vegetables. I fix attractive little snacks, as though the right nutrition might help. Fighting the monster of forgetting, I put numbers on the jars on the bathroom counter, (1) face cleanser, (2) toner, (3) moisturizer, (4) toothpaste, and (5) contact lens solution. The idea is that Janice should go through her routine in order. We practice. She thinks this is a great idea.

I pretend to be a TV personality as I perkily ask, "How can tell you tell the difference between (1) cleanser and (4) toothpaste?"

Janice points to the cleanser and proclaims, "You can't eat it!" The next day I remove (5) contact lens solution, because it's too hard for Janice to wear her contacts, and, after one awful attempt when I removed them, I put them aside. Tom or I help her go through her self-care routine. She is sleeping at night in their upstairs suite, but rests in her study all day. She can come to the table to eat.

We practice how to remember appointments on the calendar. Tom and I write all appointments on a big calendar in the kitchen. "See, Jannie, everything you need to know is written down here."

"Great!" Janice responds. "This will make it easier for me." Janice retains her desire to appreciate anything that people do for her. She never checks the big calendar. I know with my gut that this memory lesson will ultimately fail.

I write in my journal:

January 8, 2004, my room in Janice's house:
What my sister is teaching me:
That there is no end to love
That being with someone is sometimes all I can do
That it's good to sit down and rest
That I can bear sorrow—I will not die from feeling grief,
although I fear that I will.

We are each born with an essence. With Janice, it's kindness. She inquires hopefully whether I've gotten some work done, and tells me she is sorry I have to do so much for her. I am currently scheduled to lead my annual winter woman's retreat, this year in Costa Rica, on the southern tip of the Osa Peninsula. I have left all my materials for preparation home in Missoula—CDs from which I make playlists of songs, books of poetry, articles and handouts—though I bring my laptop to Arkansas. I have not yet realized that the decision about whether to cancel the retreat will approach so quickly. My assistant at work helps me cancel client appointments. My friend Sally offers to help me lead the retreat, or even to lead it. I don't yet know whether I will go to Costa Rica or stay here in Fayetteville. My usual life seems very far away; I live here with Janice.

When Janice continues to worry about my not getting to my work, I ask her to imagine how she would want to do things for me if I were as sick as she is. I'm counting on Janice's empathy and imagination to relieve some of the concern she feels for me. She nods gently, "Yes, I would want to."

Tom, Janice, her nurse friend, Paula, and I go to the oncology appointment on Monday. Paula serves as the medical translator for us. Janice's oncologist, a young man with a blithe manner, reassures Janice and the rest of us in his office, "I expect to see you next fall when you go back to teaching." He sets up a course of radiation and chemotherapy. I note with alarm the dubious expression on Paula's face. I hold Janice in my arms in the back seat on our way home. She cries, saying "If I make it through this, I'm *not* going back to teaching! I'm going to stay home and write. I have at least one more book in me." We do not know how much or how little time to expect to hold Janice. Her primary doctor Sarah calls us, having spoken with the oncologist after his visit. She tells us that a cluster of doctors in the hall conferred with each other on the day we took Janice home from the hospital, admitting that they had never seen a worse brain scan. This explains the look on Sarah's face when we left the hospital.

I call my parents at their winter home in Grand Junction, from the comfortable suite downstairs, sitting in a rocking chair that Janice acquired when she was a professor in Boulder. Colleagues may not have known we were sisters, given our then-different last names. Janice has made the guest room beautiful, with a cream-colored duvet, numerous pillows, and red-and-cream-plaid pillowcases. Large colorful Southwestern pots sit in the corners. Down here I feel slightly separated from the drama unfolding upstairs, surprised that I am able to fall in bed and sleep at night.

"Janice is probably not going to survive this illness," I tell Mom and Dad, reporting everything we've learned so far. My parents remain silent for a while.

"I'm sorry, Joycie," Dad says. He knows how hard it is for me to make this call.

"Should I call Ed?" I offer.

"No, we'll do that."

"I'm so incredibly sorry that I need to tell you this," I say, with a strong sense that I am failing everyone. I want to sob to my parents for comfort, yet I know we all need the same comfort.

"We appreciate everything you are doing," Dad says. He speaks with the royal we for the two of them. "Let us know when we can come."

At the end of the call, I sit in the corner of my room in the daylight basement and cry. The lavender twilight turns gray as I watch the bare trees and the western sky.

A line in Gary's email, after I tell him about this call, reads, "How many times can our hearts break?" I have no idea, yet, but this call to my parents again brings me to my knees in tears, as I rest my arms on the bed and cry. I am anxious and scared, as though I have done something wrong. I should not have caused my parents such pain, I tell myself. At the same time I find myself holding on to my feelings so I can try to be a calming presence, especially since Tom is coping by making lists of what to do and reading them to Janice, who cannot follow their sequence.

"OK, so tomorrow at 2:30 we have to get you set up for radiation. Then we'll stop by the store and get some food, then by 4:00 we can get you a nap . . ." Tom rehearses the day to come.

"My radiation starts tomorrow?" Janice asks.

"No, we'll just get you set up for it," Tom clarifies. "The actual radiation starts Friday."

"What is today?" Janice asks in a soft voice.

I ask Tom to come into the living room with me. "Tom, the lists help you organize in this awful time, but they are confusing Janice, I think." I am hoping he will not take offense. "She is trying to memorize what's coming up, and she can't," I explain. "I think it might be better for you and me to confer, but just tell Janice what to expect in time for her to get ready."

Tom's face crumples. "I see that. I guess it's for me." He takes a deep breath. "I can change this," he promises; he does.

That night Janice lies on the forest green couch in their living room. A curved walnut-and-cherry desk that Gary made backs up to the couch. Janice likes to grade her papers there, looking out at the peaceful view of the hills and trees. The five-foot-tall walnut mirror with dentil-carved molding that he also crafted reflects the light of a single vanilla-scented candle on the red pressed-glass plate on the coffee table. We listen to Bach, the Goldberg variations. Bach helps me think clearly when I feel muddled; I wish this precise harmony would heal her the way it unscrambles me. Janice dozes off, her head in my lap. Tom passes me his handkerchief. I stroke her head, longing for supernatural healing powers.

Soon I take her to the beauty salon, where her kind stylist cuts off her long hair, to lessen the shock when Janice loses her hair to chemotherapy treatments. When I urge the stylist to put highlights in Janice's short hair, she looks at me with compassion and says, "Let's do that later." I'm trying to make everything perfect just as everything is falling apart.

Janice is delighted with the new short cut. She looks luminous. She declares, "When I get better, I'm going to keep my hair short like this. All that time messing with my long hair!"

"You can wear it any way you want to," I assure her.

We go to a shop and pick out a wig. Janice asks what this is for.

"You are going to lose your hair because of the treatments, sweetheart. This is in case you want to dress up and have hair for a while."

"I'm going to lose my *new haircut*?" Janice can't comprehend this.

"I'm so sorry, but yes."

"Oh, I didn't know that." Janice never wears the wig.

Tom and I try to manage everything. Her friends Jean and Joel set up a meal and transportation schedule. Jean is practical and helpful; she and Joel, Tom and Janice, and other friends spend each Thanksgiving together. Janice is famous for her enchanted broccoli forest, which she makes with mashed potatoes and broccoli florets as trees, posting tiny signs on toothpicks which point out fairy-tale locations, like "this way to the magic castle," in a winding path through the potatoes. Jean tells me how they have all come to anticipate what mythic journey Janice will lead the guests through each year. Joel is quiet, kind, and calming. I obsess about trying to find someone to go pick up the eyelid primer Janice is running out of, because Janice wants it. She is still applying makeup each day; her appearance matters to her. Jean gently reminds me that any one of a dozen people would love to perform this small service; she organizes the people who want to help, freeing me to be with Janice. We receive welcome and wonderful evening meals—meatloaf and potatoes, fried chicken, hamburger and macaroni casseroles, with more banana cream pie, chocolate cake, and bread pudding than all of us can eat.

I lose perspective about what actually is most important, placing appointments, laundry, vitamins, and emails in the same category as making snacks and reading to and talking with Janice. I feel calmly crazed. From Missoula, Gary calls me in my comfortable bedroom downstairs. I look out over the winter-bare trees at the pink and purple twilight, taking in the framed pictures of all of us in the 1980s; one shows us wearing our "Big Hawk Seven" T-shirts, commemorating a grueling backpack trip with our step-children. That's the trip when Janice and I huddled in a small tent to escape the mosquitoes. I remember Janice looking intently at me, with her bug-bitten, splotched face, saying, "Do you think we're being punished for the sin of divorce?"

Downstairs seems like my apartment where I live now. I sleep well here, where all is quiet and my sister is upstairs. When I do wake up in the night, I wander around the moonlit house, a night-time ghost, touching the furniture Gary made, straightening the woven throws Janice and Tom picked out in Santa Fe, picking yellow leaves off plants. I look out the living room window over the trees to the far distance. I lie on Janice's couch under the fleece throw. Sometimes I kneel on the small ash meditation bench Gary made for Janice and pray. While I normally don't believe that God specifically intervenes in human events, I revert to earlier theology and plead with God to help my sister since I cannot help her. I ask for wisdom and courage before going back downstairs to sleep.

When Gary asks me if, when I talk with him on the phone, I could be less official sounding, I snap at him. "I can't just drop into an intimate tone with you when I am doing so much organizing." I can hear my craziness through my manic, pressured speech. "I'm doing the best I can. I can't do anything more!" I insist. I hate feeling far from Gary; what he is asking for seems reasonable and yet, at the same time, I feel it as criticism.

Janice wants me to read the last chapter of her book aloud to her. She is proud of it. I scoot the desk chair close to her couch, her manuscript in my hands. Mollie settles on Janice's stomach while Janice strokes Mollie's gray fur. Earlier in her career, Janice wrote that she had for many years identified with Athena, daughter of Zeus, who sprang fully formed from Zeus's forehead, making her a true daughter of the patriarchy. Athena's symbol is an owl. Janice described herself as "formerly a brainchild," but no longer a daughter of the academic "daddies" she tried to please and fit in with earlier in her career.

An owl perches on a branch right outside the sliding doors. I point it out to Janice, and she nods, not seeming surprised.

Trying to keep my voice steady, I read her story relating a transcendent dream she included a few pages before the end of the book. In the dream she recounts that she is bored by speakers at an academic convention who aren't really saying anything; then she flies out of the building, feeling free and ecstatic. As she flies above the convention hall, she sees a small blonde girl running below with her arms held up. She feels like Janice's child. Janice flies down to pick up this precious child, knowing that she will hold her to her breast forever, even though it's hard to fly this way. She ends the dream, and her book, "In my family all the girls' names start with 'J.' My parents thought these 'J' names sounded strong. My mother is Jean, my sister is Joyce, and I am Janice. This little one will fit right in. I think I will name her 'Joy.'"

"Oh," she breathes as she smiles. "That's wonderful." Janice appears not to know I've read her own dream. She eats her snack, and I help her sip her mint tea. I carry her manuscript upstairs, placing it in my suitcase, knowing the whole book is backed up on her computer.

Our mom picks up the theme of memory. From Grand Junction, she emails, "We would like to do something as a gift for you, Jannie." Mom knows that Janice is having trouble remembering things; she wants to do some of the remembering for her. She writes that she and our dad will talk about some of their favorite memories, "when you became a Hocker." Reading our mother's email, I am grateful that she will take on this memory project. As a family, we are partly defined by our memories. Remembering that Janice and I memorized the 1938 TCU football lineup and the verses to many of the old camp songs, I know that for our mother, forgetting seems impossible, so she will help her daughter.

Mom outlined sixteen episodes, writing intricate details from her memory for precise sensate recollections. Tom and I read them to Janice—we complete five readings. Mom writes, "By the time you were in Mrs. Todd's third grade class in Vernon, you were on your way. She wrote on one of your papers, 'Have you considered being a writer? You really have the knack for it.' Your years as a child holed up in your chest of drawers (you took the drawers out to read your favorite Golden books uninterrupted) really paid off."

Mom is a fine, careful writer. Janice acknowledged her more than once as her first writing teacher. Our mother is experiencing pain and has been for some months— physically with undiagnosed abdominal pain, and emotionally as her daughter suffers. Undoubtedly, as she writes her memories for Janice, she comforts herself as well.

As I read this vignette to Janice, I remember carrying a plate of supper to her when she was little. "Janice can't come to supper," I explained more than once. "She's in the chest of drawers." I recognized passion when I saw it. I see Mrs. Todd's note on one of Janice's papers: "I've run out of ways to say excellent, superb. I know I'll be reading your books when you grow up."

In her second vignette, my mom writes, "In the spring of 1952, I learned that a downtown department store (in Charlotte, North Carolina) was sponsoring a children's style show. All the dresses had to be made by the mothers. Your dress, Janice, was a traditional one of that time: small brown-checked tissue gingham with a full, short skirt and little puff sleeves. But it was a perfect foil for the frilly, fussy white organdy pinafore, which showed off your chubby little legs and blonde curls. When it came your turn to model, you balked, and your big sister held your hand and walked with you. You were the darling of the show!'"

Our parents and brother want to come to Arkansas from Colorado. Still feeling that I am waiting for some time when Janice is feeling better, I haven't given them clearance to come. I think we have months to be with Janice. Looking back, I realize that I liked being special, and I still thought I could manage the unfolding medical chaos. Ed warns me clearly and gently on the phone, "She may not get better." His words painfully remind me of how I put off coming to see Dianne last year. "We would like to come," he says. I feel guilty as I keep barring the gate for a while longer. I don't know how Tom and I will manage more people in the house, yet these are our family. I think maybe I'm still trying to fix everything before they come, which puts me squarely in the realm of denial. Am I living out my vow as a three-and-a-half-year-old big sister, "I will never let anything happen to her?"

Feeling torn, I decide to go to Costa Rica to lead my retreat. I prepare in a haphazard fashion, relying mainly on a book of poems that Gale, Janice's best friend in California, gave her for Christmas. I've led these and other retreats for thirty years. Preparing binders for each participant, with a photo and theme on the cover, is part of my routine. I like to print out all the poems, songs, and exercises I plan to use on different colors of paper for their use. I tell myself this degree of advanced preparation spares me the chore while I'm in Belize, Honduras, Mexico, Costa Rica, or Montana, so I can devote myself to what unfolds during each morning of psychological discussion. I tell myself this—and I also know that I feel pride in my careful preparation. It's part of my carefully constructed persona.

This year, I'm winging it, trusting that evocative themes and questions will come to me. Gary assures me that I could get on the plane with no preparation and lead skillfully and well. Agreeing, I don't believe this is true. I want to share ideas from several of Janice's chapters with the women. When I tell her my plans, she wonders if they will be interested. My psyche and heart are so tied to Janice's life and her coming death that I assume others will be interested in her work, but I don't really care. I cannot imagine embarking on this Costa Rica retreat without my dear sister's writing. Janice assures me that she wants me to stick to my plans. Remembering the one retreat she attended with me, Janice wants me to go.

Janice joined my women's retreat in 1995, when we journeyed to Belize. Later, I will read in her journal that she felt a presence say to her, on the beach in Belize, *Let it go, my child, let it all go.* I remember the look of pure joy on her face as we danced with Garifuna women in Belize, the men and women, originally from West Africa, singing call and response songs. We women formed a line of dancers under the full moon on the beach, with a bonfire at edge of the water. The drums and voices sounded out over the Caribbean.

Janice was in the middle of her midlife transformation on that retreat. In one of her morning poems, she wrote, "My angels have died. Maybe they are composting." She imagined that animus figures from the first half of her life, whom she called "the daddies," were now dead and transforming into other psychic material. We met with Rosita Arvigo, an apprentice to a Mayan healer. When Rosita read to our group from her dream journal, explaining what the dreams meant in the Mayan world, Janice grabbed her notebook. Ever the ethnographer, she quickly wrote notes detailing the two dream systems, Mayan and Jungian, while I led the group. She gave me a big smile, and I knew we would delve this work. We planned to write about dreams from the perspective of the two mythic systems. In her book, she has written about a woman's own Self animating her life, rather than projecting on men as animating figures.

From California, Gale announces that she is coming to Fayetteville, especially when I tell her that I am going to Costa Rica for ten days. Gale knows that Janice needs her. She comes to Fayetteville after I leave, informing Tom, "I'll stay in a hotel if I have to, but I need to see Janice." Tom welcomes her visit and in days to come relies on her good sense and her long love for Janice and for him as well. Tom and I ask my parents and Ed to travel when they can arrange the flight. Ed accompanies our parents, driving to Grand Junction, mitigating the difficult plane trip for people of their age. They will all arrive to help and visit right after I leave. I plan to fly to Montana, pack my tropical clothes, and get back on the plane.

Before I leave Fayetteville, I ask Janice if she is afraid.

"Sometimes, but mostly not," she replies.

Her answer surprises me. I don't know what else to ask.

We will have time for conversations about her dying, I assume. I plan to return to Fayetteville when I return in two weeks.

I don't know yet that people do not usually talk about their actual death. The afternoon before I leave, the winter sun slants through the sliding doors of Janice's writing study, illuminating her blonde hair and the red and turquoise of the Navajo fleece blanket covering her. Mollie snuggles on Janice.

She asks me, "Would you take my journals?" She looks directly into my eyes.

"When?" I ask. Does she mean now?

"Oh, whenever you want to." I assure her that of course I will.

"They are all right there," she says, pointing to her closet in the study. I look and see all the spiral notebooks and binders. My younger sister is way ahead of me. Janice and I have both kept detailed journals for many years, especially since we've been in analysis with Anne. I know without her saying so that she does not want anyone else to read her journals. Janice also knows I serve as the family archivist.

Once, looking through an early scrapbook, she said, "That's my fourth-grade report card! How did you get it?" I didn't know; I've been collecting family pictures and documents since I was in grade school. I know now she is not asking me to do anything public with her journals, though we don't discuss this. She trusts me to do whatever I know should be done with them. She knows that I will prize her privacy.

I ask her if I can take something of hers to Costa Rica. Janice looks at me sweetly. "You can take anything you want to." I pick out a pair of sparkly, dangly black jet earrings. I wonder if this is all right, taking something of hers.

"Will you be hard to find?" Janice asks.

"No, you can reach me by phone." I wish I had read the nuances of this conversation clearly, but I did not.

In Costa Rica, I meet my co-leader Gayle, from Oklahoma City, at our favorite hotel in San José. We greet the retreat participants and make the adventurous trip to the Osa Peninsula—first boarding a small plane in San José to a banana plantation airstrip, then traveling in two battered minivans through the plantation and old United Fruit Company villages, and finally piling in an open boat down the Sierpe River for a wild slamming boat ride across the ocean headland. We arrive to the beauty of the resort we have stayed in several times before. They greet us saying, "Welcome to Paradise," and while I know they say this to every guest, I think, *Yes, this is Paradise.*

I sink into the care, fresh fruit, and seafood provided by the resort staff, while feeling guilty relief at being, for a while, away from death. At night I sit on the balcony high above Drake Bay and gaze at the Southern Cross, the stars and planets vivid in the dark night sky. In the mornings, we women share dreams and ponder the questions of our lives right now. I have chosen the four elements to guide our discussion, around the theme of "Deep Peace."

"How can we live out the fire of our passion? How can we welcome emotion as water, flowing through our bodies? Where might our feelings be dammed up and stagnant?" I ask the participants, and myself. Our morning ritual of sharing dreams, journal writing, and responding to songs and poetry feels deeply healing to me. The participants bond with each other, and we become close.

I invite anyone who wants to join me for several optional afternoons as I read from Janice's book. She becomes part of the retreat in this way. I tell them that Janice wondered if anyone would be interested in what she has written; they shake their heads incredulously. Many of them are or have been women in academia, the group about which Janice has written.

Someone takes a picture of me asleep in the hammock on our deck. I relax into the tropical weather that loosens my anxiety and sorrow. Having been raised in Texas, the warm, moist air feels like home. The women treat me with tenderness. The arduous hike up stone steps cut into the hillside presents me a welcome physical challenge. On the steps, inhaling so as not to lose my breath, I slow down and climb, thinking nothing.

Our group goes by boat to Rio Claro, a cool clear river flowing out of the jungle of Corcovado National Park. As the rest of the women swim up the river, through floating fallen flowers, I lie on my back in the sand right where the river flows into the ocean. Tension drains from my body as the river flows around me and the sand shifts under me; I realize I can do nothing to change the flow of Janice's life. I lie in the sun and surrender.

In my journal I write, "I want to write in a memoir style." I feel inspired by Janice's arc toward more personal writing in her book. I can track this change through the book, from rhetorical and qualitative analysis to a personal storytelling style, still informed by myth, but alive with her own lived experience of being a woman in academia. I know that my time of writing social science in a purely academic style is over. Janice has invited me into a new way of writing; I feel the old academic order shifting, like the sands under me at Rio Claro.

When I reach San Jose after the retreat, anxiously calling Gary, he tells me that I should hurry home. The medical situation has worsened quickly in the last week. I call Janice from the lobby of the hotel in San Jose. I can hear her breathing as she holds the phone.

"I am so sorry I have been out of contact, Janice, I am so sorry." Life swirls around me in the hotel lobby. She does not speak, but I hear her breathing.

"Do you know how much I love you, Jannie?" I entreat.

"Oh, yes," she says. These will be her last words to me. I fly home.

Our mother writes more memories, but Tom tells Mom that Janice can no longer understand. The radiation treatment has done nothing but terrify her each time the technicians bolted the mask over her head. The tumors have not shrunk. Gale, with her long love for Janice and with Tom's trust, stopped the one chemotherapy treatment before midway, registering Janice's extreme anxiety, calling the nurse and saying, "This cannot go on." The ill-advised chemotherapy treatment seems to have taken away Janice's fragile physical and mental reserves. After I fly to Missoula, Gary and I fly to Arkansas. My clients know I have a family emergency, and my assistant helps me shut down my practice for now.

February, 2004: Fayetteville Vigil

My parents and Ed, on a quick turnaround from their earlier trip, return to Fayetteville from Colorado. Gary and I arrive on the same day as they do, on February 8. Stace brings us all back to the house in two shifts. We all thought, because the oncologist told us so, that we had more time. This must be the cry of all who lose a beloved other to death quickly. As we enter together—our parents and brother, Gary and I—Janice lies in her writing room in a hospital bed. Tom has asked for hospice assistance, which he and Gale sorely needed in the last few days. An IV delivers morphine, but no nutrition; the time for that has passed. The white down couch she lay on before is shoved in front of the bookshelves. She faces away from the winter view, the birds and the owl that has remained perched on a low branch outside her sliding glass door. She flutters a little, trying to reach out, when she hears our voices, but she is gone to us. I can tell her hearing still functions, because she responds to sound.

"That is *not* Janice," Mom tells me, in the living room, shocked at Janice's appearance. I want to say, *Yes, it is, she is still there*, but I refrain. Mom looks stunned and vacant. We all feel disoriented and traumatized by Janice's rapid decline, her loss of hair, her inability to speak or respond. Tom warned me on the phone in Costa Rica, but nothing could prepare me for seeing my frail sister who seems to be in a coma. I sit by her bed, talking with her and holding her hand, while all settle in. If I talk with her she will recognize me, I think.

Friends weave a net of care and practical help. Gale, who cancelled her trip back home to California to remain in Fayetteville, calls us all the "Divine Ensemble," as we play our parts in the chamber music of love and caring. Paula interprets medical information. Ed and Gary go outside to build a rock retaining wall in the backyard when they need to escape life inside. They call it "Jannie's wall." The backyard slopes down; Tom told them soil erodes down the yard from where Janice has built a small garden. Janice loves this garden, planting flowers that she has been told might be deer-resistant. Gary tells me, "It's a symbol of retaining life instead of letting it wash away." He and Ed work mostly in silence, close to the black oak forest behind Janice and Tom's house. Ed and Gary shore up what they can; Ed's masonry skills come in handy. They feel close to each other. Gary tells me, "I know he is losing his sister." They also build their brother-in-law relationship with each other, silently. They must think about their walk up Willow Creek when Ed confessed he didn't know how to attend Dianne's dying. They must remember the climb up Mt. Harvard when they wafted Dianne's ashes in the late afternoon sun, while the mountain goats watched. With an excess of pent-up energy, Gary attacks the vines that twine around the oak trees. A few days later he is miserable with poison ivy and must seek a soothing lotion to help him stand the pain and itching. When they arrive inside, I gain strength from these good, dear men who have been together before in the rituals of death.

Gale meditates in Janice's room early each morning. A wise old woman from the country, a dedicated hospice volunteer, sits silently in Janice's room. She coaches us to talk with Janice, she watches out for pain, notifying the nurse when she doesn't like what she sees or hears. We wonder about increasing the morphine because we are worried about pain control. The hospice nurse gathers us in the living room to talk about this idea. She asks if we have told Janice everything we need to. "I don't see signs of pain," she firmly asserts. "We are controlling Janice's pain." Is it *our* pain we are not controlling? She continues, "This is *her* death. You can't know what she is working on, or processing." We listen carefully. "I think you should let this death take its own course." So we do.

I sit by Janice, holding her hand and stroking her head, sometimes moistening her lips. As I talk to her, I tell her what we are all doing and that we love her. She is unconscious now, with a morphine drip. I tell her stories about camping, about our imaginary boat on Spring Creek, how we hauled water and sawed wood. I tell her through my tears of pulling her out of our double sleeping bag in the morning, how I didn't want her to suffocate. I tell her she is beautiful and relate stories of her friends and responses to her writing. Tom and I promise her we will see that her book is published. I feel drawn to the distant past, as I tell her about wheeling her up to the kitchen table in Charlotte, tucked carefully into my wicker doll carriage.

My assurance, "I love you so much, Jannie," does not create any change in her expression, but I need to tell her this, over and over. I recount my memory of holding her on my lap in Charlotte, and how I loved my baby sister. I tell her that I have learned more of how to love from her, that we have shared our distresses and joys and loves together, that she is greatly loved beyond all she might know, that I will accompany her as far as I am able. Not how I will miss her. I remember my life before Janice, and dimly realize that I am imagining my life after Janice.

We of the Divine Ensemble close ranks as we come and go. We feel better when everyone is there. When others want to visit, we say no.

Gary plays the flute while, crowding into her study, the rest of us sing hymns and camp songs. My last mental image of her before this current devastation reveals Janice on the white couch, wan but smiling, with her lovely short hair, Mollie on the fleece that covers her. I hold this image superimposed on the Janice who now rests in her hospital bed.

In the healing room, as Gary terms it, Dad requests hymns from his reservoir of memory. He spent sixty-eight years as a minister. I page through the hymnbooks in Janice's piano bench looking for ones Gary can play on his flute. I look for Dad's favorites, knowing these hymns with lifelong resonance for him will bring some comfort. His mother played the organ at their church in Lampasas for fifty-nine years; Mom's mother directed the choir and played the piano for her church choir in San Antonio and San Marcos. These hymns live deeply inside him and my mother. In my memory, I can hear Janice adding her improvised piano accompaniment to "What a Friend We Have in Jesus" and "Steal Away." She left the church, but the music stayed with her. We return often to "Abide with Me," and spirituals such as "Jacob's Ladder" and "Swing Low, Sweet Chariot." We sing the songs we sang as a family of five around the campfires in Colorado: "There's a Long, Long Trail," "With Someone Like You," and "You Are My Sunshine," which ends, "Please don't take my sunshine away."

"That makes me sad," says our father, so we don't sing the sunshine song again. He and Mom hold hands. He blots his eyes with his embroidered handkerchief.

"Please play one more," I entreat, until Gary says he has no embouchure left to form the notes. We all sit in the room for a while in silence, not wanting to leave.

We take turns sleeping on the couch in her room, waking each other up for the next vigil. I suffer a torrent of tears one night when I sleep while keeping watch, still deluding myself that the power of my attention can make a difference.

A friend prepares a generous Southern meal of tender brisket, mashed potatoes and gravy, green beans, corn on the cob, tossed salad, homemade crescent rolls, apple pie, and ice cream. She brought butter, which we'd forgotten for days to buy. "Comfort food," she says when I greet her at the front door. This former student has tears in her eyes as she hands over the welcome food. We all, except Mom and Dad, who sit with Janice and hold hands with each other, feel an inexplicable kind of comfort as we gather around the antique beech wood dining table. It's good to be together. The candles shine on Janice's red crystal glasses filled with water, and on the red wine in her Lismore Waterford crystal goblets. We serve the friend's food on Aunt Lillian's ivory plates rimmed with gold, the ones Janice used on Christmas Eve six weeks ago. Janice could easily enjoy casual dining; we are our mother's daughters, though, and enjoy setting a lovely, formal table. As I place the silver, china, and crystal, I imagine Janice's hands setting her table. We do this together as sisters. This is a night for candles and beauty.

On the night of February 19, the wild wind blows as some of us finish our meal. Gary and Gale bundle up and go for a run, cold though it is. Mom is the first to notice that Janice's breathing has changed. Joel, their steady friend, summons us to Janice's room. Mollie, who'd taken to sleeping in Gary's duffel bag upstairs, bounds down the stairs responding to some unknown signal; she begins to knead Janice's chest. "Better not let her do that," Ed admonishes, until he realizes that nothing can hurt Janice now.

Tom and I climb on Janice's bed to hold and stroke her. I whisper that I will travel with her as far as I can. We kiss her.

We lose Janice to the windy, starry night.

Again I find myself, as happened when I heard the terrible diagnosis, with no conscious thought, on the floor, on my knees, my head on Janice's belly, wailing, "Mommy, I'm sorry. Mommy, I'm so sorry." This regression plunges me back into my earliest big sister years. I am wailing, pleading with "Mommy" not to be mad at me. A tiny observing ego watches, with shock but no power, this unconscious backwards journey, but still I wail until my mother puts her arms around me to comfort me, saying, "Joycie, you did everything you could. It's not your fault. We know how much you love her." Everyone is quiet except for me as my sobs slowly subside. Clients of mine have regressed and reported such experiences. Now I know how they felt.

The hospice nurse arrives soon after we call her to certify the time of death and to dispose of medication. Someone calls the mortuary. Gale and I dress Janice in clothes in the colors she loved—black, crimson, and turquoise. We want to dress her in her cowgirl dancing boots, white with blue embossed butterflies, but the mortician reminds us that everything we want to keep should remain at home. We slip on socks; I don't want to imagine her small feet cold. It's so hard not to adorn her body with jewelry. Tom removes her gold and diamond wedding ring. Ed and Gary carry Janice to the hearse. I ride with her body to the funeral home, as Tom and Gale follow. I sit in front with the driver.

"Is this your mother?" inquires the driver.

I am shocked that he thinks she is this old. "No, my sister," I reply, "my younger sister." Tom, Gale, and I stay with her body in the quiet room. Eventually we kiss her face, I stroke her head one last time, and we go. I cannot comprehend that the time has come for me to leave her. The steps away from her are the hardest I have ever taken. The house is dark and quiet when we arrive back. As I slip into bed beside Gary, the music and words of Bach's "Oh sacred head, now wounded," accompany me as I weep myself to sleep.

February 20: The Stillness After Death

I retrieve her journals the next morning, tucking them all away in my suitcase. Because of her request, I knew she wanted me to take possession of them "whenever I wanted." Now is the time. I pile the spiral-bound notebooks into most of one bag. I feel a sense of urgency as I protect her privacy. At home, the notebooks will fill eighteen inches on my shelf. The next day, I go to her office at the University of Arkansas, to begin to clean out her files, remove everything from the bulletin board, and arrange academic journals, article reprints, and books for students and colleagues to take. As I do this, I begin the work of remembering, the labor of grieving. Each book, journal, reprint, and file creates resonances of our shared and separate past academic lives. I marvel at the evidence of her long writing life as I neatly stack reprints in chronological order on the long bottom shelf of the built-in bookcase in her office. I feel pride in what she accomplished, and I want the people who come into her office to see all she has done.

I want to be sure no personal files remain on her computer, only work-related documents. Her private life took place at home. This task of clearing out her academic artifacts takes several days. As I reread handouts we shared through the years, especially for her conflict management class, a class I used to teach, I hope the next teacher will take advantage of her perfectly organized files. Knowing how each new teacher establishes her own academic priorities, I can't know whether anyone will use her work. If I were still teaching, I could integrate her files and teaching materials into my own.

I place a sign on the door which I leave open, inviting students and colleagues to come in. I feel fiercely determined to honor her with my listening and with an orderly dismantling of her office.

I smell the dusty books and feel the cracked brown leather of the big couch on which she took naps. I fold away the plaid blanket she covered up with and take home the red velour pillow she used. I see the white concrete block walls that Janice has warmed with her red shag carpet, framed posters, and leather couch.

Many of her students and colleagues come in and say good-bye to her spirit in this room where they felt so warmly heard. I listen to their stories. Many tell me the same thing: "She found the best in me and brought it forward," or "I didn't know who I really was until she helped me find out." "She was really tough," several remind me. She upheld high standards and held them to those standards, while finding the core of Self in each student. All the time I'm thinking she did the same for me. In my work, I am used to listening to stories. These are one-time, full of heart, and they all are about goodbye. Finally, I leave her office with only a few pieces of university furniture remaining, and the books Tom doesn't want, which I invite students to take. I know that soon anything of value will end up in other offices. I close the door and unscrew her nameplate, which I take home with me.

Several days after Janice's death, we hold a small memorial service in the living room. Our parents need to attend to their move to Colorado Springs, where Ed lives, and give attention to our mother's undiagnosed pain. They are in the final transition of their lives, but I don't know that clearly.

Just a few days after her death, Tom asks Gale and me to sort through all Janice's personal belongings. I ask him to wait until I come back next month for the memorial service on campus, but he wants to remove personal items from his everyday life now. I don't think of suggesting that I store her clothes and jewelry in my downstairs room, although some of her clothes are already in that closet. Tom and I work as a team, and I don't want to cause discord, so Gale and I begin what seems like a huge project. I am extremely upset by Tom's urgent hurry, but I don't know what to do other than to comply. Gale and I remember Janice in all these clothes and jewelry. Gale, size two like Janice, chooses some of her loveliest clothes for herself.

I distribute jewelry, keeping most of it for myself, after asking Mom to take a few things she wants; she doesn't want anything. I give a silver-and-sapphire ring to Gale and a faceted garnet ring to Paula. Tom brings me the stunning platinum-and-diamond ring he gave to Janice, a gift from one of his aunts in Oak Park, years before. A while back, Janice tried to give it to me, teasingly saying, "This looks ridiculous on me!" And it did: a large dinner ring of many diamonds on her slender finger. Tom didn't know about this conversation. I accept it now with tears and thanks.

Upset and yet energized with the mission of giving Janice's things away, we continue. She was petite, so I can wear almost nothing of hers. I cannot bear for her delicate camisoles to go to Goodwill or the trash. Gale takes many personal items home, including Janice's elegant long teal wool coat. She will share some of the clothes with one of her daughters. We give many items to a young woman I meet in Janice's office, a former advisee.

Tom and I will talk into the night, eight years later at a convention in San Antonio, when I will tell him about my pain and upset at this time, and he will tell me about his need at this time, and I will forgive him, and he will understand me.

The Work of Remembering and Honoring Begins

I go home and plan the service for late March with Tom and Gary. Some of Janice's best-loved colleagues plan to attend. Mike, who called Janice "Miz Myth," created an award for teaching and service that Janice will receive posthumously in a few months. A group of colleagues in her region create an early career award for young scholars in her name. They all love her, and I will find their presence comforting. My first husband, Rick, will give the benediction. Rick met Janice when she was fifteen; she served as my maid of honor. Gale, Tom, Gary, and I make our plans to speak.

March 26, 2004: University of Arkansas

While I meet with my clients when I am back in Montana, in the interim before we return to Arkansas, all my energy is caught up in planning. Gary and I fly back to Fayetteville. I feel completely at home in my downstairs bedroom, living room, and bathroom. Gale and I confer on what to wear to the service. Gale stays in the main floor guest room, where not long ago Mollie slept in my suitcase as we both sought comfort. Gale and I confer like sisters about our dress.

The ghosts of the Divine Ensemble still inhabit Janice's home, but we are drifting back to our other lives. I speak at the service, giving the first of my several talks about Janice. Gary's prayer turns into a lamentation, as he tells a story about himself and Janice when they took a bike ride in Montana. At the base of a hill ahead of her, he got off his bicycle. Looking back up the hill, he realized that her momentum was such and her speed so great, that she would probably fall when she reached the gravel at the bottom of the hill; he could not save her. He watched helplessly as she slipped and fell in the gravel. She arrived back at our house, bleeding and shaken, Gary feeling terrible. He prays, "Though we loved Janice, though we made the best medical decisions possible, though we prayed for her, though we sought to comfort her, though we needed her, we could not save her from the wind that swept her away from us on the night of February nineteenth. This means that a husband loses his companion, his collaborator in life, love, and research. It means that two sisters will not go on long walks together making sense of their overlapping worlds. It means that we will not hear her voice on the phone, will not see her entering the classroom or convention hall beautifully composed. It means that we will not benefit from all the thoughtful questions and genuine affirmations that made us feel like better people than we were before we knew her . . . We come together to give thanks for this woman we loved, to celebrate who Janice was in the world, and to honor all that she expressed during her brief and intense sojourn among us."

While we all talk too long, everyone seems to understand that this grief can't yet be contained in short speeches. We project a slideshow with images of Janice, with "Bless the Road" playing in the background. I am suspended in time, completely in Janice's time, our time. At the service, Rick sits on one side of me, Gary on the other. My middle husband, Bill, who loved Janice, with whose children we spent many summer vacations, attends with his wife. Rick gets excited when he sees pictures in the slide show of our wedding, and of Janice at sixteen. "That's us!" he whispers loudly. Rick and his wife have stayed close to Tom and Janice. The service spills over into a reception and dinner. Taking refuge in my role as hostess at the reception and the dinner Tom gives for all the out-of-town people and close friends, I know if I sit too long and talk too deeply, I will sob. Barely present, I feel grateful to be able to stay busy.

Gary and I fly back to Missoula. It's the end of March. Spring must have arrived, but I remember nothing but overwork, dark grief, and corresponding with Tom and Gale. I have only begun the long road of grief, the trail to Tincup, to our cemetery plot in the forest. I do not know, yet, how to live without my sister.

chapter four

Living in the Lost and Found Department

Spring, 2004: Missoula

Forty-nine days after Janice died, I am home in Missoula. Gale reminds me that in the Buddhist tradition, the soul travels for forty-nine days before it reaches the other side. It's Maundy Thursday as well, a dark night in the Christian world. Barely able to sleep, although exhausted, my weariness increases each day. My mind seems porous and scattered. The hospice bereavement group begins next week. Their receptionist urged me to wait a while to join, but I called my friend who will lead the group and begged him to add me to it. I need a new group; I miss the people who surrounded Janice with love in February so much that I write them all a group letter. The psychological container of the Divine Ensemble helped hold me together when the light drained from Janice. My letter reads:

> *Dear Friends:*
> *I want to reach out to each of you and hold you in my mind's eye one more time, as we were at the house in Fayetteville.*

I feel humble gratitude for each of you and for our spiritual connection around this event, never to be repeated. We are blessed. I am amazed that Janice has been gone for longer than we knew she was ill. So fast, so very fast. . . . I always said that the worst thing that could happen would be if something happened to Janice. Now I am living into that worst thing. I did not know anything about grief before this. I am strong and will grieve my way through this loss, but oh, it is hard. I still live in liminal space—part of me there, part here. I am a heart broken open. Deep peace of the gentle night to you / Moon and stars pour their healing light on you / Deep peace to you.
Love, Joyce.

Peace escapes me. I wander through our house when I can't sleep, my restlessness reminiscent of my nocturnal wanderings in Janice's house last month, as I searched for somewhere to light, to settle. I cannot read, a lifelong activity I could count on for solace and peace. Sometimes I sit in the corner of my study, the smallest room in the house, where I light a candle on a small inset shelf where I have placed a string of pearls with a carnelian heart attached. My Christmas gift to Janice one year, she later loaned it to me for my wedding with Gary; now the pearls and heart remind me of her. Next to it I place a gold pre-Columbian Costa Rican design of "Butterfly Woman," who is revered as the mediator between heaven and earth. The torn-out page from January fifth with the quote from Joanna Macy reminds me that "the heart that breaks open can contain the whole universe." One of the haunting black-and-white professional photographs of Janice sits in the middle, in front of the mirror. For now, this small space serves as a makeshift altar. Sometimes I gaze through the candlelight to see if I might catch just a glimpse of her in the dark mirror or I sit wedged into the corner on the floor and cry. While I long for deep peace, I find no peace. Lightfoot shadows me; if I sit still long enough he settles on my lap.

I do, however, find a welcome focus sitting with my clients, listening to their stories, asking questions, grateful for compassion that connects me to them. I have begun to inquire about their losses in a more searching way than before. Losses carry layers of meaning for them, and for me. Tom and I email almost every day, comforting to us both. I write to him, *I always thought that in some distant future Janice and I would have more time together. It's what Gary calls the loss of a future and a hope. My main identity, other than being my own self, odd as this might sound, was "Janice's sister." I feel lost and very lonely.*

Tom and I make plans to go to Shalom in early July to bury Janice's ashes at the Tincup cemetery. Tom, Ed, and I write about our deep concern for both Mom and Dad. Mom still does not have a working diagnosis for severe pain. Dad experiences debilitating headaches. Somehow Mom and Dad move from their Grand Junction condominium to an assisted living duplex in Colorado Springs. This way they can be closer to Ed. For all these reasons, they did not join us in Fayetteville for Janice's memorial service at the end of March. Toward the end of April, I write Tom that I no longer cry every night; I've entered into a flat period of grief. I confess to him that I miss the sharpness of my grief, that I feel dull all the time.

With grief as my constant companion walking with me day and night, I felt oddly alive. I needed only my love for Janice, my memories and nightly dreams connecting me to her. Eating, shopping for groceries, creating order in our house, all these activities happened in the only reality that mattered—memory, grief, and love. As acute pain dulls, however slightly, I feel more loss, the raw edge of grief that bound me absolutely to Janice. I don't want to feel anything else. This doesn't seem crazy to me.

Obsession with Things

Tom tells me that he is obsessing about financial issues; he worked with a trustee to make a new will, taking account of their joint assets. He sends me the notarized copies so I will have them. He is sorting everything out at the house, he tells me—I overreact with panic and criticism when he tells me he just cleaned out the hall closet. I cringe when he writes me, *Take it easy, Joyce, it was just the gift paper and boxes in the small closet, nothing of Janice's.* I still mourn the loss of Janice's clothes and personal items, way too soon for me after her death, and the thought of losing anything else of hers unhinges me. Tom finds some comfort in small rituals he has developed; he changes the flowers in the purple, red, yellow, and aqua vases from the Metropolitan Museum that she and I gave each other. They are on the altar shelf in Janice's study that we created during her last days. On that shelf he placed on a linen handkerchief her wedding rings, and next to them a small enamel jewelry box holding some of her ashes. One of the black-and-white pictures, taken at a friend's wedding last November, serves as an organizing icon. I know what he is going through; the altar in Fayetteville shimmers just out of sight for me in my mind. My obsession with physical objects fills my days and nights now.

Gale and I disassembled and dispensed all of Janice's personal things. Each item of her carefully chosen wardrobe brought smells of sandalwood and Tatiana, part of her essence, to me. I keep items I cannot release. I become the lover of things, much like the poet Rilke in the period in which he wrote of the dear and particular things of the world. As I handle and smell Janice's clothes, I remember Janice in childhood, wearing the brown-checked, organdy dress Mom sewed for her. I visualize her changing, growing body, the clothes she wore as a teenager, hairstyles, school pictures, her words, moods, and accomplishments. A slideshow runs in my memory and in my dreams. I visualize only what I can remember. I will not acquire more images or new experiences with Janice; sometimes this thought alone brings me to sobs. I understand the loss of a future and a hope. My women's group invites me to show the pictures we assembled for Janice's memorial service, kindly asking for stories about her so they can know more about who she was and how our relationship formed.

Saved by Stories

A friend I don't know all that well invites me to come to her house for dinner, with pictures of Janice.

"I want to know about Janice," she states with a warm look into my eyes.

"Oh, thank you, Jerri. We can go to coffee . . ." I don't want to be a bother.

"No, I want to make dinner for you, Joyce," she says. "My husband will be somewhere else, so we'll have privacy." Hers is an invitation I know to trust; she lost her brother a few years back; she knows. At the end of our dinner, talk, and time looking at pictures, Jerri says, "I don't think we are done." Her tenderness triggers more tears. "Let's do this again." While I do not write out narratives yet, compassionate friends help me begin to shape stories I will live with, stories I can carry for the rest of my life.

Openhearted listening helps me bear my grief. For a while, I am able to bring my sister to life as I recount my memories. These stories begin to save my psychological life. Freud wrote that we identify with the lost person, that we integrate them into our ego so they become part of our psychic makeup. We intuitively perform this reshaping of our own ego so we can withstand the loss of finally letting them go. The process of incorporating the lost loved one creates a new psychological reality. Each conversation with a receptive friend forms a new piece of my life with Janice.

Friends and fellow mourners in my hospice group ask, "What did you love about Janice? How did the two of you develop such a close sister relationship? Did you ever fight?" These questions help me ponder our relationship instead of solely grieving her loss. Questions evoke memories; these stories of my sister, imbued as they are with delight, amusement, wonder, interpretation, poignancy, and specific details, help me bear her loss. As I verbally shape her life, at least her life that I remember and knew about, into stories for others and for myself, I gain a wealth, a treasure chest, of burnished story memories. The memories live inside me until we make them into stories. The stories take on the life that Janice now does not live.

Sometimes I inundate friends with stories whether they ask for them or not. Gary patiently listens to my memory stories and adds his own to the collection growing inside me. Sometimes I become uncomfortably self-aware that I insert stories about Janice into conversation to help myself rather than to respond to a request.

On the sidewalk outside my building on Higgins Avenue, I run into a colleague. "Oh, Joyce, I've been thinking about you," he says warmly. "What a hard time. How are you doing?"

"Thanks, Richard," I reply quickly. He looks interested. "My sister's husband and I are getting her book edited for publication," I rush on. "She finished a book on women and men and mentoring just before she died . . ." I stop myself from continuing. I seem not to be able to contain myself, assuming that people could not know me unless they know Janice. My sister and I are merged psychologically at this moment in time. Unconcerned about my own life apart from my sister, I live only to remember and magnify Janice. Comrades in my bereavement group report much the same obsession. I leap into any conversational breach that leads to a Janice story.

Things of Her World

Tom and I saved her dress from her first wedding, a navy-blue-and-white hippie dress made by our mother. As I look at an oil painting of her first wedding in Colorado, I remember her gleefully swinging on the rope at the Carters' cabin. Don, her tall lanky first husband, stands on the other side of the small stream. Time compresses as I remember our family camping circle. At that wedding in 1972, our extended family grows as my first husband performed the ceremony with Dad. Now Don is added to our circle. We hold the ceremony in the Carters' forested yard, on the banks of Spring Creek. I see a picture in my scrapbook of Janice looking up fondly at Rick, who wears a large-collared, red-and-white print shirt and a leather strap with a rough cross around his neck. His hair is long; they look at each other with deep affection.

Janice and I picked yellow daisies and purple asters to hold and put in our hair. Tom also preserves her Victorian-style ivory satin dress in which she married him, the one in which she danced the Cotton Eye Joe at the Moose Lodge up Boulder Canyon in Colorado. I picture these dresses hanging in Janice's study back in Fayetteville, her boots, along with Tom's, set out together in the living room. I exist in between there and here. I live nowhere. I am lost.

Grief plunges me into a time of madness as I hoard and sparingly use Janice's OmegaBrite fish oil capsules that should have helped her brain but didn't, eke out the vitamin C lotion that I rubbed on her head when she lay on the sofa, head in my lap, listening to Bach. I remember humming the Bach melody to "Oh sacred head, now wounded." I knew the difference between Janice and Jesus, but this confabulation did not seem strange to me.

Continuing Conversations

Each day I wear a piece of her jewelry, misplace pieces, find them, lose them again—frantic in my distraction. Gale—visiting us in Missoula from her home and university duties in Oakland—and I frenetically searched the grass looking for one pink-and-silver earring we later found in my jewelry drawer. These months, like the pink-and-silver earring, I seem to exist in the lost and found department. The objects connect me tangibly to the living Janice, and I fiercely protect them, even though I could not protect her. The hair conditioner that made her hair curly and smelled like lemon balm, the shampoo that carries her scent of spice and sandalwood, the special oil that she used on her feet, the skirt into which I can barely fit, all the photos, the newspaper clippings, the nail polish remover, the perfume.

One morning I sit on the hearth in front of our gas fire, massaging Janice's foot oil into my dry feet; I exclaim out loud, "Janice, I can hardly bear to touch and smell your things. I miss you."

In my imagination, I hear her reply, *Joyce, we loved these girly things. Feel me with you when you use them.*

Smiling with the realization that our dialogue continues inside me, I resolve to talk with Janice in my imagination and to write to her in my journal.

I change my perfume back to her Tatiana, which she originally adopted from me. I use her sandalwood bath salts, her fifteen percent alpha hydroxy lotion to make our skin young, her small flashlight that we laughed about when our middle-aged eyes couldn't focus in a dark restaurant.

"Where is that damn light?" Janice exclaimed with a laugh in Miami. "I can't even find the thing that is supposed to help me see!" I hook the little light on my keychain. Each last dab, each spray, each pour, each tablet reminds me that soon this, too, will be gone.

On a dark day in late March, back home after the memorial service in Arkansas, I sit on the floor of my closet, stroking and smelling her ponytail, cut off before chemo started, remembering the growing-up days of playing beauty shop and spraying her hair with "Summer Blonde" when Mom wasn't watching. I remember the compassionate hairdresser who lessened Janice's trauma of losing her long lush hair, her kindness as she gently suggested that the highlights I insisted on should be applied later. I sob into the blue T-shirt she is wearing in the last pictures. I swallow the last of the OmegaBrite, gulping them down, knowing they will not ultimately save me either, that even with very good self-care, excellent medical attention, and the possible luck of avoiding a major disease, I will die.

I develop an entirely new relationship with her things, seeing through them as if they are transparent, understanding in a new way that the objects— and we—all disappear. I hold her delicate, gold filigree earrings in my palm before I put them on. I remember a pair of yellow-and-silver, art deco earrings with a matching necklace that Great-Aunt Letha gave Mom to distribute to nieces. As a teenager, I did not treasure them; I gave them away, not appreciating old jewelry. Now I wish they had taken their place in my jewelry box. All these objects will wear out, deteriorate, or disperse, going to friends, family, or strangers. Yet I am comforted by these transitional objects, which relate me to my sister.

I fold the last "Big Hawk Seven" T-shirt, remnant of an arduous trip our family group made into the Jewel Basin in the Bob Marshall Wilderness in the 1980s. I had the T-shirts made to commemorate the brutal and beautiful backpack trip. In January, Janice laughed as we found yet another one in her bottom drawer. Over the years, all of us passed them on to Janice as they shrank.

"Not another one of those damn things!" she teased. "I thought I used the last one as a dust rag." Holding it to my face, I remember Janice's blotchy, insect-bitten, sweaty face as we huddled in a small tent, escaping the bugs and our adult responsibilities. I continue my ongoing dialogue in my mind with Janice: *Do you mind if I use this up? It's so hard to pour the last of this oil that smells like you.*

I can almost hear her say, *Joyce, these things help you let go. Since I left so quickly, you need these reminders. I know I am in your heart. Use it all up. I'm here.*

I am mad with grief. I focus on my clients when I'm in my office, grateful to enter deeply into their traumas and stories instead of my own. One of my clients lost two brothers to death from a genetic illness that she did not contract; she talks about her guilt and grief that she remains without them. While she tells me her story, I find it easy to feel deeply with her, saying, "Tell me what you remember and love about them," and "How is your life different because they were your brothers?" Then I come home to try to make it through another night. Usually I start to cry when I drive into our driveway. Often I reach for a glass of red wine. More than once, a painful marital interaction unfolds.

Last year Janice gave us a CD of soulful, resonant classical melodies. Most nights we go to sleep listening to *Night Tracks*, the slow music a ship sailing us into the safe harbor of sleep. What a prescient gift. I often awaken in the middle of the night, though, permeated with grief, not able to soothe myself. Erupting from sleep already gasping with sobs, I say to Gary, "Please, I need you to hold me."

"I can't, hon. I was asleep," he says. "I need to sleep," he continues wearily, staying on his side of the bed. Sometimes I go to the guestroom to try to sleep, or play CDs at the far end of the house so I won't bother him.

Bonnie Raitt's "Valley of Pain" and "Wounded Heart" reflect my own state. I play the CDs repeatedly, like I played Sinatra's *Blue* album on my portable record player when I was fourteen. Our family had just moved in the middle of a school year. During that displaced time my sophomore year I first experienced what I now know was a clinical depression. Back then I learned to soldier on. This time, I don't have Janice's tender solicitude, as I did in our shared bedroom in our Fort Worth rental house. The church board dismissed our dad from his small-town church in North Texas, this time because of his progressive stand on integration. Our family would move on to the next parish after Dad completed a postgraduate semester back at his seminary. Paschal High School, a big-city school of three thousand students, intimidated me compared to the five hundred back in Vernon, where I enjoyed popularity and acceptance. At the temporary high school, the girls competed to join sororities, just as in college. I went through rush, knowing we would relocate before next year. I pretended that I belonged, that I had a future in the school. Janice would come over and sit on the side of my twin bed in the early morning, gently asking "Are you OK, Joyce?" Knowing my younger sister cared made my situation just bearable. As in that difficult semester in Fort Worth when I would make myself get up and go to the school where I didn't know anyone, I am lost. My future appears murky to me. Just as I forced myself to wake up and go to school, now I make myself get up and go to work.

Repeatedly, Gary and I talk about our interlocking complexes. I crave comfort and physical warmth; he needs to feel distance from the pull of a woman in emotional distress. As I was a firstborn child, my mother did not hold me when I cried as an infant, because she was in the generation admonished by Dr. Spock not to spoil their babies. I know she loved me, but hers was more of an anxious, unsure manner of caring for me as an infant, from what she has told me. In Gary's earliest memories of his mother, she is crying with physical pain, as well as emotional pain, as he later learned. The child Gary stood on the threshold, thinking he should do something but not knowing what to do. He learned to stay far away from what he feared to be a woman's bottomless well of tears and uncomforted pain, because, as he explained, he felt helpless and trapped. He knows now that his father might have helped him manage his outsized responsibility, but he did not. I can't imagine my husband not wanting to hold and comfort me. In my view love expresses itself through voiced compassion, comfort, and touch.

"I can't stand to feel so alone. Please hold me for a little while," I persist. I know in my mind that I suffer a grievous attachment loss, but this intellectual knowledge means nothing. I need what I need.

"I need to sleep," Gary insists. "You will have to learn to find your own comfort." Once Gary tries to teach me a meditative chant that comforts him. I yell at him to just stop. We go back and forth, alternately trying to feel compassion for the other's safety and comfort needs. I do not want to suffer my middle-of-the-night grief alone, and Gary does not want to feel responsible for soothing me when he needs to sleep. I think he cannot bear my grief, and I feel even more alone. Gary and I are trained in a form of couples' therapy called Dialogue Therapy, in which we map the unconscious emotional communication habits of our clients. We talk about our experience of serving as Polly Young-Eisendrath's and Ed Epstein's demonstration couple ten years earlier during our intensive training. Although we know quite a bit about our partly unconscious emotional longings, we don't seem to be able to heal ourselves, or rather, our complexes. The truth is—we both are suffering from grief, fear, and loneliness. Of course we should have sought couples therapy for ourselves, but did not.

During this time, I write another active imagination dialogue with Janice in my journal. I begin by writing what a challenge this time of grief is in our marriage, and how often I am hurt at Gary's lack of warm compassion. In my imagination, Janice responds, *Joyce, Gary is very sad. He lost me, and now he feels like he's losing you to grief. Could you be nicer to him? He's suffering, and he's doing the best he can.*

I want Janice to take my side, not Gary's. I sit quietly for a while, then write, *OK, Jannie, I'll try. You're still coaching me about being kinder, just like when you were the little cherub at church, and everyone liked you a lot better than me. I watched and learned from you then; I've been learning from you all these years.*

Janice replies, *You just get stressed and sad, and then it's hard for you to be kind. But you can do it.* I did not expect this kind of advice, but I recognize the truth of what my imaginary Janice wants for me.

Janice always found the tiny speck of best in me and everyone, even when we were at our gnarly worst. Gary benefits, as do I, from Janice's coaching in my imagination. I know this voice; I hope to internalize this quality of my sister's.

Years later, Gary will tell me that he failed me during this time, and I learn that forgiveness can and does reach backwards into time. I failed him and myself as well by not learning how to use time-honored tools of self-soothing even during my desperate nights. During the day when I'm not working, I write in my journal, work with my dreams, talk with friends, and correspond with people who loved Janice. Many of my friends are therapists; they offer me wonderfully compassionate listening. My analyst helps me learn from my dreams. But my attempts to contain my grief often collapse at night. I avoid waking to each moment of re-experiencing the loss of Janice. Loneliness looms large in the middle of the night.

When I was a child, I heard my father tell a story in his sermons. In the story, the father tries to comfort his child by telling her that God is with her when she is afraid at night. The girl replies, "But Daddy, I need a God with skin on." The child in me wanted comfort I could *feel.* This season of wild grief plants a toxic seed that will grow into distance and conflict as we travel through our grief differently. We demand that the other meet our needs. I want comfort and companionship and Gary wants safety and quiet.

Searching the house for any spot to endure the middle-of-the-night hours, I light candles, crowd into a corner of my small study, searching for proof in Janice's journals that she loved me. I know that she did, except during times when I disintegrate with doubt and grief. During these fragmenting times, my adult memory and resilience failing me, I forget that the human ways I irritated, disappointed, or annoyed Janice did not cancel out her love for me. When I am most porous to my unconscious shadow, I cannot remind myself of my worth, of her love, of our human sister relationship.

One night I walk into the dining room to hear on *Prairie Home Companion* a full choir, with harmony, singing "Abide With Me." I feel as though we three children have wandered in the forest and come upon a lighted place, and opened the door where someone is always singing. I wonder if death is like this.

In the morning, I enter my other reality, my quiet office. Arriving early, I look at the Japanese prints of irises, the picture of the open gate leading into a Central Texas field of cactus, limestone, and bluebonnets. Janice's photograph is tucked beside my door, so I can look at her face when each new person enters. I want my clients to ask about that beautiful blonde woman, but they usually can't see the photograph, and I remind myself not to ask for comfort from those who come to me for help with their own sorrows and concerns. Through the healing practices of listening and sense-making, my conscious ego helps me remember who I am. This happens quietly as I remind my clients of their worth and goodness. When I want a different kind of human connection, I run down to Butterfly Herbs for a cup of coffee and a chat with the people I know who work there, or I walk down to the bank to make a deposit, enjoying the warm connections with people on my downtown block.

Grief disrupts my sense of self. My normal human flaws grow into a sense of guilt larger in proportion to the whole relationship than makes sense. When I am a couple of minutes late to greet my next client in the waiting room, I over-apologize. Several times tears seep down my face when a client tells me something sad. When I apologize to a woman who is describing the recent death of her mother, she interjects, "Please don't apologize. I see that you know what I am feeling, and I don't feel so bereft." My therapy practice deepens and becomes richer, more real. Fearing nothing,

I take risks; I ask everyone about their losses, wanting to hear all the details, without talking about my own. My personal grief merges with other stories as I join the ongoing human drama. I inquire more deeply than ever about my clients' lives, traumas, hurts, and losses. More than ever, I want to help.

For a conference presentation on internal dialogues with Janice, I begin by writing in my journal: *Jannie, I'm not sure if such a personal paper will be meaningful to other people.*

After a pause, I write her imagined reply: *Joyce, this is what you have been living, and you live deeply. Write it the way you are living your feelings, and people will learn from it. They need to know about grief. Remember the paper Tom and I wrote on how people in academia are afraid of the downward pull of grief or depression? I'll help you.*

I wish you were here, I write.

I am. Read what you write aloud to me. I'm always here, Janice responds in the interior dialogue. The voice I imagine sounds like Janice's voice inside me. Hearing is one of my strongest senses; I take time to listen within.

My friend Sally invites me to join a group of women friends who gather on Sunday nights at her house for a potluck dinner and a viewing of *Sex and the City*. Although I can't follow the plot, I am grateful to be included in a group of women who are celebrating life and laughing out loud. One night at Sally's, I surprise myself with my head on the table, crying with heart-wrenching sobs. "Bless the Road," one of the songs that accompanied the slide show of Janice's life at her memorial service, is playing on the CD mix. Again, without intervening thought, I collapse.

Sally gently explains to the women, "Oh, not everyone knows what's happened to Joyce." Her hand rests on my neck. "She has just suffered the loss of her sister." My friend finds the words for me.

Ritual Spaces

A year later, ritual spaces mark love and grief in our home. Mary Oliver's poem "In Blackwater Woods," printed out on exquisite paper by Gale, now hangs in our home gallery in the hall, the piece at the end. The first piece in this gallery, a framed, black-and-white abstract rose, invites me to gaze into the center where I imagine seeing into the deep feminine. Next, the eleven-by-four-teen-inch haunting black-and-white picture of Janice, taken a few months before Janice died. One eye looks bright and clear, the other smaller and clouded. She was already ill, and yet so beautiful. Next to Janice's photograph, an abstract red and black acrylic I found in Lewistown a few months after Janice died. A black gash divides the thick palette swipes of red and black. I came up with my own title, "Heart Broken Open." Next to "Heart Broken Open" I smile at a picture of our mother, looking like Ingrid Bergman in 1943. The Oliver poem ends, "To live in this world/ you must be able/ to do three things:/ to love what is mortal;/ to hold it / against your bones knowing/your own life depends on it;/ and, when the time comes to let it go,/ to let it go." I hold on to these words, which I have spoken in each memorial service, trying to embody and impart their wisdom to myself and to others. Altars and sacred space in my home help me contain my grief. I stand in front of each piece, touch them gently with my fingers, and remember. They invite me to pause.

I let go a hundred times after holding the thing, the memory, the image, the voice, the fabric, the jewelry, even the smell to my bones. They evoke Janice, but Janice is out of my reach. She is gone, as I relearn many times every day.

In the sixties, Janice performed at an oral interpretation of poetry event at a speech festival in San Marcos, Texas, while she was in college. In Robert Frost's poem, "Wild Grapes," a young girl hangs stranded at the top of a tree, not heavy enough to keep the limb of the tree and her feet on the ground. Her older brother urges her to just let go. In the poem, Frost has the girl argue in her head that it may not seem far to him, on the ground, but to her, it's an impossible distance and she can't imagine letting go. He muses about monkeys hanging on to trees. As her brother exhorts her, the girl hangs on even more tightly. In the girl's voice, Frost ends the poem saying that she had not yet learned to release the grasp of her hand, and does not need to let go with her heart.

I saw her charm the judges, who clearly could see the five-foot-tall college sophomore in the role. Janice won that contest.

I don't know how to let go with my hands of Janice's things, much less imagine letting go with my heart. Remembering the poetry contest in San Marcos, I write another internal dialogue:

Janice, how can I let go of the things that are yours, but not let go of you with my heart? I long for her reassurance.

Janice's voice sounds firm in my imagination: *You have to trust that your heart will always know where to find me. Or I'll find you. I asked you if you would be hard to find when you went to Costa Rica. You said no. You will be able to find me.* I can tell instantly when her imagined voice is spot-on and sounds like Janice. Sometimes the practice for me is trancelike. The more I can let go of my observing ego, the more likely I am to hear Janice within me.

But I still feel attached to her *things*, and sometimes I can't find Janice in my heart and mind when I am paralyzed by grief.

When her voice seems silenced during journal sessions, sometimes dreams arrive at night to teach me. One night I dream that Janice and Tom arrive at our house in an old pickup truck, driving from the opposite direction from which they usually approach. Janice is hot, disheveled, and tired. She comes in our door saying, "Sometimes we can come through the back way." I cling to this possibility. My unconscious seems to be telling me that my closeness with Janice may come from unexpected directions.

Gale tells me of a dream she has in which the Divine Ensemble is preparing food in Fayetteville. Janice appears among us. Gale, delirious with joy, clings to Janice, who gently admonishes, "Not too tight." I think of Mary Magdalene clinging to Jesus in a resurrection scene, when he tells her not to cling too tightly. We all want to touch and feel our beloved person who is gone. Gale and I talk about whether this is the Janice inside us, or the Janice out there. Of course we don't know.

In the fall, I still live in the lost and found, like Janice's jewelry, but no one is finding me yet. I have learned, barely, to let go with my hands, but not my heart. Music has left me again, except for Janice's gift CD from a few years ago. I am scattered like the wind that blew the night Janice died. A dream helps me.

In this dream, my psyche creates an image of Janice helping us find the right key to our grief: *Gary, Tom, Ed, my dad, and I are singing in a living room. Dad is weak, but still part of the group. He rests, his head back in a recliner. I think I'll put a curved travel pillow under his head, but Ed tells me I already did. We begin to sing a folk song from the sixties, but can't quite get the words or the music to the poignant song. We falter. Then Janice appears at the piano. She finds the key we're looking for and confidently leads us in the melody and the words with beautiful, improvisational accompaniment. She sings in a heartfelt voice, and we follow along. She seems to be guiding us as we find a way to sing.* My memories of Janice help me as I reflect on her way of gently helping people find harmony, among each other and inside themselves. The dream reminds me that we do have the words and music, which I think of as emotional accompaniment, to help us find meaning.

For Christmas in 1986, I presented Janice with a framed print of Renoir's painting of two girls at a piano, the blonde one playing, and the dark-haired girl leaning over the music. The picture shows in art the way Janice opened up music to me, as I learned from her. My analyst helps me connect my associations to that picture with this current dream. The time period of the song we seek in the dream points to the sixties. This was a time when our family was under tremendous stress because of our father's stands on civil rights and the early anti-war movement. Yet we were together. The dream reminds me that we still are, in spirit, and some sure note in me will help me find the key to the sorrow I feel.

April, 2004: Open Book with Missing Pages

These days my life, as Nancy Griffith sings, "is an open book with missing pages that I cannot seem to find." I am blank, empty, with no emerging story that I can recognize yet. I am not writing. Looking back at 2004, I find almost nothing in my journal that is not associated with memorial services or emails to friends.

Gary builds me a cherry dressing table with an intricate sliding drawer to hold my jewelry. Many days now I almost forget which was hers, which she gave me, which Tom presented to her or bequeathed to me after Janice died. The evocative pieces belong to *us*. All the OmegaBrite is used up. I buy more Tatiana. Her journals, pictures, and school papers and notebooks, which I brought from Fayetteville, fill a shelf in my study. These artifacts often draw me on dark nights of longing and insomnia. "There aren't any secrets," Janice assured me when she asked me to take responsibility for all the notebooks, back in January. "I just want you to know how I feel."

One night, searching for something of Janice in her writing, I do find a secret. From a letter she wrote to herself in 1963, when she was a ninth grader and I a busy senior, she writes:

> *I see Joyce now about three hours of every week, four if I'm extra lucky. It will be the same all summer and then I will never really be with her again. This summer I want so much to be with her. Just doing things at home, like sewing, planning, and anything! I love her so much. I guess no one could ever know how much, not even her. She has so many faults, but so do I, and I guess maybe that's why we're such good friends.*

My heart cracks open. My faults back then stand out clearly: a self-centered teenager who tried to do too much, keeping the lamp on late in our shared room, talking on the phone to my friends, leaving Janice out—but I can't think of any of hers. Even during that time, I thought my little sister was wonderful. Now I could be any age, ten or sixty, and Janice is beyond age. I want the same thing. I just want to be with her, doing anything.

In addition to all the frequent trips for work, I fly to see my parents in their new duplex in Colorado Springs in early May. During that visit, I find myself unprepared for my parents' need for care. They are in their mid-eighties now. I help them unpack as they organize their medical, physical, and practical needs. Dad wants to be ready to "hightail it to the high country" soon after Memorial Day, when they will move to the cabin in Gunnison National Park for their summer stay. I am concerned about the impact of their needs on Ed, who lives in Colorado Springs and helps them with many tasks.

One day I ask my dad if he can help me deal with my grief about Janice. I am thinking of all the days I tagged along with him when I was a child during his pastoral visits in hospitals and homes, and remembering some of the many funerals at which he has officiated. He is still my minister/father. But Dad looks miserable in the wake of my question.

"No Joycie, I don't know what to recommend for you." Tears form in his eyes. Was I expecting him to give me helpful books to read, or some quick spiritual guidance?

Later, he comes to me. "I feel so bad that I don't know what to tell you," he says, "but I don't. You and Janice were so close. Jean and I have each other to talk with, but you have lost your best friend. We always were so proud of the way you gals took care of each other." I am gratified that Dad knows she was my best friend. He pauses. "I feel that I've failed you, that I don't have anything to suggest. Anything I said would be inadequate." He sighs. "I know you won't always feel the way you do right now, but that's no comfort for you. I know that grief becomes bearable because I've gone through it myself," he assures me, "but that doesn't help you now."

We hug, and I realize I have asked an impossible question. For a moment, I was focused only on my own grief and loss. I wanted him to be my daddy instead of my dad. The last thing I wanted to do was add to his sorrow, and now I have. We hug again, and he pats me on the back, a little too firmly, as always. He's not comfortable when he cries. He has to work hard to keep control of his deep, resonant voice when he reads something from the pulpit that moves him. Janice and I teased him about sounding like the voice of God. Right now he sounds like what he is—an elderly father and worried husband who is experiencing many layers of grief.

I am not used to feeling needy and vulnerable. I'm usually the strong one, the older sister, the therapist, teacher, and comforter.

I certainly have felt vulnerable many times in my life, like when I was sick and getting a divorce in Boulder, and since Janice died, but my default position is "helper." Now I feel guilty for having asked my dad to help me, but since I have always seen him as strong and helpful to others in their grief, it makes sense that I would do so. We are in this together, my father and I.

While Janice was dying in Fayetteville, Mom spread out brochures promoting the assisted living campus where they have now moved. Mom talked with a sense of urgency unusual for her. "I must make the phone calls to sell the condo, then set up our move. Oh, and I have to call the appraiser." I was no help to her at all. *Can't you see we're busy here?* I thought, but thankfully, did not say. Now I realize that Mom knew something dire was wrong with her health, and she felt fiercely determined to organize this one last move for her husband, so he would be close to Ed.

Mom had organized thirteen complicated post-retirement moves from their winter home in Grand Junction as they took up interim posts with churches that were searching for a minister. Dad sought interim positions, making it clear to the prospective churches that they intended to return to the cabin in Colorado when summer began. Mom kept two sets of dishes and utensils, one for the condo in Grand Junction and one for interims. She decided thirteen different times what items to pack into the camping trailer and what to count on the parishioners to furnish. I visited Mom and Dad in one of their interim posts in Brownwood, Texas. Somehow Mom, drawing on all her years of making a home with too little money for extras, had created a warm home in the parsonage, with her fabric hangings, quilts, and family pictures. Dad sought these thirteen temporary posts in places like Salida, Grand Junction, Aurora, and La Junta, Colorado; Galveston, Brownwood, and Laredo, Texas; Fremont, Nebraska; and Casper and Sheridan, Wyoming. He wanted to make more money before he stopped working entirely to pay for the cabin in Colorado and to leave his beloved Jean better off financially.

He confessed to me in Fayetteville that he felt ashamed that their frequent moves and a lifetime of low-paying jobs left his wife vulnerable financially. He wanted to take care of her. Now I see that she is organizing this relocation, even as she is grieving for her daughter, because she wants to take care of her husband. They even join the church in Colorado Springs that fired Dad in the early seventies for his anti-war activities. This is her last act of caring for her husband, whom she worries will not survive well without her.

Mom is way ahead of me.

Memorial Day, 2004. Back Roads of Montana

Gary and I head out on a "back roads of Montana" trip as a way to restore closeness with each other and claim quiet time away from Gary's end-of-semester pressures. We need to recover from working while grieving. Since Janice died in February, I have continued to see clients through my miasma of grief, rescheduling an afternoon or morning here and there when I could not imagine being fully present. I am truly exhausted. Like a medieval mystic living in a small hut attached to the larger cathedral, Gary has mostly stayed at home, an anchorite for our partnership, keeping the vessel of our marriage from floating away and wrecking as we navigate grief, my insomnia, unrelenting work pressures, and too much travel. I am glad to reconnect with Gary as we explore state highways and small towns.

I need to see the first green signs of spring on the eastern slope; I need vast landscapes and the enduring contours of the mountains. I need to walk across the Missouri River Bridge where steamships reached their destination at Fort Benton. I need to emerge from my recent past into a larger history. I need to unfold into life. I need to feel the wild thunderstorm and the light-filled sky in the Little Belt Mountains.

Somehow I will survive the interior storm of grief that still shakes me awake and out of bed most nights to walk through the dark house shadowed by Lightfoot while I wail, or try to find something to read, contemplate, or listen to that will help me make it through the night. I had always loved my nocturnal solitude until grief filled up all the space that used to feel like home.

Janice often made tapes and CDs of songs for special occasions. As Gary and I drive east from Fort Benton through the almost empty Montana landscape, past the Fort Belknap reservation, we take the state highway from Havre, heading ultimately toward Lewistown. Gary and I listen to Janice's gift of *Driving Music* as we plumb the meaning and enjoy the intricate connections of her choices. We try to read the tea leaves of her gift, knowing that the web of associations between the songs was known only to her. We ponder "All that Heaven Will Allow," Steve Earle and Emmylou singing "I Remember You," and her attempt to brighten me up in the winter with "Here Comes the Sun." In my mind, I continue my internal dialogue with Janice:

Janice, I wish you and Tom were riding in the back seat looking at this astonishing rainstorm over the mountains and listening to your driving music. I imagine Janice in the backseat, rapt with the beauty around us.

Joyce, I'm here. This is all amazingly wonderful. I hear her quiet voice in my imagination. She would absorb the sight of the mountains and wild rain with awe.

We let the moods sweep through us like the rainstorm sweeping over the plains through the Judith Mountains. A rainbow appears, in the kind of sky painters can never capture. The wild Montana skies.

In Lewistown we settle into our historic bed-and-breakfast. Montana people function as though we live in a small town; we talk with our hostess about people we know in common across the state.

Back in cell phone range in Lewistown, I return three calls from Ed in Colorado from the serene upstairs bedroom. Mom has been in the hospital for more advanced diagnostic tests. As I listen to one of his messages, my stomach contracts as I grope for a chair. When we talk, Ed sounds slow and somber.

"It looks like advanced pancreatic cancer," Ed says.

"We thought maybe colon cancer," I say, trying to turn back this new truth.

"Yes. This is worse," Ed confirms. Ed and I are talking on the phone, again, as we did from the Big Hole about Dianne, and from Fayetteville as Ed reported on the kind of small-cell lung cancer Janice had, after I told him about our meeting with her oncologist. Recoiling at the confirmation of something I already intuitively know, I ask for more details.

"The treatment options are not good," Ed adds. We let silence gather. Something medically serious has been going on with Mom for months. She had been in pain as we kept watch with Janice. As Janice lay in her final coma, Gale overheard Mom, a normally unsentimental person, whisper to my sister, "I'll be with you soon." Mom never talked about heaven or an afterlife, so I did not know what to think. Maybe her whisper was a reassuring comment to her daughter.

I remember back to Thanksgiving 2003, when Mom and Dad visited us in Missoula. We parked in front of Bernice's Bakery to pick up the Thanksgiving rolls. We were also stealing time away from Dad, who likes Mom to stay with him. Mom told me about her unremitting abdominal pain. Incredibly frustrated and irritated at the lack of good medical analysis of her pain, I wonder if her doctors listen carefully enough to this elderly woman. We talked about how she could assert herself with her doctors, to help her find a diagnosis. I offered to come to Grand Junction to visit doctors with her. "No, we can handle it," she replied. Then she surprised me. "I think I have cancer," she said quietly.

"What makes you think that?" Mom was crying softly as I questioned her.

"I don't know what else all this pain could mean."

"We have to get more answers," I insisted. I was missing the point of her resignation and sorrow. Comforting my mother seemed new and untried to me; problem-solving came more naturally. I promised to help her, thinking that indeed I should come to Colorado to talk with her doctors. Then Janice received her diagnosis on January fifth. Mom's active pursuit of diagnostic exploration went on hold. Our sad Christmas season came and went, and we all gathered in Fayetteville. She began to plan their move to Colorado Springs.

Now we know what was wrong. I am unaccountably angry at the interruption of my recovery trip. I am not ready to let go of our wandering, not yet willing to return so soon to that now-familiar world of illness and grief. Feeling childish and rebellious, as if my protest might stop the drama in Colorado, I am embarrassed. Abandoning the blue roads for a more direct route, we head home on I-90.

May 28, 2004: Journal Entry

Mom has stage IV pancreatic cancer. I feel so many mixed feelings— heavy and wooden. I feel none of the sense of I must go do something that I felt when I heard Janice's diagnosis. I realize that Mom is dying, and I feel extremely sad. She has always lived her life with such resilience. She has been almost unshakable, and always practical. I am so grateful that she and I have come to understand, or at least accept, each other. We both feel affection. She told me this year, for the first time, that she loves me.

I feel safe and supported in the hospice group. Our leader, Tom, an experienced chaplain, tells all of us "grief is love." He means that the work of grief is part of the work of love. He encourages us to talk about all the details of the deaths and memorial services. I feel grateful relief at not being the leader and not having to keep my persona intact. We don't pretend in this group. One other woman has lost a sibling, her brother, in a skiing accident. We bond immediately. Everyone else is dealing with the loss of a spouse or parent. I feel a sense of intimacy and freedom with this group of former strangers. Loss, especially the sudden loss of siblings that Karen and I share, brings us very close to each other. Loss unites us as human beings.

We work, in the group, with many individual ways of addressing some final tasks—the task of saying thank you, I love you, and grappling with necessary forgiveness of others and of ourselves. We write and read our writing to each other. I write a short piece I call "Sister Grief," describing that loving Janice the way I did made me aware that potential grief always hovered close by. I held her close, and in living with such unbounded affection,

I left my life open to grief. If I could have chosen a relationship of more distance and reserve, I would not have. I have learned that fully loving anyone will almost inevitably lead to deep grief. They will die first, or I will, but grief will come. "Sister Grief" is my first piece of reflective writing, other than my journals and words at Janice's memorial services. The group listens respectfully.

The hospice group provides a liminal space for love and grief. Karen and I often talk in the parking lot after the group, as the late spring sun goes down. We repeat the details of our losses, understanding some of our shared coping strategies.

"If Sam had not gone out in that storm at Big Sky, he would not have crashed into the field of boulders, and he'd be alive," Karen tells me repeatedly.

"I know. Why did he go out, anyway?" I ask.

"Damn! He always saw himself as the rescuer and such an expert that he didn't know he might crash. Or I guess that's what he thought. I miss him so much," Karen says again. I can listen to her as long as she wants, and she does the same for me.

We rehearse in detail how she will go to his apartment close to Big Sky to get his things.

"I'm not ready yet. They can sit there for a while. I have his dog, Buster, and that's the most important thing for now," Karen says.

I talk with Karen about the cemetery service we plan for Janice in July. I tell her about my struggle with letting any of the things that belonged to Janice go. She understands.

Just as Janice's brilliant intellect could not save her brain, so Sam's nationally renowned expertise as a ski rescue team member could not enable him to rescue himself. Karen and I give each other all the necessary time we need to talk through all the tiny details that matter to us. We call each other whenever we need someone who understands. This connection brings us each great comfort, we tell each other often. While Karen and I are not in a shared group of friends, at this point I seek her out more than any of my other friends.

At the hospice group Wednesday night, after Gary and I return from our shortened back roads trip, I tell the group what is happening with my mother, of her diagnosis of pancreatic cancer.

I confess that I am not ready to step into this present crisis. Some part of me knows that I am in denial again, trying to dive under this next wave of loss that is breaking upon me too fast. *No fair*, I protest to myself. *I'm not ready. I am exhausted.*

"I shouldn't feel this way. I'm not ready. I am so tired," I say to the group.

"Of course you aren't ready. You'd never be ready, and given what you are going through with the loss of Janice, you must feel awful," Roberta replies. During the break, Roberta, whose husband died, comes up to me to ask when I plan to go to Colorado. I equivocate, citing work and saying I plan to go in mid-June. She looks at me with a steely, but compassionate gaze. "I think you should go see your mother *now.*"

I explain that my clients have put up with many absences and that I need to stay here for a while. Roberta is not impressed. She pats me on my upper arm and gently, firmly says, "Go now, just for a while. I really think you should go see her."

Roberta is still looking at me. She doesn't speak, but pats my arm again and nods. She speaks with authority. That gentle pat gets my attention.

"I was just there three weeks ago. I can't leave again so soon," I insist. With the unreason of grief, I somehow think that the trip I made to my parents' new duplex in Colorado Springs a few weeks ago should count. I'm regressing again, to the psychological level of ten-year-old morality, which leads kids to insist, "No fair!"

Observing my childlike response within myself and to Roberta, I go back to the group and tell them I am going to Colorado. I plan another trip, put my therapy practice on hold again, and tell Gary I am going. My clients are tough, or gone. Gary seems far away, resigned. He doesn't want to make another trip, and I don't know that I ought to ask him to come with me. I pack my bags again, hug Gary goodbye a few days later, tell him and Lightfoot to take care of each other, and get on the plane. Ed picks me up in Colorado Springs and fills me in on what is happening. Ed and I function as a team now, the way Tom and I did with Janice.

A heart that breaks open can still hold love. Like the girl holding on to the tree branch, I must let go with my hands and my mind of what I thought I needed, to open my hands and heart to what I now need to embrace—my mother's dying.

chapter five

Turning toward Tincup

June 2004: Colorado Springs, Visiting Mom and Dad

In the new duplex, I see order and harmony. No clutter mars the serene atmosphere. Even though Mom, Dad, Ed, and I have much to do, and many decisions to make, I can rest here. I sleep, once again a child in my parents' home.

I accompany Mom to her first—and, as it turns out, only—consultation with her oncologist. As I struggle to maneuver her into the hospital in her wheelchair, I feel clumsy, inept, and alone. My role as oldest sibling prepared me to pitch in and get things done, even though I don't necessarily perform this role peacefully or skillfully. My father and I sometimes clash over how to plan and make decisions in the family. Both headstrong, we occasionally stumble into a power tangle.

My dad and I shared a rich intellectual life as I grew up, resulting in a more intimate relationship than my connection with my mother, although my mom and I are changing our decades-long relationship. At a family reunion in 1999, I experienced a new sense of teamwork with Mom, a partnership we sorely need right now. I traveled to Colorado to be with some of our extended family as Mom, her two brothers, and their families planned a Lightfoot family reunion at the cabin. I could not imagine my eighty-year-old mother doing the physical work of cooking, cleaning, moving furniture for seventeen guests, climbing steps, and managing without a right-hand woman. She loves to entertain, planning food weeks ahead of an event, freezing desserts and entrees, and mapping out which tablecloths and tableware to use. All this organizing presents a daunting challenge, even for routine family visits, because of the cabin's location an hour and a half from a grocery store. Janice and I confer about this reunion; she and Tom decide not to attend. For Janice, being with a lot of people in too small a space, on her summer vacation no less, sounds appalling. She comments wryly but truthfully, "It sounds like one of the rings of Hell. If you go, you will get all kinds of stars in your crown. Just don't mention me." She wants to stay home and write. She seems guilty but clear. I decide to act on my impulse to offer help and call my mother from Montana.

"Mom, I think I will come help you with the reunion." She has not specifically invited me.

"But they won't know you," Mom replies.

"What do you mean, they won't know me?" I don't quite grasp her meaning. "Aunt Mary and Uncle Fred, Uncle Malcolm, and their kids and grandkids are coming." I name all the attendees, my relatives. Uncle Fred and I maintain a good relationship, communicating about family history and staying connected on email. I don't understand what my mother is telling me.

"But you're not a *Lightfoot*," my mother insists.

I have to think about this a moment. I don't know quite how to take this. "I'm your daughter! I must be at least half a Lightfoot." I am grasping for some levity as I reel from her comment. "I have known many of these people all my life or all of theirs." I want Mom to tell me she was kidding. She is not.

"You won't know what to talk about with them," she counters.

I'm having trouble with this conversation.

"I know how to talk with people. It will be OK," I manage to reply. "I talk with people every day in my work." I don't know whether to be angry or sad, and I know this conversation is not about my communication skills.

This interchange about sums it up. My mother and I come from different tribes. One of the turning points in our mother-daughter connection came near the end of the reunion when she said, with some surprise, "We *are* a team. We did really well." I had cooked vats of pasta sauce and planned with Molly, her best friend across the road, how we might store food in Molly's extra refrigerator. With no dishwasher, I recruited cousins to help me wash dishes so Mom and her brothers could linger out in the meadow, catching up with each other, watching the weather over the Sawatch Range. Ed built tables on sawhorses and rigged up tarps for shelter from sun and rain. Now at the hospital, more than anything, I want to be on her team, and she is letting me. Tribes don't matter much when her need for help is so dire.

Dad does not to make this trip to the oncologist. Time, analysis, and my siblings' coaching have mellowed most of the old tensions between us, and only love remains. We express our love often to each other. When Janice was dying, none of us in the Divine Ensemble struggled with each other over anything. We dealt with our inner and shared grief without stepping on each other's needs. Now, Dad is physically weak, scared and sad, and more than ready to accept all the help I might provide. I don't know whether I can help Mom in any tangible way. My role must be to help her die well, to experience a death with quality and dignity.

We finally reach the oncologist's floor, and I push Mom out of the elevator. Dr Moffatt ushers us into his office, not an exam room, quickly. With compassion and courage, he tells Mom that her treatment options would offer at best only a five percent chance of success. I hold my mother's hand as we talk. A deep rush of tenderness and concern for Mom wells up inside me. This doctor takes time to ask her if she has questions, to explain his thinking, and to express his sadness that she has to make such a difficult decision—whether or not to ask for treatment. I want to kiss him, thinking of my sister's blithe, young, chipper oncologist who told her that he expected to see her periodically for checkups after her successful treatment. I cannot separate my sister's experience of being treated kindly, but dishonestly, from what is happening now.

My mother says, "I think I'll just let it go, but I need to talk to my family." I feel immense admiration for her clarity and courage. Our side-by-side connection seems essential and natural. As we leave I am heartbroken; I don't have to do anything heroic. My mother just did.

At home that night, Mom says that she doesn't want to let us down by not seeking treatment. Dad hugs her as he says, "Jeannie, I support whatever you want to do. Do what you need to do for *you.*" Through the years they have spoken in such a royal we voice that I am surprised by Dad's ready acceptance of Mom's decision. They have been married close to sixty-three years. Ed and I accept that the worst we have dreaded is happening—our dad will outlive our mother, who has effectively provided assisted living for him for the last four or five years, shielding us from how much he has declined physically. I have tried to interest him in yoga and more walking, but Mom tells me that he seems engaged for a while and then "lets it go." Culturally and temperamentally dependent on his wife's provision of food, social life, and planning of living arrangements, Dad will be bereft. He loves her dearly; he tells us often that marrying Jean was the best thing that ever happened to him.

At eighty-three, Mom has begun the hard work of detaching from her husband and her physical life. She eats almost nothing. Her body grows even more thin; she can walk, but tires quickly, so she spends most of her time on the couch or in bed. She seems not to initiate conversations with Dad, at least not in my hearing. I am slow to accept what is happening to her body.

"Mom, eat some of this applesauce. No? How about some of these potatoes?" I urge, reversing the mother-child relationship.

"Joyce, don't push," Ed interrupts my efforts at supper. "She isn't hungry." I realize that I am taking care of myself. Maybe I can get Mom to eat. Maybe I can help her live longer. I am still haunted by thinking that I should have insisted that Janice see her neurologist back home for a CT scan. My doctor friend in Missoula has helped me release some of my miserable sense of responsibility by coming to my house with Janice's medical chart and reviewing it page by page with me, pointing out that no neurological signs showed up in Janice's record. I must learn to accept my mother's decline.

I am pushing too hard, and it's too late for good nutrition to help my mother. Mom needs to contemplate more important concerns than applesauce and potatoes. She needs to do the difficult work of life review, acceptance of her death, and communicating those few things that still need to be said. The topic of treatment does not come up again, and Mom agrees later this evening that we should call hospice.

The next night I help her out of the bathtub, wrapping her in a big blue towel. I dry her rough, cracked, painful-looking feet. Sitting her on a chair in the bathroom, I massage her feet with some of the Shea butter that Gale had brought Janice in February.

"You're really pampering me," she says, seeming uncomfortable with all this physical attention.

"I like doing it. I'll do this every day." I think, but don't say, *It's about time you got some pampering.* Her feet feel rough at first. They soften with the Shea butter and massage.

She sighs, "That feels so good." Mom has never treated herself to a professional massage. I wish I had given her gift certificates for massages.

Tom makes plans to come help care for Mom, tag teaming with Uncle Fred and Aunt Mary, Mom's younger brother and his wife. Ed keeps track of everything. I admire his calm, steady, intelligent involvement. He manages medications and appointments, shops, hires and supervises in-home help, and keeps our parents company, all while working full time. Somehow he manages to do this without making them feel too dependent. I will go home to Missoula for a short while and then return for as long as my mother lives.

I no longer assume that I am obliged to work no matter what; in the past months I have come and gone from my psychotherapy practice as my family has needed me. Clients know about Janice's death and now, my mother's diagnosis; they express understanding and compassion. With so many absences from work, I have not tried to maintain the recommended nondisclosure about my private life. While I do not discuss any details, I have shared my family challenges with my clients so they do not wonder whether I am ill myself. In some cases, I refer them to colleagues who fill in for me if needed. Others assure me they can wait until I return. As I accept once again that death breaks rudely into life, I contemplate my powerless place in the master drama. All I can do is respond as my intuition leads me; my clients see me as the family member that I am, not only as their therapist. Their responses to my crises leave me humble and grateful. My assistant tells my clients I will let them know when I return from Colorado. We don't set a date.

One morning I settle my mother back in bed after her bath. Her new bedroom in the duplex offers a view of the Front Range of Colorado Springs. She can see the mountains and gaze at the clouds. Familiar colors of teal, tan, and green make up the pattern of the quilted bedspread on her bed; she loves these colors, which complement her reddish-auburn hair. Despite all the moving around in their work and retirement lives, Mom manages to create a sense of familiarity and home wherever she is. Their new duplex seems familiar. I recall the many environments she made home for us, her quick assessments of new parsonages and her practical first changes. She needed to work with the parsonage committee; sometimes they vetoed her color choices, because the next minister's wife might not like them. I recall our enthusiastic choice of soft teal for the Dallas living and dining room, and how disappointed she was when we ended up with neutral, boring gray. Now, I hope *she* feels at home here.

Quiet and reserved at breakfast this morning, Dad knows Mom is making an important decision, whether to go to the cabin or stay here. He looks still and sad as we eat quietly together.

When Mom is resting as comfortably as possible on a pile of pillows in her bed, I pull a chair up beside her, holding a mug of rose hip tea, supporting her head for small sips when she wants to drink. We talk long and deeply. She tells me of her experience early that morning, around 3:00 a.m. She woke up wondering "if the time was now. I became very peaceful, and I prayed."

I ask, "What did you pray?"

"Mostly gratitude," Mom replies.

"I watched the clock," Mom continued, "and then I realized that I was playing God."

"What do you mean?"

"Part of me wanted to die and get it over with. But that's not the way it's going to happen." Mom nods slightly as she tells me this.

"Are you reviewing your life?" I ask.

"Oh yes," she replies. She raises her eyebrows, apparently surprised that I needed to ask.

This is sacred ground. I want to respect her privacy, yet Mom seems open to talking with me about reviewing her life. I wait.

"I have some regrets," she lets me know. "There was a woman in Corpus Christi who did some things my mother should have done." She frowns slightly, remembering the period when she worked in a church in Corpus Christi, and also planned her wedding.

"What did she do, Mama?" Mom almost never criticizes anyone. Her views emerge indirectly. Now she is remembering her own mother, whom I knew as often stern and distant.

"Gave my wedding reception." Mom's words come out clipped and short. "I don't think I thanked her enough."

"Mom, you are always gracious. I'm sure you thanked her a lot."

"Maybe not enough," Mom replies. I don't know the details of this story, how she came to be married in her place of work in Corpus Christi instead of at home in San Antonio. In 1942, economic times were difficult during the war, but I'd never before wondered how this decision was made. I'd seen pictures of her parents and brothers at the wedding in Corpus Christi, but I realize with an ache today that my mother may have felt abandoned by her mother as she married away from home.

Not for the first time I ponder how little in the way of traditional mothering her overworked chiropractor mother was able to give her. My compassion grows as I see our lives converging. I have barely extricated myself from chronic overwork to care for her. I remember that only a few days ago, I thought I was needed in Missoula and couldn't afford to come to Colorado right then. How grateful I am to Roberta for insisting that I visit my mother *now.* I imagine that my grandmother must have also worried about how to balance her work, which supported her children during the Great Depression, and their need for her domestic presence when their father was often on the road. Grandmother employed a housekeeper to cook and care for the children when she needed to stay overnight in the towns surrounding San Antonio, where she drove to work with her patients. It must have been exceptionally unusual for a middle-class mother to work and employ help at home in the 1920s and 1930s.

Mom states very clearly that in the last few days, objects have begun to glow. "There is so much beauty around us that we don't notice," she declares.

She appears to live immersed in a heightened sense of gratitude and an acute awareness of beauty. This must be a state of grace.

"Please tell Gary how beautiful the grain is in that second drawer of the jewelry box." She stares at the box he made for her. "Gary and I have a connection, you know," Mom says. "Not magical, but a deep connection."

"I've noticed that you do. Do you know what it is based on?" I ask. Gary and I have only been married for eleven years, and he has missed a lot of years in Mom and Dad's lives. I wish he had known them earlier, when they were adventurous and active.

"Yes. Beauty." Mom sounds definite about this.

As we discuss the experiences of people who have almost died and then come back, and how universal the experience of being helped by those already dead seems to be, she remarks, "I'd like to help people who haven't quite made it."

Confused, I clarify, "After you die?"

"Yes, all of you," Mom states. "Something is really bothering me, though."

I can think of quite a few things that might be bothering her.

She explains, "They think I believe in traditional ideas, but I don't, and I don't want to disappoint them."

I'm not following this.

"I mean about Heaven and the afterlife. I don't want to let them down."

My mother has lived the role of minister's wife for sixty-three years, experiencing her life in the fishbowl of each congregation. I assure her that "they" will not know.

"You have the right to believe whatever you believe," I assure her.

"I know. But I don't know *what I* believe," she replies.

This is a new conversation for us. I feel immense gratitude that she feels free to think for herself. She's so used to acting as the role model in their churches that she may have little sense of her private life.

Mom ponders whether to ask us to take her to the cabin. Their summer home, which they built in 1980, feels like their central home.

Thinking of the cemetery outside of Tincup reminds me of a summer visit in the 1990s, long before Janice became ill. Dad said he wanted to show me something. We drove in his rattling old Scout to the Tincup cemetery, the one Janice and I explored with such delight when we were children. Dad led me across the wooden bridge up to the Protestant knoll, overlooking upper Willow Creek and Napoleon Pass. We pass the grave of the Chinese cook, China Jim, whose name is etched both in Chinese and English. I doubt if this man was Protestant, but someone made a choice that he belonged here. The Catholic knoll lies up a trail to the right, Boot Hill is farther to the right, and the Jewish knoll, with three graves, sits across the creek to the left. I've always thought it was odd that in a rough mining camp, people still wanted to be buried with their own kind. Dad points out the graves of contemporary men who apparently wanted to be remembered as ornery residents of Boot Hill. I recognize some of the names. Signs point the way up the Protestant knoll.

"I want to show you the plot Jean and I bought. It's for all of us, if you decide to use it."

We've moved around so much as a family that no hometown

exists. While we didn't grow up here except for camping, our hearts settled long ago in Western Colorado. We walk to a pleasing spot on a hillside overlooking the creek, about twenty feet from where Janice declared, "When I die, I want to be buried here."

"Oh, you talked with Janice," I say with delight.

"No, what do you mean?" Dad asks.

I tell him the story of the long-ago time when we sisters explored the ghost-town cemetery.

"I never knew that," Dad says.

I wonder whether time sometimes unfolds in a spiral, rather than in a linear way. We sit on a log, looking out, for a while. Wildflowers bloom in the meandering meadow. I remember watching Mom and Dad fish, a memory that remains clearly present as I sit with my dad.

"I wanted the site next to us, but the Todds have it." The Todds live across from Mom and Dad in their summer home; Molly and Morris are their closest friends. Dad always wanted to camp at the end of the road, with few neighbors. If he has to endure neighbors, the Todds will be the best neighbors of all.

Now that they have built their retirement cabin and sunk their roots into the Tincup community, this choice of a cemetery site makes sense to me. As I remember this talk with my dad, I recall imagining the look on Janice's face when she visits next. Dad and I quietly soak in the beauty of the summer day, the distant mountains, the beaver dams, and the meandering stream. Lupine, columbines, and phlox cover the hillside between where we sit and the creek.

"I love this place, Dad."

"I feel peaceful knowing where we will all be someday," Dad discloses. Our family circle brings him joy.

Later that day I talk with Morris, across the road. Morris, a bit stooped at eighty-nine, with a full head of white hair and twinkling, mischievous blue eyes, jokes, "We *have* to get along, Joyce. We're neighbors for eternity."

"You're pretty hard to get along with, Morris, but I think we'll manage," I tease back.

"Hey, I've got that twenty-five cents in my pocket. You gonna fix me this summer?" This is an old joke between Morris and me. I always tell him he doesn't have enough money for me to fix him, *or* that he is too healthy for me to bother with. He was a prisoner of war in World War Two, incarcerated with other airmen in a camp in Germany. He and Molly are two of the most resilient people I know. Morris and Dad used to walk every morning. Older now, sometimes they simply sit on one of their decks, drink coffee, and talk. Morris quizzes Dad on matters of faith. Dad refuses to play preacher with his friend, but he tells me he takes Morris's questions seriously.

New Closeness

For much of my life, Mom and I were friendly but not close. Janice and I often talked about how I was closest to Dad, she was closest to Mom, while Ed connected easily with both parents. Our dad saw similarities between Mom and Janice. Janice was a sweetheart in Dad's eyes. I identified with our dad's social justice activism, liked to read theology, and spoke out more than Janice did in our earlier years. Mom appreciated Janice's delicate tact.

Who knows all the reasons that a daughter and mother don't bond closely? I don't, even today. But Mom is eighty-three, and we have both evolved into a new relationship. We touch lightly in our conversations in Colorado Springs on my mother's interrupted scholarly life. In 1941, she dropped out of seminary after completing one year, to work at a church in Corpus Christi. Later, when she married a minister in 1942, she probably could not consider a separate professional life; she would have been isolated and misunderstood by the congregations my dad served. She now asks questions about my work. She seems to have forgiven me for two divorces that I know gave her great pain, as she lost sons-in-law whom she had grown to love. In her generation, they married "till death do us part." My generation, marrying in the sixties and seventies, did not rest on the bedrock of that social certainty. We demanded more freedom, and sometimes that freedom led to divorce. My mother did not understand this, although she did not openly criticize me for what she considered failed marriages. I often wanted Mom to assert control over her own life more than I thought she did. We will draw on this more seasoned acceptance of each other in the remaining weeks.

Mom seems ambivalent about traveling to the cabin. Ed and I know that the door of opportunity is swinging closed for this trip. We believe she wants to live her last days at the cabin, but we both wonder if she is afraid to be so far away from hospice care. At this point, we are clueless about what this choice will require. On Sunday, Ed tactfully asks, "Have you decided whether you want to go to the cabin? It's OK with us either way."

"Yes, I'd like to go," Mom states clearly.

Ed and I look at each other, knowing that we must act quickly. We call the Colorado Springs Hospice nurse. "Yes, there is a *small* hospice organization in Gunnison," she replies to our question.

I can hear the doubt in her voice. She is a caring and excellent nurse, an attractive, midlife woman who dresses in her own casual clothes rather than a uniform. She must wonder why we are making this move. Gunnison is more than an hour down the mountain from the cabin. Gunnison Valley Hospice accepts her over the phone, warning us that they have very little staff available. The Gunnison nurse promises at least one visit on Tuesday. The Colorado Springs team faxes medical notes to Gunnison, Mom is discharged from Colorado Springs, and the hospice nurse in Colorado Springs makes a final visit to Mom, arriving at the duplex on her day off. She seems kind and concerned, trying to operate as hospice does, which is to follow the wishes of the patient when possible, while assessing the wisdom of our choice. When we explain the location of the cabin, she looks thoughtful. "Are you sure you want to do this?" she asks Mom, directly.

"Yes, that's where I would like to be," Mom calmly answers. In the living room, away from Mom, the nurse continues to instruct Ed and me. "Here is the morphine I think you will need," she quietly says, showing us how to use the syringe and the vials. "I'll be thinking about you. Call me at any time if you have questions."

Ed and I don't have any idea what those questions could be. With all the staff in Colorado Springs wondering if we are clueless or neglectful, and perhaps feeling baffled that we are leaving their excellent care, they bid us goodbye on the phone and in person. We call Dr. Moffatt, the oncologist, thank him for his kindness, and tell him what we are doing.

"Do you have any questions for me?" he asks. We don't. He too says we can call him if we would like to, which I register as unusual generosity on his part.

Ed and I hurry to pack two vehicles with clothes, food, all the medicine for our parents, a rolling tray, syringes, and pillows. Overtaken by a sense of excitement, in a bizarre way we all feel liberated to be packing up and going to the high country, to the banks of Willow Creek, to the place that has come to be home. It's late June; the grass will be green and the columbines will be blooming.

Home to Shalom

The next morning, we carry Mom in a desk chair to the green Chrysler, pad her lowered seat with pillows, make her comfortable, and begin her last journey to Shalom. Ed drives his old navy pickup with Dad and most of the gear, food, equipment, and clothes. I drive the Chrysler with Mom. Ed and I worry that we won't know how to control her pain on the three-hour drive. Any minute I expect some authority figure to question our right to take our mom to the remote cabin. When I tell Ed my apprehensions, he answers, "We're the grownups."

Mom calls out landmarks, smiling. "Oh, there's the hat," a rock landmark that locals named, marking the transition from suburb to true country environment. Mom is alert and interested, even excited.

"Wilkerson Pass—there's still snow." Mom and Dad have been driving this highway to Western Colorado since the 1960s. Each landmark means she is closer to her destination. They always made a rest stop at the top of Wilkerson Pass, accepting a cup of coffee and a cookie from the volunteers who staff the site; but we don't stop today. The first long look to the mountains of the Continental Divide provides information about how wet or dry it will be in the high country. Snow in June means we will have a good crop of wildflowers, which Mom loves. Snow shines in the sunlight on this day in late June.

"Look, here's South Park." Mom continues her place-naming. I've heard the stories about several trappers' rendezvous in South Park. The trappers, for a brief time while the beaver trade was still profitable, would gather at a location passed from native trader to trapper for a spring rendezvous, where horse racing, betting, games, and drinking relieved the boredom of winter in a solitary trapper's cabin. Several took place here, along the South Platte. The road aims straight toward the Rockies. Today, I don't drive my usual eighty miles an hour to get closer to the cabin fast. I follow Ed's truck; we both keep to a sedate level of speed. Mom doesn't want a rest stop. I pass her some water in a bottle, but she can't hold it to her mouth.

"Here's Florissant," Mom exclaims. She greets each familiar milestone with joy, childlike in her excitement. I think of how many times she has made this trip, earlier in her life when the family lived in Colorado Springs, and later when she and Dad drove to the cabin with Ed. Her face looks young and happy; my love and admiration grow with each hour. I feel a mix of sorrow, knowing this is the last time she will see these familiar places, and awe as I learn that joy can overtake sorrow, even shortly before one's death. She does not comment on last times. She lives in the present moment.

In Buena Vista, we stop for hamburgers before we drive over Cottonwood Pass. Ed and Dad sit on a park bench at the city park, outside the car, and I eat my hamburger in the car with Mom. "Umm, that smells good," she hints. Surprised, since she has not been eating, I feed her in tiny bites from my burger. "Pizza," she proclaims definitively. "No, that's hamburger," I reply.

"Nope. Pizza." She seems to enjoy it, whatever it is.

Driving over the pass, I ask her if she wants to nap. "No, I don't want to miss anything." As we wind over Cottonwood Pass, on the paved side, I slow down at the summit, 12,400 feet. Looking out over the Taylor Valley, she sighs "*There it is*," with a deep exhalation, as we catch the first glimpse of Taylor Reservoir from the top of the pass. After a forty-five-minute descent over the gravel road, we arrive at the cabin to the warm embrace of Morris and Molly, who have been keeping watch for us. We haven't considered how to get Mom up the stairs, so Dad and Morris walk upstream to find a neighboring teenage boy who, with Ed, carries Mom's ninety pounds or so up the stairs in a deck chair.

As we settle her in on the couch, she looks out toward the Sawatch Range and names the birds. "There's a Rufous. A Stellar's Jay, and look at the Junco! There's a Gray Jay—a camp robber!" She has always fed the birds at the cabin. Ed takes on that service the first thing every morning while we are there. She would not let us take down a mostly dead lodge pole pine a few years ago, because it's her birdhouse tree. The tree is hung with different feeders for the different birds—black flaxseed for the pine siskins, a mix of larger seeds for the other birds, and puppy chow for the chipmunks and jays. Mom says, referring to the Asian-style bird feeder that Gary made a few years back, "I always liked that feeder." Looking toward Ice Mountain she exclaims, "It's so beautiful here." We arrange her so she can see the birds and the mountains.

Ed sleeps upstairs in the room next to Mom and Dad, installing a baby monitor so he can hear any cry for help. He reverses the roles; the youngest child now monitors his parents. Ed tells me that one night he hears Dad say, "Jeannie, I love you." While he tears up next door, he knows he is not needed at this moment. I think about Mom telling me that she wants Dad to show her that he loves her, and I know he is doing that the only way he can now, by holding her and keeping her company. We agree that Ed will pound on the floor with Dad's walking stick, which he carved years before from a Ponderosa branch, if he needs me to come upstairs quickly from where I sleep on the ground floor.

We learn how this remote high country community says goodbye. Many friends live nearby. They built their homes at about the same time and share a history of potlucks, four-wheel-drive adventures, and sitting around the campfires at various building sites, drinking coffee and sharing stories. Now all these original residents are old, and our generation is moving into responsibility. Chris, a good friend up the creek, sends a beautifully arranged fruit salad, kiwi fruit and strawberries placed just so on a green crystal plate, but she cannot bear to visit to say goodbye. Sam, a psychiatrist, now in his nineties, cannot walk up the stairs. He stands at attention outside, hand over his heart. He served as a doctor in the Coast Guard in World War Two. I go out to talk with him.

"Thank you so much for coming, Sam," I say. He keeps his hand over his heart, holding his wide-brimmed hat in his left hand.

"She is a great lady. She means the world to us," Sam tells me, tears in his eyes.

"Do you want Ed to help you up the stairs?" I ask.

"No, I'll stay here." He does, standing at formal attention, while his wife Dorothy visits, speaking gently to her old friend Jean.

Dorothy touches Jean's hair, saying, "Someone's made you all pretty." She strokes Mom's cheek and they look into each other's eyes. I notice that no one says goodbye in words; they indicate their love and respect in touch, gestures, and tone of voice. The community's minister, Newton, a retired chaplain who preaches at the Tincup Community Hall on Sundays, comes by often. He will officiate at the cemetery service we already have planned for burying the ashes of Dianne and Janice.

Molly brings a bouquet of wildflowers—flax, lupine, and prairie roses to put in Mom's white milk glass vase, one of Mom and Dad's treasured wedding presents. She refreshes the wildflowers when they need it, and makes chocolate chip cookies for Dad since she knows he has a sweet tooth. Molly served as a WAVE in World War Two, and she's about as no-nonsense as my mother. They saw each other every day during the summer seasons for twenty-five years, collaborating on brunches for the sewing circle, drinking coffee together, going on jeep trip adventures with the other founders of the summer home group, and sewing quilts and clothes together.

At a remote site high in a mountain valley, the web of kindness keeps us from falling too far from human connection. While Molly sits reminiscing with Mom, Ed and I can take a quick walk outside. Molly mothers us.

"You be sure and get some sleep, you two," she admonishes Ed and me.

"We are," Ed assures her.

"Well, you may be, but I see your sister's light on late, as usual. She likes her books." Molly knows me; when I can't sleep, I read in my downstairs bedroom until sleep arrives. My journal rests by my bed, but I don't write any dreams during this time. When my mind is actively and emotionally engaged in my waking hours, often I do not remember my dreams.

Meanwhile, by our third day at the cabin, Ed and I panic. We did not realize that we would have almost no access to practical help beyond one nursing visit and one volunteer from hospice. The volunteer, who admits she used to be a nurse, shows us how to change the bedding while Mom is in the bed. I hear her nursing experience as she counts, "One, two, three . . . go, go," when we lift Mom back on the bed. Hospice volunteers are not supposed to make their professional skills evident, so no confusion exists about who is supposed to do what, but Ed and I take comfort from this former nurse's skills. She knows we need her help, to learn how to care well for our mother. The role of hospice volunteer is to provide conversation, emotional comfort, and wisdom about dying. She realizes we are also desperate for practical assistance and, as did the hospice nurse in Colorado Springs, she gives Ed and me her phone number and invites us to call if we need to. No one else is available to come help us; we spend time quelling our anxiety by making calls, trying to find practical nursing help. The two hospice staffers in Gunnison call friends and everyone they can think of. No one can come now; maybe later, after the Fourth of July.

Ed and I are trying to plan a future in which there will be orderly help, and we might take the role of the support staff. But there is no orderly help, only a rapid disintegration toward death, and we *are* the help. We learn one more life lesson: death moves with its own trajectory, while we witness the process. We don't know that we don't have weeks to plan. By about Tuesday, we realize we're alone. We *are* the staff. We are still trying to administer the regimen of many medications and vitamins, which are increasingly difficult for Mom to swallow.

"All she really needs is your love, sips of water, and morphine," the hospice nurse in Gunnison gently instructs, after I've called her with my anxious questions. We put all the rest of the medicine and superfluous vitamins in a cabinet. I realize I'm still clinging, as I did with Janice's OmegaBrite, to the magic of . . . something.

We learn how to measure the morphine. The nurse instructs me over the phone how to use a morphine suppository. I recoil, but there is no one else to perform this intimate act. At one point, while Ed and I are changing our mother's bed and diapers, Ed wryly comments, "Well, *you* never had a baby, so I guess this is all new for you." I don't mind Ed saying this. He is right; I feel out of my league. Good thing that Ed is here. He not only nursed Dianne, he raised his daughter Katie on his own from the time she was six. He knows what he is doing.

Surprised at the physical strength required to bathe and move our ninety-pound mother, Ed and I lift as a team; I rely on his physical strength and ask him to tell me what to do. I call the hospice nurse again, upset and confused about how much morphine to administer. I don't want to make a mistake resulting in Mom feeling pain. Again the experienced nurse cuts through talk about milliliters and measurement to urge, "Give her what she needs. Use your own judgment. Keep her comfortable."

We are nursing without a net—no more fine lines on the syringe to measure, only our own perceptions of her needs. Mom must have felt this helplessness when I, as an infant, screamed between feedings. She told me once that she regretted not trusting her own instincts about feeding.

"You know those baby packs women wear on their stomach?" she asked me a few years ago.

"Yes, of course."

"That's what I should have done, but I didn't know what to do." She looks pensive. "I regret that now."

My mother had to learn to be a mother—she was not warmly physical with me, the firstborn. She did what she knew to do. She told me stories of dressing me up and walking me—"the baby"— around our Atlanta neighborhood in the stroller, hoping that people would think she was being a good mother. During that conversation, she doesn't seem to connect me, the adult, to the baby she didn't know how to mother.

Babies were supposed to get fresh air. She bore me in the forties when childbirth had become the province of the medical system instead of women helping women at home. The basic instinctual mothering that woman had relied on for eons atrophied, and mothers received little help at home. Drugged while delivering, she and countless other 1940s mothers must have felt what I am feeling now, complete confusion about what to do. I feel compassion for her, and for us. I have never borne this much responsibility for a person's physical care and comfort before. When Janice died, we had every kind of help available. A hospice nurse came every day, and a hospice volunteer sat with us and gave practical help and good advice. She told us how we would know when Janice was actively dying—that her feet would get cool and her breathing would become shallow. Gary and Ed turned Janice, and even washed her. I am shocked that I did not provide this service. I learned late.

Today I remember my mother's regret and turn it into gentle encouragement for me to do what seems best. She unknowingly helps me now because of what she told me about her own experience. I don't want to overdose her, and I don't want her to feel pain.

Now, we are attending a home death without a trained midwife.

Ed and I talk about how this way of dying at home, like birthing babies at home, prevailed until very recently in Western culture. With Janice, we were more in the hands of the medical system, even though she died at home. She endured radiation, half a chemo treatment, and as a result went into a coma, sustained only by saline and morphine in a drip. Completely grateful for the pain relief of morphine for Janice, at the same time I deeply regret submitting her to chemo and radiation. We followed the best advice we were given at the time. Now, as a family, we are assisting in a hands-on death. We want to give our mother what she has asked—her last days to be spent at the cabin, without intervening treatment that ultimately would not help her. She made her choice, and we agree with her and carry out her wishes. In the remote mountains, we return to the old ways.

Our dad's medical and emotional needs coexist with our mother's dying. One morning I am scrambling for clean sheets. We wash linens every day. Even though Mom loves to be on the couch so she can look at the birds and mountains, she wants us to move her to her bed at night so she can rest with Dad. When she lies on the couch, she tries to stay awake and look outside, only occasionally talking with us. During what was the last move of our mother from the sofa to her bed, Dad comes into the hall while we are supporting Mom on our interlocked arms, her arms around Ed's neck and mine as we balance her for the transfer. She trusts us to carry her.

Dad, carrying his empty cereal bowl, says, "I need some breakfast. I haven't eaten yet." Looking back, I know he felt panicked and desperately sad. Mom prepared almost every meal he had eaten in their home for sixty-three years.

I snap at him, "We're busy. Fix your own cereal, please." Finishing the move and tucking Mom into the last set of clean sheets, Ed asks me to come outside on the deck. We stand looking out at Ice Mountain in silence for a while. Ed counsels, "I know it's irritating. He can't help it." Ed manages to teach without shaming. "He just needs us to be kind to him." I am embarrassed at my outburst and feel grateful that Ed models calm, and that my father maintains his forgiving nature. Each day I discover more lessons I must quickly learn. The child in me wants Daddy to help, and he can't any longer.

July 3: At Shalom

Mom rests in bed. I bathe her and put Shea butter and a trace of makeup, blusher, and soft coral lipstick on her face. I wash her reddish-gray hair with a washcloth and a little baby shampoo, using my curling iron to restore the appearance that she prizes. Mom has taken good care of her body, clothes, hair, and face. Until a few months ago, she looked much younger than eighty-three. She mostly sleeps now. Ed and I put liquid morphine under her tongue when she grimaces. Like the birds she loves, she opens her mouth only for this mercy of pain relief. We are not counting the milliliters. We spoon eyedroppers of water into her mouth although she can't really swallow. We help with elimination, keep her warm and clean, keep her company, and talk to her.

The morning light comes into the east window of their bedroom, illuminating the objects she has placed on the windowsill. The pewter candy dish that always held candy in our home now holds rocks Mom has collected. The green pottery ashtray that Mom kept even though no one ever smoked, because Ed made it in seventh-grade shop class, holds more rocks. The sixties-era, gold-and-red stained-glass angel I gave her filters gold sun into red beams. A pottery owl with enormous, blue, fake-gem eyes that Janice discarded long ago rests on the sill. Mom must have rescued it. A picture of the family sits where she can see it. A light green Depression-glass dish that belonged to Grandmother Freddie needs dusting.

As I massage cream into her face, Mama opens her eyes and smiles into mine. "You're sure beautiful," she says. Tears leak from my eyes. Today my mother tells me this for the first time. I remember beauty pageants I entered during high school years along with the hours Mom spent making clothes for my sister and me so we would be "in" with the other girls. Our mother, without any doubt, supported us in our desire to be accepted and admired by our peers. While I longed in the past for her to see me as beautiful, I am moved by her appreciation of me as an older woman today. My youthful yearning for my mother to see me as beautiful has passed. What she tells me today resonates powerfully—she recognizes something in me that is deeper than physical beauty. She knows that I love her. Our intimate connection is beautiful.

I have dressed in a forties-era, yellow, sleeveless shirt with red sprigged printed cherries, and button-style red earrings. One moment, I learn, can erase years of longing for a closer relationship. Mom once disclosed that she had been jealous of my advantages. She recounted her poverty-tinged teenage years in San Antonio, when she studied hard to become valedictorian of her large class so she could go to college with a scholarship, edited the newspaper, and wanted to be seen as a brain. She confessed that she often thought if she had been given just *one* of my offices and advantages, she would have been satisfied. She told me she had sometimes seen me as spoiled and ungrateful, but felt embarrassed that she envied me.

Daughter-envy forms the root of the wicked stepmother complex in fairy tales; I know that women who envy their daughters often think something is wrong with them. I have experienced the uncomfortable emotion myself, of women with children, and now that I am older, of young people with their lives ahead of them. As I remember Mom confessing her envy, I join with that seventeen-year-old, now my mother. Just as she forgave me for sometimes being a difficult teenager, I find my forgiveness for her lack of understanding of me follows easily after I experience deep empathy for her. Now her story and my story come together in a moment of recognition and compassion. She does not speak again except to let us know "hurt."

I ponder that one of the important things that happens before death, if one is very fortunate, is that we forgive each other. I have already asked my mother to forgive the ways I made my growing-up years stormy and rebellious. A few weeks ago, recalling that period in our lives, she said, "I just saw you and Janice as . . . different from each other." That was putting the matter mildly. Janice took in the situation with her older, acting-out sister and decided, as she later told me, to be the "good" one. In the fairy tale books Janice and I shared, we found the story of Snow White and Rose Red. When we claimed our roles, I chose Red, the passionate sister, while Janice yearned to be pure and good as a child. Mama not only forgave me, she didn't seem to remember the problems I'd created for her.

The morning of July 4, after an arduous time of cleaning up Mom with Ed, getting her clothes changed, sponging her face and chest, and trying to make her comfortable in bed, I sit at the dining table eating breakfast. Looking at Gary's well-crafted oak table that he delivered three years ago for their sixtieth anniversary, I realize that they did not enjoy much time at the new table. I am looking out the window at Ice Mountain when Ed touches me on the shoulder.

"I doubt if she is going to last the day."

"How can you tell?" I get up quickly.

"Her breathing is very irregular, and . . . I can just tell," Ed says quietly. Although we have witnessed the daily decline, I am shocked that the end is so near. Dad surprises me as he walks quickly across Camp Bird Lane to tell Mollie and Morris, perhaps to receive their comfort. I sit on a chair by her bed and begin to sing, in my hoarse, allergy-ravaged voice. I think, *I'm no choir, but I'm the only choir she has.* I hold her hand and sing camp songs, hymns, and old popular songs. Dad sits on the other side of the bed, holding her other hand. Newton, the chaplain, stands quietly in the doorway. Occasionally Mom shifts a little. I sing the TCU *alma mater*: "Mem'ries sweet, comrades true. Light of faith, follow through . . ." TCU was the emotional home for Mom and Dad, the place where they met, where Dad fell in love with the pretty redhead cashier in the cafeteria. Dad wipes his eyes with his handkerchief.

Although I think Mom is unconscious, tears seep out from her closed eyes. Then Mom opens her eyes with a startled look and coughs up dark blood. She is actively dying. Distressed that this time we cannot clean her up without disturbing her unduly, Ed and I simply place a towel over her chest. Dad, Ed, and I touch her. I sing, "There's a Long, Long Trail a-Winding," Mom and Dad's favorite song, their song. I think maybe Dad will sing with me, but he can't. Mom slightly shifts her body toward Dad. She stops breathing. I find myself speaking a spontaneous prayer of commitment for the recently dead, the way my dad did for Janice right when she died. I could not speak then. Now, he is not able to.

"God and all the angels, Freddy and Belle and Janice, accept Jean, a lamb of your pasture, a sheep of your fold. Guide and help her . . ." I continue a prayer from my heart. Newton blesses her, touching her forehead and cheeks, then kisses her forehead, saying, "Bless you on your journey, Jean."

We sit with her for a while. Molly walks to Mom, kisses her forehead, saying, "You had a good life."

Ed and I dress Mom in clothes she made, a teal, A-line skirt and short-sleeved print blouse. We choose pearl earrings that Dad gave her, and her favorite liquid-silver-and-turquoise necklace, a Christmas present from Janice and me a few years ago. We know that we will need to remove these shortly, but for now, we want to adorn her in objects she loved. She looks beautiful to me, her face smooth, lines erased. I call Tom.

"It's Joyce," I tell Tom.

"I thought it might be," Tom replies. "She's gone?"

"Yes, about noon."

"I'm all packed, Tom says. "I'll get on the road." Tom has been waiting for this call to begin his travel. "I'll call you when I get to Hays." Tom and Janice usually stayed in Hays, Kansas, on their way to the cabin. Later, Tom will tell me that he places the container of Janice's ashes on her side of the front seat. Sometimes he talks to her, but he tells me that he felt too sad to keep up any patter.

Although it's July 4, the mortician arrives in a little more than an hour. His hair shows the comb marks of a recent cleanup. I imagine he was having a picnic with his family. Respectfully stepping back, he requests that we remove all jewelry. We remove the earrings, the liquid silver, and her wedding rings. She has not taken off the wedding band since Dad put it on her finger in Corpus Christi in 1942. I put them in one of her gold-banded china cups in the red oak sideboard.

The mortician and Ed manage to get the gurney down the steps where we recently struggled to get Mom *into* the cabin. I ride in the front of the hearse to town, as I did with Janice; Dad and Ed drive behind in the Chrysler. I don't want to leave her body at the mortuary. Something seems incomplete, as though a crucial task or ritual has been left undone. Dad comforts me with a gentle hug. "Joycie, it's hard because you did the same thing with Janice so recently," says my father, thankfully taking charge. "But we can go now." We leave in silence.

Sitting in the car, we decide we don't have the heart to go home and make supper, so we get Chinese food, feeling relieved to be out of the cabin for a while. We drive back up the Taylor River Canyon, naming each campground. This is a family ritual: One Mile, Rosy Lane, Lottis Creek, Cold Springs. These places ground us as we remember countless trips up and down this canyon.

Ed points at Cold Springs. "That's where you tried to kill me with a stove," he teases me.

"I did *not* try to kill you. It was a pillow fight."

Ed smiles as we remember the panicked trip into town to get Ed stitched up when he was three. He's balding now, and I can see the scar.

"Do you want to stop for water?" Ed asks. Long ago we decided that this cold spring water is the best water in the world. It tastes of minerals, granite, and memories. Ed brings a water bottle from the car. We pass it around as he dips it deeply into the rock opening at the base of the rockslide. This is communion; we drink our fill.

"That's good," Dad says. Ed holds his hand out to help him over the rocks.

Later that night, I sit in front of the wood stove with Dad. I tend the fire; he talks about their marriage. Their time together was the great gift of his life. I will sit up with Dad as long as he wants. Finally, we both can sleep. He tells me all the stories that make up the narrative of their love—the sign near Marble Falls, Texas, an advertisement for Aransas Pass, claiming "They bite every day!" This is the spot where he proposed (for the second time, I find out) and she said "yes." Dad reveals something I did not know. "I asked her once before, but she said she wasn't ready," he admits with a small smile. "She wanted to work on her own for a while." He tells me about sleeping on the sand on the beach in Corpus Christi where Mom was working as a director of religious education before they married. He needed to save money. "We had a *wonderful* marriage," Dad says again.

"Do you want to sleep on the couch, or the small bedroom?" I wonder if he wants to avoid being in their room.

"No, I'll go in there," Dad gestures to their bedroom. We hug, and I go downstairs, where I stay awake a long time, getting up twice to look at the stars before I go to sleep.

Three Memorials at Tincup

On July 7th, family and friends have been notified that we will hold a service at the cemetery for Mom, Janice, and Dianne. Tom and Gary arrive the day before. We plan a full memorial service for Mom in Colorado Springs. As we prepare to go to the cemetery, I remember something.

"Do you have Janice's ashes?" I ask Tom.

"Uh, no. Guess I'd better get those." Tom retrieves the ceramic blue-and-green vase containing Janice's ashes. Ed brings a small box containing some of Dianne's ashes.

We all drive the rocky road to the Tincup cemetery. Walking past the spot Janice and I discovered as children, we gather at our plot. Mom and Dad's summer friends join us at the Tincup cemetery to mourn and honor Jean. Her brother Fred and his wife Mary place a rosebush with white roses behind her spot, knowing it won't last the winter. I love seeing the roses, as I know Mom would. Mollie and Morris sit on the bench at their site next door.

First, we honor Jean, whose friends have come to be with us. Not knowing whether he will be able to stand, Dad sits in a deck chair that Ed's best friend Clyde has brought for him, while others sit on logs or stand. At the right time, Dad rises and tells the story of the day Jean said "Yes" to his proposal. His voice sounds strong and firm. We bury Jean's ashes, pouring them directly into the hole Ed and Clyde dug. We hadn't found the right container in the short time since she died. I wish I had thought of one of her quilted pieces to wrap around the ashes.

Not knowing whether people will want to stay for the service for Janice and Dianne, we create a break and give friends a chance to leave, but they all stay. Many friends seem stunned at the experience of burying three family members at one time. We hold abbreviated, separate memorials for each in turn. Ed reads what he wrote for Dianne's service in Colorado Springs, about the wildfires in the forest and the fires of their love. Gary plays a song for Dianne on his Native American flute. I read a poem for Janice, Thomas Centolella's "In the Evening We Shall Be Examined on Love." Tom reads a rewritten John Denver song for Janice. Gary plays "Morning Has Broken," and prays. Newton gives a benediction. His dignity and love for Mom and Dad help us.

The two marker stones are made of dark red granite, with white incised letters. Dianne's marker reads, "Not all who wander are lost." Ed has told us how much it meant to Dianne to be welcomed into our family circle after a life that felt like wandering. Janice's stone reads, "Born of love, bearer of the light of kindness." We agreed that Janice's essence was kindness. Mom's granite stone will have to wait until next spring to be ordered and set. We place Janice's and Dianne's stones directly on the ground, with plans to build the concrete pads and set a large family stone next Memorial Day.

Ed, Tom, and I only half-jokingly decide that we'd better build our concrete pads pretty soon while we are still young enough for the physical labor. We water the wildflowers and take a last look, not knowing when the next thunderstorm will arrive.

chapter six

Things Fall Apart

The day after the service for Mom, Janice, and Dianne at the Tincup cemetery, all of us at the cabin pack quickly to go back to Colorado Springs. We will hold a full memorial service there, but I don't want to think about that now. Tom and Gary offer to pack Mom's clothes in bags for donation. Like Tom with Janice's clothes, Dad needs us to remove all her personal items from the cabin—he feels too much pain seeing her clothes hanging in the closet.

"Joyce, do you want any of these clothes?" Tom calls from Mom and Dad's bedroom at Shalom. I'm cleaning up in the kitchen.

"Just a minute. Let me come see," I call back from the kitchen. Ed is helping Dad pack to go back to the duplex in Colorado Springs.

The first dress I notice in Gary's arms is the teal dress Mom made to wear to my wedding with Gary. She looked beautiful that day in 1993 at the lunch reception that followed. A picture in my scrapbook shows her delight in the event, and in her outfit. She restrung blue-and-gold art deco beads I brought her from England to wear, adding small green beads to pick up the colors in her dress. With her red hair and big smile, holding a champagne glass of orange juice, she looks young and vibrant. Do I want this dress? No, I want my mother.

"I don't want to give them away, but I don't know what else to do with them," I tell Gary and Tom. No one offers any better answers than donating the clothes. Again, I am stunned by how quickly a person's life objects may or must be eliminated in a few days. I'd like an old family home with plenty of closets and an attic, so I could preserve Mom's clothes for a while, touch them, find people to give them to, and let them rest in peace, undisturbed. I wanted the same thing with Janice's most personal items. No one lives that way anymore; maybe we never did. I recognize my need to preserve what cannot stay—life and the accouterments of life.

Six days after Mom's death, we all drive back to Colorado Springs, retracing the path we took with Mom and Dad two and a half weeks earlier. Driving by myself, I look at Mom's place in the Chrysler as I navigate Cottonwood Pass. Contemplating in reverse the landmarks she loved, I name them out loud for her. When we arrive at the duplex, Gary and I move into the guest room I occupied in June. The process continues—taking apart our mother's thoughtfully constructed wardrobe. Her dressy clothes, except for that one teal dress she wore to our wedding, remain in the closet in Colorado Springs. Her casual clothes are at the cabin. We save her small-sized outer jackets, vests, and sweaters for visitors to the cabin; I am relieved that a few items she wore stay behind. After a while, I ask Gary not to inquire about any of Mom's clothes since I find the repeated questions too painful. For now, I pack the oak jewelry box with her earrings, pendants, and necklaces into our Honda to take to Missoula. I plan to return the jewelry box to the cabin next summer, so I can see it and use it when I visit.

We organize a meaningful service for Mom at the church in Colorado Springs; however, I struggle with my resentment of some of the people there, the same people who seemed to be Mom's friends decades ago, but who turned their backs on her when the elders fired our dad. I was long since married, Janice safely at college, but Ed moved in the middle of his senior year—another inconvenient and painful dislocation. In the early 1970s Dad spoke against the war in Vietnam. His opposition to the war, in Colorado Springs—a city full of active and retired military personnel—proved unpopular.

When he joined Clergy and Laity Opposed to the War, some judged him as unpatriotic. He also went on tour in the state, speaking against the death penalty, debating the state attorney general. At the same time he was preaching and teaching about these and other social issues, the church was in the process of planning a new sanctuary. Dad provided leadership on the design of a new, contemporary sanctuary that would reflect inclusion by organizing seating in what he called a gathered plan. A skylight beams light onto a central table. This is the location for Mom's memorial service.

I remember my mother's shocked incomprehension that people she considered good friends turned against Dad and asked him to leave. "These women were my *friends*," she told me in phone conversations from Colorado to Austin, where I was attending graduate school. Rick and I were married in the old sanctuary; later we camped out in the education rooms when we led groups of teenagers from Austin on backpacking trips to Western Colorado. While decades-old resentment against these people still simmers in me, Mom and Dad rejoined this same church when they recently moved back to Colorado Springs.

Yet just as hospice staff honors the wishes of their clients, Ed and I decide we want to honor Mom and Dad's choice not only to rejoin this church, but Dad's desire to hold her formal memorial service here. I ask Dad about this, and he replies, "We know the people and we feel at home there." Mom's service provides an opportunity for me to learn from Mom and Dad's generosity of spirit. However, I ignore Mom's former best friend, not having forgiven her for her betrayal, although clearly my mother had. Given her nature, Mom probably remembered their neighborhood connection and their time in the women's fellowship, and not her devastation when the board fired her husband.

Again, as at Janice's service, Gary sets the tone for Mom's memorial with a reflection on her life as a quilt of experiences, a life beautifully pieced together with friends, family, moves, service, and good work.

Exhausted, Gary and I leave Dad to embark on the hardest time of his life, living without Jean. Ed tells me he will spend as much time as he can with Dad. Preparing to drive home, my now-familiar sense of guilt that I am rejoining my life back home rides along with us. Maybe guilt overshadows my more primal experience of sorrow. Dad, Ed, and I hug each other in the living room of the duplex, but Dad does not come outside to wave goodbye. Ed stands and watches us drive away.

The Long Way Home

Gary and I drive over back roads in Wyoming to Montana. We find some measure of peace and reconnection, taking the trip slowly, talking, stopping often, avoiding a fast trip north on the Interstate. We talk through my hurt and dismay when Gary appeared reluctant to drive to Colorado after Mom died. Gary tells me how weary he is of our chaotic married life. I think of how recently our back roads trip in Montana ended with the call from Ed saying Mom had pancreatic cancer.

"It's not my fault," I insist.

"I know. But I am weary," Gary repeats. I do not feel forgiving. We turn west at Ranchester, Wyoming. The high mountain meadows are spread with lush wildflowers, more than I have ever seen in this part of the state. We wander and hike close to the Medicine Wheel, on the Red Grade Road in the Big Horn Mountains. Walking slowly through the flowers, I think of Mom's assiduous study of Rocky Mountain wildflowers. Returning from her walks around Shalom she would head directly to the wildflower books to identify any flower she didn't know. Some stumped her, and I could hear her reciting "little yellow flower" in frustration. She didn't like to give up on identification. She would relish the columbines, lupine, prairie smoke, arrowleaf, balsamroot, and clover in bloom. My internal dialogues with my mother do not yet form easily in my imagination as they do with Janice. I'm not working with my loss yet; I'm only enduring more grief.

Gary asks what I would like to do for my birthday, coming up in mid-July.

"Nothing," I reply. No sense of anticipation, or any desire to mark my birthday, breaks through my flat, absent-spirited mood. Gary persists and offers to call a few friends to gather at a restaurant and then on our deck. He'll get the cake. I agree, touched by his determination to honor my life.

When I arrive home, I contact my clients to schedule our meetings. I had referred some people in critical personal situations to other therapists over the past few months. Many clients have told me that they are waiting for me to return; they don't want to start over with someone new. I've been in private practice for almost twenty years; deeply committed to my clients and their healing. I am moved by their compassion for me as I come and go. I haven't taken on any new clients since Janice became ill, so I'm facing the need to reduce my waiting list. Gary and I work with couples in a form of conjoint therapy in which we combine communication coaching with analysis of difficult underlying dynamics. He worked with some of them on his own during weeks when I was gone.

I wish we knew someone who provides this kind of couples counseling. We are dealing with grief and separation differently and as a result, we are not easily and readily granting each other slack, compassion, and forgiveness.

Layers of Grief

At home, a startling dream awakens me. In the dream, Mom appears in desperate trouble; I have forgotten that she is in distress and still needs us. Anguished that we are neglecting her, I awaken to set up a place at home to remember Mom. The mid-summer view out the east window toward the stream in the back seems appropriate. Mom slept in this room last Thanksgiving; I imagine her sitting by the bay window, watching the fawns and the birds. Again, the need to build an altar, a place for remembrance, emerges. Soon, one of her pins in the shape of Texas, with an enamel picture of bluebonnets, rests by a picture of Mom at our wedding. A heart-shaped pink box made of quartz composite, which she chose for me one birthday, holds some of her jewelry—a gold Texas pendant with a star in the location for Dallas, a pin with *Jean* spelled in cursive, and a spherical watch on a gold chain. When I was a child squirming in church, she used to hand it to me so I could gaze at the watch workings and calm down until the service was over. I once judged the heart box as too sweet and sentimental for me, but now I love having something she gave me to hold a few pieces she prized.

Gale is praying for Mom. In her Buddhist religion, the soul of the departed arrives at a gateway to reincarnation on the forty-ninth day after death, which will occur on Mom's birthday. While this is not my own belief, I appreciate Gale's meditations on Mom's behalf. Gale meditated for Janice in the same way. The dream tells me that I have moved quickly into caring for Dad's needs, from a distance, and I am not taking the time to grieve for my mother. Frazzled and distracted, emotionally numb, I keep my emotions under the surface, even at our hospice group meetings.

Gary officiates at a wedding of a midlife couple. The ageless, achingly beautiful language, "to have and to hold, until death do us part," finally loosens a wave of sorrow, as I think of Mom and Dad's long marriage, and Dad retelling me their love stories before the wood fire at Shalom the night Mom died. Fleeing the celebration as soon as I can, I head home. On our deck in the warm July night, lavender and pink fill the western sky as the first stars emerge. I begin to cry out loud. This seems to be the first time I've been alone since Mom died. No one can hear me but Lightfoot who comes to sit in my lap. I weep for Dianne and Ed, whom death parted with cruel speed; for Janice, who left us so breathtakingly fast; for Dad, who lost his wife of sixty-three years; for Mom, who lost her life; and for my own broken-open heart. Lightfoot's weight in my lap comforts me as the light fades. Finally I mourn privately for Jean Lightfoot Hocker.

So many tasks consumed our time just after Mom died. The haste leaves me swamped with deep regret at how quickly Ed and Gary bundled up Mom's carefully chosen clothes, gifts from Janice and me, along with so many meticulously tailored dresses and jackets she made for herself. I wish I had kept that teal dress and had taken the time to choose some clothes to keep tucked away. Now I grieve for those clothes—a rust-colored wool suit, small print blouses with matching jackets in her favorite green, blue, rust, cream, and tan colors. Mom delighted in fabric and color. I washed the red-and-white-striped, sprigged-pattern cotton pajamas she was wearing when she died, placing them downstairs in the cabin under a big pile of handkerchiefs she'd saved from the forties and fifties.

"I don't want people to think I'm a clothes horse," she explained. "It's just that we had so little to wear growing up that now that I can make things for myself, I just keep going." In the duplex in Colorado Springs, as I was sorting files, I uncovered correspondence between Janice and Mom as they collaborated on jackets and skirts that Mom sewed for my sister. Janice's carefully sketched designs, with snips of fabric glued to the letters, communicated what she wanted. Janice, I read with surprise, completely adapted to Mom's sensate nature by writing about things Mom loved. She wore two jackets Mom made from the same pattern for her, one deep red and one teal. These fit her petite body so much more attractively than the boxy blazers of the day. The jackets nipped in at her waist, and featured small puffed sleeves, tapering to a closely fitting wrist. I saw Janice wear these jackets for years, but I had not known the exquisitely coordinated planning Mom and Janice gave to the design and fabric. I am relieved that Gale took those jackets.

I place Mom's oak jewelry box in my bedroom so I can touch it as I pass by. I know I will wear the gold aspen-leaf earrings and pendant, her sweet-sixteen silver heart, and the necklace made from tan-and-pale-green jasper. I will enjoy the silver-and-turquoise dangly earrings and silver feather-patterned earrings when I visit Shalom. While I now keep most of Janice and Mom's jewelry at home, I left some of Mom's jewelry behind at the cabin. Dad left his jasper bolo tie that I gave him for their twenty-fifth anniversary hanging on a nail in their closet. It's still there with his other bolo ties. They will remain there. I look forward to rediscovering

Mom's jewelry every summer. My regret feels familiar; I've been here before, with Janice's things.

Since I'm missing my mother intensely, I find and read the letters she wrote me when I went away to college. I have placed them in three-ring binders, with quilted covers she made from scraps of dresses she sewed for me in junior high and high school. She incorporated a small blue print for one part of the design on the binder now holding my junior high mementoes; I recall the rickrack around the collarless neck. She added purple cotton print fabric from a shirtwaist dress I wore into my college years to make up the Texas Star pattern. Mom kept these scraps for decades, organized in her sewing chest of drawers—the same furniture that Janice crawled into when she was a small girl so she could hide away and read. When Mom asked me what she might sew for me, I mentioned my journals and scrapbooks. Mom created four journal covers before her pain and Janice's death put an end to recreational sewing. An appliquéd red rose, for the San Antonio Rose, decorates the cover of a journal from my high school years.

In the letters I read about her concern for my clothes at college—the emerald-green, raw-silk suit she made and sent to me reminds me of a date who said, "You sure know how to dress." Mom helped me fit in with tasteful clothes she made, along with items she found at good consignment stores. She must have thought of her own high school years in San Antonio, her mother unavailable to help her dress well, and no extra money for fancy clothes. Mom carefully scoped out the best consignment stores in San Antonio, found dresses that would fit me, then altered and prettied up the dresses, many of which had probably only been worn once. The San Antonio Rose scrapbook holds pictures of three elaborate formals she found for my high school dances. One was an extravagant, deep-red velvet dress with an explosion of red net for the skirt, worn over hoop-skirt petticoats, a brief reprise of the antebellum period in the South. She applied hundreds of rhinestones to the skirt with a device that she squeezed to affix the rhinestones to the velvet to make it sparkle. I wore a soft lavender net strapless formal to my junior prom; she embellished this one with dozens of tiny velvet bows on the horizontal seams of the tiers. She scored a short cocktail dress in brilliant orange organza that made me feel daring. Mom did all this while substitute teaching, filling many roles at church, helping us all with homework and sewing for Janice as well.

When I went to college, Mom worried that I did not have a good coat, so she shopped for a new pale-pink wool coat and mailed it. I was thrilled to find the yellow slip in my post office box, notifying me that I had a package behind the counter; soon I was gasping with pleasure as I unwrapped the soft coat in the lobby of the campus post office. I read a letter asking if I've received it yet and if I like it; I loved it and wore it with pride through college. In a letter from October 1963, Mom asked if I would mind if she altered my hot pink organza and white lace formal, which she had crafted with a spray of hand-made, silk chiffon roses down the back, so Janice could wear it to a formal dance. I had worn this in several pageants, but I wouldn't need it in college. Just recently, I delighted my great-niece Keira with this pink-and-lace formal, and the lavender-checked flounced hippie dress I wore to Janice's first wedding. Keira paraded through the cabin, playing dress-up all those years later. When she's older I'll frame pictures of Aunt Janice and Aunt Joyce for her room. For now, she loves pretending she's a princess.

In another letter, Mom asks if I would like a cream-colored, whipped cream blouse, a popular fabric in the sixties, with or without a bow. She kept me up on life in San Antonio. She writes to me that after the family left me at Foster dorm in Fort Worth, she found herself walking around the house, thinking, "You'll never really live with us again," and she writes that she found Janice crying in our room. She writes that she will send the blue-and-lavender-plaid, taffeta bedspreads and curtains that Janice and I shared, since my roommate and I don't have any, and she will make some new ones out of fabric that Janice chooses. These letters comfort me. Mom made sure we were provided with both sustenance and beauty. Reading the letters binds me to her with threads of care woven through the fabric of our mother-daughter relationship.

I call my dad, reaching him at the duplex in Colorado Springs. I try to tell him about my love for Mom and how carefully she tended to me, but I can tell he is flattened by his own grief and can't hear mine. Reminiscence about Mom's attention to fabric and color means nothing to him; my words can't penetrate his sorrow. When I suggest a hospice bereavement group, Dad's replies seem distant and polite. I think of the time in May when I asked him for help with my grief for Janice. Next Sunday Ed calls me and tells me that Dad went to church but could only see Jean; when he came home, he panicked and called Ed. "I saw our pictures on the wall. I wasn't expecting that," he gasped, sounding anxious and breathless. "I don't know what to do. Can you help me?" Dad was referring to formal portraits of previous ministers and wives on the walls of the church. The portrait pictures Mom in the 1960's, with her short, layered haircut and cat-eye glasses. She is smiling, wearing a pink, pleated blouse. Dad wears a black suit; the picture was one that a photographer took of them when the church compiled a photo directory. Ed spent the afternoon with him.

I ponder the great gulf between love and someone else's grief.

"Dad sometimes can't be alone in the duplex," Ed reports. "He doesn't know what food to prepare and how to do it." Mom knew this, and resented his helplessness while blaming herself for babying him. Ed continues, "I take him out for a lot of meals, but I'm worried about him, long-term. He looks scared." Ed and I both know that this sad drama is unfolding as we have feared. My concern for Dad, and for Ed who tries to comfort him, grows.

August-October, 2004: Still Lost

I've been a member of the Congregational church in Missoula since I arrived as a young assistant professor in 1976. A worship team task force organizes a retreat on Elbow Lake, off the Blackfoot River. At first I enjoy being away from town, concentrating on plans for a group larger than my family. After locating my room, I wander to the boat dock before dinner, enjoying the quiet, the still water of the lake, and the water lilies. I watch the birds and feel peaceful. Inside the old camp kitchen, we enjoy a spaghetti dinner that someone else brought and served. My journal entry from that night reads that I felt "numb, shocked, and disoriented." My roommate, Jean, stays awake to talk with me in the dark when she hears me crying. My eyes water from allergies and sorrow, a sinus infection has lingered since June, and my brain is not working right. I literally lose my way at night in the unfamiliar setting, and for a while, I can't remember how to get back to my room after going outside to look at the stars.

Gale makes a welcome trip to Missoula. She, Gary, and I create a quiet, peaceful respite for a few days, then I go to Shalom. I remember almost nothing about that trip, since my mind and heart are filled with painful memories. August passes in a daze, although I note briefly in my journal that Ed, Dad, and I are at the cabin on Mom's birthday, August 22. We visit the cemetery and sit on a rough log bench, after tending the wildflowers we planted last month. We know wildflowers don't respond well to transplanting. Determined to create a lush forest flower meadow over the ashes of our family, we stubbornly haul water in five-gallon buckets from the creek to give the lupine, columbines, blue flax, pink yarrow, and red clover some chance to survive. We humans need to pair fragile beauty with fragile lives. *See, they lived*, we insist.

Again, I write Tom, Ed, and Gale, preserving our emails for my journal, which serves as my primary written record of this time. Writing to myself no longer provides release of my grief. I need the emotional connection with those who are going through this time of grief with me.

September, 2004: Floating in France

In September I spontaneously join a trip to France with my friend Gayle, the co-leader of our years of women's retreats. We will visit Paris, then float on a barge through central France on old canals. The group of Gayle's friends that she invites seem just right to me. They are fun and kind, and I am not in charge of anything. I want to experience Paris for Janice and my mother. At least unconsciously, I want to run away from my grief. Gary kindly encourages me to go.

I unconsciously look for Janice and Mom at each new turn in the Paris streets. At the Cluny museum, I sit in the round room made to look like a stone tower, taking in the Unicorn tapestries, sensing Janice beside me. I imagine my mother sewing.

In my imagination, we experience the art together. *Jannie, look at the last one. The Lady is outside her tent, looking so calm. What do you see?*

The tent is titled "For My Soul's Only Desire." I think she has found the solitude and interior life that allows her to go inside and then expand into her true life, I imagine Janice replying.

I realize that the beautiful Lady on the tapestry reminds me of Janice. She has entered timeless space, away from distractions. In my psyche, Janice has entered archetypal, eternal space. I see and experience her in art, dreams, music, and landscapes. I remember Mary Black's song we played at Janice's memorial: "You stand before that open door, and you must soon walk through. O beautiful, my own, my soul companion, bless the road that carries you."

Janice, are you with soul companions? I long to know.

It is full of light, she answers.

I am projecting beauty and timelessness, which I associate with Janice, into art and the natural world; I don't need to withdraw these healing projections. These interior projections help me heal as I experience the essence of Janice in art. It's another way of finding her in my ongoing living world.

My barge trip through Central France seems like a dream, both during the trip and after I return. My inconsolable crying one night forced my roommate to the upper deck to nap on the cushions in the lounge. The group of women extends kindness to me. Ungrounded, floating, dissolving with grief, I try to navigate my shifting life.

Fall 2004: Writing Begins

Since Janice recruited me back into my former field of communication studies, I renew connections with former colleagues from the seventies and eighties with whom I've lost contact. Tom and Art propose a special memorial edition of the *Southern Communication Journal* to honor Janice's academic work. Art coached Janice to write personally rather than academically; now he is shepherding her book into publication. He and his wife Carolyn had developed a warm collegial and friendly relationship with Janice and Tom. They invite scholars to write about the influence of Janice's work on their own, asking me to provide a biographical introduction. Gathering and creating stories about Janice provides a welcome focus for me. Some of the same scholars participate in a tribute panel for Janice at a national convention in Chicago, where I meet Tom and room with Gale. Tom and I go out to dinner to talk about Janice before we join other colleagues. This will become a ritual. I wear the diamond ring that belonged to Janice, given to me by Tom the morning after she died.

At a tribute panel in Chicago, with five of Janice's closest colleagues speaking, I end the panel with a few comments and the slideshow that her chairman at Arkansas organized for the memorial service last March. The projector jams at a certain point before the slideshow is complete. Technicians fail to restart the machine; I am unreasonably upset when we must end the slides before we reach pictures of Janice in the last month of her life, before we stopped taking pictures. I want the large audience to see her radiant face with her short hair. I begin to cry as colleagues filter out, needing to get to their next program. I wanted the ballroom of people to see *all* the pictures. I could not finish her life story for her.

Ghost Apartments

By mid-October of 2004, Ed and I have enlisted home health care providers from an agency in Colorado Springs to help our dad in the duplex. One woman does light housekeeping, and the wonderfully named aide Hope makes lists of needed supplies for Dad, prepares his lunch, and sets out food for his supper. Ed organizes Dad's medications each week. Dad suffers from extreme headaches, and his shoulder pains him. None of the medications, even lithium, help his headaches. Unless Ed comes over, Dad often will just heat up canned soup for supper. Once when I visit, I over-hear Hope asking what he would like for dinner.

"Oh, anything," Dad answers.

Hope keeps trying: "There's some meatloaf, or some of that leftover chicken, and I can cut up some veggies for you to steam."

"Whatever you think," Dad replies, listlessly.

I suspect this will be another canned soup night, since Ed needs to get me to the airport before Dad eats dinner. We talk on the way. "I really don't want to make him feel guilty, because I can keep doing what I'm doing," Ed says. "Sometimes he tells me he's sorry he's so much trouble, and of course I always tell him he is not trouble for me, but it's bound to be weighing on his pride."

Ed and I discuss the extra care needed for Dad. We think it may be time for Dad to move to assisted living on the same campus Mom found for them. Dad wanders or sits for hours in the duplex, not reading or even watching television. The duplex is inhabited for Dad with Jean's absence. He tries attending a hospice bereavement group, but he cannot hear well enough to take part in the discussions, and he seems even more depressed surrounded by other grieving people than before he began attending. After one session on his own with the leader he stops attending.

"I'm so grateful to you," I continue with Ed, "but you have to travel a lot for your work." We drive in silence, not knowing what to do. Dad almost never leaves the duplex. "At Skyline (the assisted living center), he would meet people at meals and the staff would encourage him to go to the gym," I offer hopefully. This hope is mildly delusional.

We both know our introverted father in his deep grief seems unlikely to initiate exercise, socializing, going to the library or even attending church on his own. Mom had always accompanied him on his calls to parishioners, prepared his food, and urged him to walk with Morris at the cabin. In addition to his undiagnosed headaches and bursitis in his shoulder Dad suffers from diabetes not yet requiring insulin. I provide Dad with a green Nalgene water bottle and ask him to drink two full containers a day to help with the diabetes. He calls me at work one day to report proudly that he did it—drank all the water. Then when he tells me that he made coffee and soup with it, I realize that he's having trouble remembering how to care for himself. I recall stories about his crippling eyestrain and headaches in college. All our growing up years he took a nap in the early afternoon to deal with eyestrain and the pressures of an extraverted job on a deeply introverted man. Things are falling apart for Dad.

By mid-November, Ed and I are out of realistic options. I consider asking Dad to live with us in Missoula, but he would know no one, and Gary and I work every day. I maintain this fantasy for a while, but Ed and I agree that another move out of town would be disorienting for Dad. I worry about how Gary and I would manage as well since grief already takes up so much space in our marriage. Gary feels as though he gets my leftover energy and he is right. While I feel like a failure as his daughter, I don't issue the invitation to Dad. I have the same sinus infection I've nursed since June and I am depressed, even though I know the difference between grief and depression. Only the diagnosis differs; I feel flattened.

After Thanksgiving, Dad tells Ed, "I am ready to move. I need more care than is practical here at the duplex." This surprises Ed. When he tells me I am relieved, although I know this will be a difficult move for Dad. Ed assures me that he could have continued to care for Dad but he, too, feels relief.

In early December, Ed and I choose the apartments we think he would like the best. We know we are employing denial—Dad won't like any apartment, and furthermore, he insists that we choose one for him, refusing to look at them. We select a third-floor apartment with a clear view of the mountains of the Front Range, and extra space for a TV alcove. Dad is too swamped with grief to care about his next living environment. Ed and I worry about his increasing passivity and depression. We hope we can help Dad feel at home in the conveniently planned apartment. We will set up the furnishings to closely duplicate where he is now.

I try not to think about the limited library down the hall from the new apartment, containing few books of any substance, where dust coats the pink-and-blue silk flower arrangement on the coffee table. Dad has loved libraries all his life. He won't love this library.

December, 2004: More Falling

Christmas of 2004 is a sad, quiet affair in Colorado Springs with Ed, his daughter Katie, and Dad as well as for Gary and me. Ed sends me a picture of Mom's handmade quilted ornaments he strung on tinsel in his living room. They do not set up a tree. Tom does not want to travel anywhere. In Missoula, I pretend that Janice has drawn Gary's name for a gift. Our extended family began drawing names a while back so we could reduce the packing and mailing at Christmas. Gary unwraps a yellow cashmere sweater with a make-believe note from Janice, telling him what he should wear it with. Gary had said the year before that he always wanted Janice to draw his name since she mirrored his desires so perfectly; that year she had chosen an olive green Carhartt jacket. I weep through part of Christmas morning, remembering Janice's call last year.

Ed schedules a truck to pick up the furniture to move to Dad's apartment.

He phones me on the day of the move, leaving a message asking me to call him as soon as I can. I remember Ed's call to me when Mom was diagnosed with pancreatic cancer. When I reach Ed, he is upset.

"Dad fell last night and couldn't reach the pull-cord for emergencies, so he spent the night in the bathtub where he fell. I called an ambulance, and we are at the hospital now," he tells me, sounding almost as though he is crying. "He hit his head and probably broke some ribs." This kind of lonely, traumatic fall has been one of our nightmares. I cancel clients and fly to Colorado Springs. Ed picks me up at the airport; we eat at our favorite barbecue place and go visit Dad. Like Fayetteville, Colorado Springs has become another home. I wonder if we expand our sense of home as we lose our family members. Dad will be in the hospital for observation so his neurologist can assess why he was having such painful headaches even before the fall. Ed and I feel miserable as we imagine what Dad experienced, waiting through the long night. Hope, the aide, found him the next morning. She checked on him when Ed could not reach Dad on the phone.

When Dad is released from the hospital, he will not be able to return to the duplex. All the large furniture is now at the new apartment, thanks to the scheduled move. I wonder whether Dad fell partly because he could not imagine another move, this time without Jean. Ed's house, a Victorian with steep winding stairs, and no bedroom on the main floor, does not seem to be a good option at all for Dad. In between Ed's work and spending time with Dad at the hospital, we get busy setting up the new apartment. I move into Ed's guest room and we move all the clothes and smaller items from the duplex to Ed's truck, then to the third floor of the assisted living complex, using the residents' elevator. The residents, many using walkers, make conversation, wondering who the new person will be. They seem friendly and eager to welcome someone new. We explain that he's in the hospital now, but when he's released he will come here. Several women promise to look in on him and make sure he knows where the dining hall is.

The social worker assures us she will introduce herself to Dad and help him get oriented. She wonders what activities he might enjoy. He does not like crafts, he never has played cards or board games and he doesn't need to go on field trips since he knows Colorado Springs well. She wonders if Dad would like to preside at the Sunday services occasionally. I can't imagine Dad doing any of these things. I enlist the help of the physical therapist at the gym, who says he will be glad to work with Dad when he moves in. Dad has never joined a gym. A sense of ominous foreboding creeps into my overly busy arrangements. One woman who lives close to Dad's new apartment brings us cookies while we are moving; this gesture is promising. Dad loves cookies. We carry boxes of photographs, books, files, simple kitchen equipment, framed pictures, lamps, small tables, linens, clothes, and medical supplies.

In between hauling all this to the new apartment, Ed and I visit Dad in the hospital. I sit with him when Ed is at work and I am not moving things. Once, Dad says something that startles me.

"You are so busy, and you are doing what you think you need to do," Dad says, "but I would rather you stay here and talk with me." Dad looks despondent and speaks firmly.

I am taken aback. Doesn't Dad know that Ed and I are doing everything we can to set up his new life so he will be comfortable, surrounded by familiar possessions?

"My life here is *desperate*," continues my father, as he points to the clock on the wall in front of him. "I watch the clock until the next pain medication, or until you or Ed come." I know that he is right. Our priorities seem skewed as Dad talks to me, but I also feel defensive. *I can't do any more! I'm doing everything I can!* The truth of his plea stabs me with guilt. I've begun to obsess over getting everything right in the apartment as a cover for my fear that nothing will be right. I let the picky details go and talk with Dad. I belong here in the room where he is now, I tardily realize. I massage his painful back, which he appreciates with a grateful moan. Dad tells me that he will try to live and that he wants to be a help to his family. I tell him that at this stage in his life, his *being* is a gift to us.

After a long pause, Dad says, "You are kind to say that." I don't think he believes me. I talk with his primary care physician about pain medication, feeling extremely frustrated that no one seems to be in charge. His primary care doctor, internist, neurologist, substitute neurologist, and various nurses come and go. I don't know what to do to help him, and we don't know why he can't walk. He's weaker, with no explanatory diagnosis that anyone offers.

Back at the elevator at Skyline, Ed and I are carrying one particularly heavy box of books. One of the women on the staff approaches with an unfriendly look. "Can your dad even walk?" She wears a nameplate pinned to her pink smock. We say no, not yet, but we expect him to be released in a few days. She reminds us that residents must be able to walk on their own to live in this wing. Ed and I didn't know this; we thought *assisted* living meant that residents would receive assistance until they were able to walk. We check into the skilled nursing option, where Dad might need to stay for a while. I'm angry at what I perceive to be her lack of compassion. Can't she see how hard we are working to get everything set up?

Crucial Conversations

I'm back at the hospital while Ed is at work. One day we talk about Dad's social activism. I ask him to clarify stories I think I know, but I want to get the details right. This is a man who invited the Negro Brotherhood of his denomination, in 1949, to meet as coequals when they held their separate state conferences in Charlotte, North Carolina. The elders at his church had passed a resolution that the visitors could be just that, *visitors*, but not equal participants. I ask Dad if it's accurate that on Sunday morning he joined a well-known Negro singer of the time, as she knelt and sang, "Let Us Break Bread Together On Our Knees."

"Yes, I knelt beside Rosa," Dad replied. "She was kneeling to sing; I couldn't stay standing under the circumstances—it would have been wrong."

"What happened then?"

"That didn't make me popular with the board. I'd violated what they asked me to do, treat the other group as visitors and not as equals," he said. "And I had welcomed them all as our brothers and sisters."

"Did they fire you right then?" At that time, I was only four years old.

"No, that took a while, and they didn't fire me, they just suggested that maybe we would be happier back home in Texas." He smiled a crooked smile. "I took the hint. That's when we moved to Dallas." This happened a long time ago; no passion remains in his recounting.

"I told you that I met Rosa again in the seventies in Boulder, didn't I?" I reminded Dad. "She made it happen for her church board to hire Rick as their interim minister." My first husband moved to Boulder with me for my job at the University of Colorado, without a job of his own. When Rosa and I met at a church conference and she found out whose daughter I was, she ordered me to go get my husband; within a week Rick had been hired for an interim job at a black church in inner-city Denver, where he worked for a year.

"Yes, I remember that now," Dad replies. "She was a fine woman. That never would have happened in the forties, you can bet on that." I believe that he means a black church hiring a white minister.

"I never knew what happened in Dallas, exactly," I said with a question in my voice. We'd moved to Vernon from Dallas when I was eleven.

"Some of the same business. They didn't appreciate my preaching about *Brown v. Board of Education* in 1954, and saying I hoped we'd be part of the solution and not part of the problem." I remembered my dad taking me to see a segregated downtown Dallas hotel, when I complained about six members of a black choir camping out in our parsonage. He knew the proprietor so he asked him if he could take his daughter to see his hotel. He led me up the stairs; we looked into open rooms, with the bathroom down the hall. The hotel did not look like the ones we stayed in on the way to Colorado. Dad remained silent. "Thank you, Mr. McComas," he said as we left the hotel.

I asked, as we were driving home, "Are you mad at me, Daddy?"

"No, I'm mad at the situation, and I want you to understand it," he clarified. I believe I did, from then on.

"In Dallas we also had to contend with their misunderstanding of communism. Some of the leaders viewed the National Council of Churches as a communist organization, which of course it wasn't." He continues, "Since I was in favor of the ecumenical movement, that made me suspect."

"We liked Dallas," Dad muses. "Some of our happiest family times took place there." I loved grade school in Dallas. Dad wrote his thesis on "Progress Toward Christian Unity Since the 1930s."

I read his thesis when I was in high school. "And of course you remember what the problems were here in Colorado Springs." I did—his support of the anti-war movement and his opposition to the death penalty.

We talk about the years in Vernon, when Dad was fired over integration in the middle of my sophomore year.

"The elders asked me if I would accept Negro members into our church, and I said if any walked down the aisle, I would give them the right hand of fellowship," he states clearly.

"I can't imagine any black people would have wanted to join an all-white church," I comment.

"I don't think they would have," Dad agrees. "I think the question was a setup to see what I would say." He goes on, "So of course, I had to say what I would do. I knew it would make them mad, though."

"Do you regret any of those stands you made?" I ask, assuming that he would say no.

He closes his eyes. "I regret what all those moves did to my family, to all of you. I can't say that I regret what I spoke about." He smiles as he adds, "But I will say that I didn't have you gals' communication skills!" He refers to Janice and me, who chose communication studies as our specialty areas. I went on to specialize in conflict resolution; Janice and I often joked that we were doomed by our past to learn something helpful about communication.

"I'm proud of you, Dad," I assure him. "You didn't take the easy way, and I love you for that and so many other things." I am trying not to cry. I mean it. I see my dad as brave and correct in his views. "I didn't suffer; I gained from moving and having to adapt to new schools." Right now, I am not recalling any past hardships as a teenager, only respect and appreciation for my father.

"I think it was hard on all of you," Dad says. "I appreciate your saying that." He is quiet for a while, napping. When he wakes up, he says, "We had a good family."

"Yes, we did." I kiss his forehead. "I'll be back in two hours— no more, I promise."

"Thanks, Joycie." Dad closes his eyes to rest.

I eat with Ed, and we return to talk with Dad again. We attempt to determine which neurologist will do rounds tomorrow morning, but no one knows. Ed drops me off back at Skyline, and I do some more unpacking, readying myself to sleep in the almost completely organized new apartment. In the same way I came to feel at home in Tom and Janice's house, I know my way around Colorado Springs and have developed preferences for restaurants as locals do. I imagine living in this apartment. I am making room in my mind and heart for Dad's next phase. Inhabiting this new apartment in my imagination helps make it a home. I tack up a picture of Mom on Santorini, one of the Greek islands. She looks radiant, slightly sunburned, their ship in the Mediterranean appearing small, far below. I can't find the mattress cover and make up the bed with only sheets, then write for a while before I am able to sleep. I want to remember the details of our conversation this afternoon, so I write in my journal:

> *January 23, 2005, Penrose Memorial Hospital, Colorado Springs. I am sitting with my dad in the hospital in Colorado Springs. He's sleeping. He has lost his wife and daughter to death in the previous months; his will to live is weak. He tells me he will try to live, but that he hears Jean calling him from the next room. I ask him if it seems like she's really there or if she's on the other side, and he says he doesn't know; I realize it's a silly question he can't answer.*

Mom said she wanted to help us all when we die. I wonder if Mom is helping Dad feel less alone, but I know she can't do that.

At Penrose the next day, my dad smiles at me when I appear.

"When you come in, I calm right down. This is a real quality in you. This is one reason you are a good psychologist," Dad says.

I am very moved by this compliment. I can remember times when I did everything *but* calm him down—stay out late on dates in high school, argue against restrictions, try to get Mom to do what she wanted instead of what he wanted. Most sadly of all, Rick and I divorced; Dad loved Rick like a son. Given my recent experience in asking forgiveness for these early failings with Mom, I don't ask for forgiveness from Dad. We say almost all the things we need to say to each other. He tells me again, as he has so reliably in my life, that he loves me. I find it very easy to tell him, each time I see him, that I love him and always have. I am returning to Montana tomorrow after a week here with Dad and Ed.

I want to ask a question before I go. Dad grew up in Lampasas, Texas, the son of a banker and a piano teacher. Mom grew up in San Antonio; her father, I knew from childhood experience, held racist attitudes. I remember him, as a developer and construction boss, talking about "my *Meskins*" who were working for him. Grandmother Freddie never said anything about race that I overheard. While she was a faithful member and choir director of her church, she also read *Science of Mind* publications, kept up with health food ideas of her time and was the first licensed female chiropractor in Texas. Grandmother Freddy may have been a closet progressive.

Dad's church ordained him at eighteen, then sent to him to Texas Christian University in 1936 to study for his BA and later for the ministry. He learned from progressive professors a wider perspective than Lampasas offered. Still, this was racially segregated Texas in the late 1930s, during the Great Depression.

Dad tells me he wishes I didn't have to go home. I feel torn. I know I will return soon to help him adapt to life at Skyline, but again I register the pull between here and home. While I'm here, I want to ask my question. Dad seems comfortable today, smiling at me and eating his lunch.

"I've wanted to ask you something," I preface my query. "You and Mom grew up in Central Texas in the nineteen twenties and thirties. It seems to me, from what I've heard and seen, that your parents weren't at all socially liberal." This may be putting the matter mildly. "Is that right?"

"Well, it was complicated," he begins. He stops eating to remember. "They were all four, well maybe all three—I don't know about Dad Lightfoot—strong Christians." Dad and Granddad Lightfoot kept up a cordial enough but definitely not close relationship. Granddad watched wrestling and boxing on TV, read and wrote about Texas history, and didn't have much to say. Remembering the bottle of Jack Daniels in the refrigerator, and Grandmother's pursed, silent mouth, I'm pretty sure that he drank a bit when we were not visiting. "But they were products of their time, so race matters were hard for them. They had been raised to keep the races separate," Dad explains. "We all grew up in the segregated South."

As Dad fills me in on some of his history, I remember the small green water fountain marked "Colored," and the larger whites-only fountain, which didn't need a sign, at the J. C. Penney's on East Grand in Dallas.

"So how did it happen that you and Mom managed not to be racially prejudiced?" I ask. I've always wondered about this. By the time I was aware of the Civil Rights movement, I knew Dad and Mom were solidly in favor of integration.

"I don't know that we were entirely free of that," Dad admits. "But we knew what we needed to do."

"How?" I ask. I really want to know.

"Well, Joycie, we had great teachers, and I just read the Gospel."

He read the Gospel differently from a lot of people.

Dad didn't have to explain what he meant; his passion and clarity made me want to study the social gospel, theology, and current social justice issues, as well as take an activist stand some of the time, as he did.

I had a great teacher, too.

Dad's New Apartment

Ed and I complete moving items into the new apartment, and I spend five nights there, feeling a mixture of hope and anxiety. Dad's black recliner sits next to the oak, glass-front shelves he brought from his father's study in Lampasas. We've placed some of his favorite books on the shelves—his shelf of worship guides and family Bible, his hymnbook, covered for protection in plastic, wildlife and environmental activism books, some Jungian books I know he hasn't read yet, and a few Barry Lopez books on the environment he told me he wants to reread. On the top sits the grandfather clock he bought because it reminded him of the one in his childhood home. I've kept the chime function off while I'm in the apartment, but he likes to hear the quarter hours ring, so I remember to turn the Big Ben chime back on. Mom's amber glass candlesticks sit to the left of the clock, with candles in them, even though I know he won't ever light the candles. He and Mom come from the generation that viewed candles as either decorative, for birthday cakes, or something to be used when the electricity went off. Small pieces of pottery Mom gathered in Egypt and Israel complete the decoration. The TV and music system sit in easy viewing distance of his chair. He loves the pictures of two howling coyotes on the opposite wall. We've stocked the simple kitchen with snacks he likes, even the Little Debbies, which are not good for his diabetes but make him happy. We've added granola bars to tempt him away from cookies with butter spread on them, one of his snacking habits. Cans of soup and stew will get him through when he doesn't want to go down to the dining room. Cereal, milk, and dried fruit will work for breakfast; Ed will bring the milk later. I hope Dad won't have to be in the nursing unit long. As I leave, I feel proud of our efforts; I take a picture to show Gary.

I fly back to Missoula, again catching up with client appointments. By this time I have a pat response, "I'm needed for family medical issues." I don't explain. After a few days, Ed phones me that Dad is still in the hospital for observation and diagnosis, and is not walking.

Gary and I plan another getaway trip, this time to a lodge on the Bitterroot River, just for the weekend. We spend a quiet evening, choosing to eat takeout picnic food rather than venture out to a café. I go to bed early and sleep deeply. It's way too cold for fishing, but Gary takes a long walk along the river before I awake. On the second morning, the phone rings early. "Dad is slipping away," says my brother. "If you want to see him before he's gone, I think you should come today." I fear telling Gary, but I must. He does not offer to come with me, and again I do not ask him to. I am avoiding conflict. I know that Gary wonders whether our life will ever return to normal, not dominated by grief and family urgencies. I am disappointed and apprehensive, but have to keep moving fast. Ed calls Delta and gets me on a flight that afternoon. At home, I remove my weekend clothes from the suitcase and repack for Colorado, not knowing how long I will stay. Gary drives me to the airport; he hugs me goodbye, but we are not communicating warmly with each other. He seems remote and resigned.

January 30, 2005: Fallen

In Colorado Springs, Ed's daughter Katie picks me up and takes me to Penrose Hospital, where she was born, where Ed and Dianne married, and where Dianne died in Ed's arms a month later. This was a little over two years ago. I know the way to Dad's room. I've been away for only a week.

Ed and I hug. He looks beyond exhausted. In his hospital room, Dad speaks in a delirious state; the neurologist explains his delirium as the result of a combination of pain medications. Ed works very hard to make sense of what Dad is saying. He leans over him, repeating phrases and gently asking questions.

"Ed, you are trying very hard to understand Dad," I say to Ed, "but I don't hear that he's making any sense, at least that we can decipher."

"I guess you're right," Ed replies. "It's hard to see him like this."

After listening to Dad for a while, I suggest, "I think you might go home and come back in the morning. I'll stay."

Ed finally agrees to get some sleep, and I settle in the best I can to spend the night in the recliner. Dad's delirium upsets me; we've always counted on clear communication with him.

Matt, a warm and effective nurse, brings me blankets and a pillow. He tells me that Dad invited him to the cabin to go fishing in the summer. Matt is a burly guy with tattoos and a long ponytail. He also discloses that he got sober, sold his motorcycle, went to nursing school, and loves what he does. He becomes attached to his patients, and I can clearly see this is true. He assures me he will be there all night, and he will check on us.

Dad told me, referring to Matt, "No amount of money can pay for what people give freely." Dad and I talked about the gift of kindness when we least expect it.

"It's a kind of grace," said my father.

Dad is not in a state of grace tonight. He speaks urgently through his delirium. At one point he commands, "Call the firemen. Call them *right now*. They'll know what to do." He looks at me and stabs his finger in the air for emphasis. I assure him that I have called all the emergency responders. He insists again, "Call the firemen *right now!*" Then I remember that as a young minister of nineteen, in 1936, while he was in college, he took the train from Fort Worth to Pilot Point and Aubrey, where he preached on Sundays. In those days, the school encouraged young ministers to serve preaching points, small churches that could not afford a full-time minister, before they even entered seminary. They reported back to their fieldwork adviser at the college. None of the college students, at least not the ones training for the ministry, could afford cars during the Depression. The train he was riding back to Fort Worth after an evening service derailed. His train car stayed upright, but the engine car overturned and caught fire. Dad and others ran to help. The engineer leapt free and survived, but the fireman was pinned to the ground by the engine. Dad held the fireman in his arms, talking to him all night as he died. Dad told us that this event changed his life; that he learned how important simple presence is when people are dying. He spoke of the mystery of one man living, and one man dying.

Ten years later, on December 7, 1946, when Dad was serving as associate minister at Peachtree Christian Church in Atlanta, a huge, tragic fire in the Winecoff Hotel claimed nine lives, many of them young people who were attending a conference. This hotel was close to the church Dad served; he and the senior minister spent all night comforting the surviving victims and waiting with families. No wonder Dad wants me to call the firemen now. Matt and I are the only firemen around tonight. I, too, learned the gift of simple presence when people are ill and when they die; I learned it from this man who is dying now.

The neurologist makes his rounds, and we decide that anything is better than Dad's delirium, so he gives him sleeping medication. He warns me this may hasten his death. I ask if there is any hope for recovery, and the neurologist shakes his head. Again I sing the old songs and hymns, many of the same ones I sang for Mom and we sang for Janice. I hold Dad's hand, telling him all the things that I want to tell him. I do ask for his forgiveness, and tell him that all is well between us, that I am not holding on to anything that I need to say. I thank him for being a wonderful father. I do not say goodbye. Matt checks on us at about 2:00 a.m., standing by me while I sing "O God Our Help in Ages Past," one of Dad's well-loved hymns with words by one of his ministry heroes, Harry Emerson Fosdick. Matt suggests I sleep for a while, so I do. When I wake up Matt has tucked an extra blanket around me.

Ed returns early in the morning with Clyde, and we talk with each other and with Dad, although he cannot respond. Clyde tells me that a few days ago he told Dad that he had been a model of a gentle, powerful man for him. Ed and I discuss transferring Dad to the hospice wing of the hospital, but we are too late. I am out in the hall, talking with my practice assistant, rescheduling clients, when Ed urgently beckons me in. While we hold his hands, Dad slowly stops breathing. Ed and I cry, holding hands over Dad's body, while Clyde stands back, wiping his tears away.

"Such a profound difference between the moment of life and death," Ed says through his tears. "It seems so lonely with just the two of us." We talk about Janice and how absent she seems. We could never have imagined we would say goodbye to our parents without the three of us being together. Ed and I stay in Dad's room for several hours, as Matt disconnects him from all the apparatus.

"I knew he was a good man," Matt says. "I could tell he was an honorable man. We won't get to do that fishing trip." Ed invites Matt to come to the cabin.

I don't know what to do now. With Janice and Mom, we called the funeral home, but now, without hospice involvement, we must wait for certification of death, and we can't predict when the coroner will arrive. I tell Ed that I won't leave Dad's body; that I want to see him into the hearse. Ed quietly explains why that is not possible. His body will stay in the morgue for a while, before being transferred to the cremation facility. Too soon, we kiss our dad, thank him for our lives and for his, and leave in silence.

Disassembling the Ghost Apartment

Ed and I devour our big sandwiches at the deli close to Skyline. Slowly the truth dawns on us. We have to disassemble Dad's apartment. We look at each other and sigh.

We go to the apartment that Dad will never see. I could not hold the space for him, envisioning him in this lovely place with views of the mountains. In my deepest heart I did not think Dad would be happy at Skyline, but I hoped he would live for a while, seeing a few friends and what family was left. I hoped he would have one more summer visit to Shalom. I hoped he would read a few books, watch sunsets, and remember. I was not ready. But he may have been more than ready, since he heard Jean calling him from another room. This diagnosis-free death caught me completely by surprise. They used to call this dying of a broken heart.

Ed and I call a used furniture dealer and arrange for him to come the next day. We agree that we don't need to keep any of the large furniture, but we do need to make decisions about everything else. Before I can face that task, I make calls to family friends in other states, using Mom and Dad's address book. Tom Carter lives in Wichita. He is one of the brothers who built the cabin close to our favorite camping spot at Grasshopper Park, where Janice and her first husband were married. Tom answers the phone and when I identify myself he interrupts, "Joyce, I guess since you're calling me you don't have good news." We talk about his friend Lamar, and I tell Tom about our plans for a memorial service at Tincup this summer. Tom tells me again about his wife who died three years ago. "I talk to that beautiful girl every day," he tells me. His voice sounds weak. "I'll be there, if the Lord's willing," Tom replies. He sounds bereft.

Again, Ed and I pack things, including donations to Goodwill and books for the church. In a box, we find pieces of a 1940s dark blue, fluted vase with white painted flowers. Mom kept this wedding gift in view. It graced the living room in their various homes. Now it's broken. We don't know when this happened, but clearly Mom didn't want to throw it away. Maybe she thought she could mend it with glue. Ed and I decide that it can't be mended and we will let it go. We place it, regretfully, in the trash. "It doesn't seem right to throw it away," Ed remarks. Next year, I see that Ed has picked up one of the larger pieces. There it remains, on one of the family end tables that Ed refinished for his home.

We box Biblical commentaries and books of theology, taking them to the church library after verifying with the minister that she wants them. When we return to the apartment to continue clearing things away, the used-furniture man comes. "I can give you eight hundred dollars for all this," he offers. Ed and I look at each other and shrug. We have no energy to bargain.

The minister visited Dad in the hospital; I met her when I was there. Now she insists by phone that we plan a memorial service at the church. When we hang up the phone, having notified her of Dad's death, we look at each other. One of us says first, "I can't do this." We call back to tell her that while we will have a service this summer at the cabin, we will not plan a service in Colorado Springs. We are exhausted and can't imagine organizing a meaningful service. We also both still feel mixed emotions about this church from which Ed was uprooted in the middle of his senior year in high school because they fired Dad. But mostly, we are tired and spent. She will not accept our decision, saying that Dad was well-known and well-loved in the Rocky Mountain region, and many people will want to come and honor him. She is president of this regional group of churches. I suspect the service she wants would serve others more than our family. I want this insistent minister out of our lives.

At the end of my emotional strength, I call Gary and ask him to intervene. With his ministerial status, he can talk to her on our behalf. Ed and I are packing and making trips up and down the same stairs and elevator that we recently used to bring household goods *into* the apartment. Gary calls the minister. That night, on the phone with me, he recalls the conversation.

"This family cannot go through another service right now," he explained to her. "You need to understand that Jean and Lamar's best friends spend the summer in Taylor Park. What Joyce and Ed plan seems best to us all." Still she would not desist. She said that she would hold a service the next Sunday before church regardless of any family involvement. When Gary told me this, I became furious. Who is being served here? What kind of too-late face-saving is going on?

"You have to do what is right for you," I tell Ed, "but I'm going to Missoula on Saturday and want no part of this service." We held a service for Mom at this church last July. *Enough*, I am thinking. Of course, the "enough" I am feeling is enough death, enough sorrow, enough serving death. I want to be left alone. My feelings are mixed up and hardened, but I feel what I feel. The minister is undoubtedly acting from values that led her to respect our dad for his service to this region.

"I feel the same way," Ed states. "I'll think about it." Ed often is less emotionally reactive than I am.

I sleep in the ghost apartment one more time before I move back to Ed's house. I cry through part of the night. My eyes appear permanently red from allergies and crying. The next day I remove all the pictures from the walls, and we pack more boxes, labeling the destinations: Shalom, Missoula, and Ed's house. We find a neat folder in Dad's handwriting giving suggestions for hymns and scripture for memorial services.

As Ed and I pack the last of the boxes and odd household items in his truck, we look at each other in our exhaustion. I'm wearing one of Dad's forest green parkas and his tan canvas work gloves. I found a pair of Mom's old tennis shoes that fit me, and Dad's itchy wool socks that are too big for me. In Missoula, I had not packed for the task of disassembling what amounts to the footprints of two lives. I can barely see; the bitter wind throws sleet and parking lot grit into my face.

"Where's Gary?" Ed asks. We are carrying heavy objects and could use his help. I am wondering the same thing. I expected that he would be with me through my father's last days. While he is help-ful on the phone, he is not here. The crack in our marriage widens.

I go home to Missoula, not knowing what Ed will do about the memorial service we don't want.

Ed prepares a well-written eulogy for Dad which he delivers at the church on February 5, the next Sunday after Dad died. He highlighted Dad's life as a minister, his quest for social justice, and his family life. Ed did not shy away from Dad's views on Vietnam. He emphasized Dad's practice of forgiveness. It was just as well that I wasn't there.

Layered Grief

Back in Missoula, I am again exhausted. I read in my journal lists of self-care advice I give to myself: cardio three times a week, weights twice a week after work, yoga class, a movie once a week, have people over. . . . I am attempting to take my own advice. For years I have asked clients to fill out a list of pleasures and to mon-itor their exercise when they are feeling depressed. I star my note to self, "limit work significantly!" I don't take my good advice, at least not right away.

My coauthored textbook revision is due March 5; Bill, my former husband and coauthor, has written a new chapter in the last few weeks that I will need to rework. We each edit the work of the other. This is the second revision after our divorce. Although we are able to collaborate on our writing, the process takes an emo-tional toll on me, and undoubtedly on Bill as well. Looking back, I am stunned to realize that I revised this book exactly during the time that Dad was declining and dying. I would never have coun-seled my clients to undertake such a killer task, instead urging them to take a complete sabbatical. Self-care was not my priority. I had to finish up all the other chapter edits, no matter how I felt.

But textbook writing, even on a topic I care about, conflict resolution, does not help my emotional life. I must go to Albuqueque for an ongoing consulting contract. My only healing comes while listening to my clients as I sink deeply into their stories, listening as never before. Stories rise up from the well of grief. As we dive together into them, my new courage encourages my clients.

Writing about my experiences of loss begins to loosen the grip of grief just a little. Tom and Art, who edit the tribute journal for Janice's work, tell me they are pleased with the biographical piece I wrote in the fall. As I edit, I experience a deep sense of satisfaction as I tell about Janice hauling water at our summer camps, getting her toes wet as she struggled back to camp. Recalling Janice performing for guests when she was six, asking them if they knew she could spell *antidisestablishmentarianism*, I refer to her as a smart girl speaking well, a twist on Quintilian's dictum that rhetoric consisted of a good man speaking well. I write that I recognize both reluctance to break Janice's privacy, and a desire for people to know more about her, referring to Janice's article about Princess Diana's death. Writing about Diana's memorial service helped Janice open the door to writing personally, from her heart and her dreams, instead of primarily academically. I feel close to Janice as I write about her and her turn toward personal writing. As I recall the three of us siblings playing on a huge downed spruce log on Spring Creek, I begin to feel again my imagination at play, and I feel some of the fun of our childhood. Early memories weave a larger tapestry of life and love than my more recent dark shroud of death stories.

My journal reflects several long, detailed, comforting interior conversations with Janice, as our sisterly conversation continues. In one, Janice urges me to make quick decisions to create a saner work life. She ends with admonishment: *Listen to my life.* She tells me to keep pursuing my own, non-textbook writing, as she made that shift in the last years of her life. No more writing for the academic "daddies," she vowed. Her courage encourages me.

From Five to Two

"We started with five, and now only two remain."

Gary dreams that he and I are in family therapy, and he silently removes three branches of cedar from a grouping of five, indicating nonverbally that our family started with five, and two remain. Even though Gary and I often seem miles apart in how we cope with grief, I realize in this dream of his that he registers the somber absence of my family. He is grieving, too, especially for Janice. He expresses himself artistically, in poetry and fine wood-working, more than in conversation about his grief. He writes a poem, "The Fate of Beautiful Women," which Tom places in the front of Janice's book. This and other poems help me feel part-nered by Gary. While he cannot easily comfort me in the middle of the night when I weep, he honors my family.

April, 2005: Writing at the Ranch

I return to a place of refuge, Rancho la Puerta, in Tecate, Mexico. Here I work out, hike, do yoga and meditation, eat healthy food, sleep deeply, and this year, participate in a poetry writing work-shop. The ranch serves as my healing retreat, and has for years. In this, my twentieth visit, I write poetry, make journal entries, and sleep deeply. Grief ebbs and flows in the nurturing, healthy envi-ronment. I write a mix of personal essays and poetry about Janice, Mom, and Dad. One day, dancing the salsa in the rock gym, with a view out at an ancient, sacred mountain, I almost see the strong presence of my mother, dancing and smiling across from me. The orange, red, turquoise, and yellow Mexican colors, the wild, pulsing salsa music, the smell of burning cedar and pine, and the adobe buildings connect my senses to my mother's early life in San Antonio. One night I dream that Mom agrees to accompany me to Europe in a few days, now that Dad has died. She would not leave him to travel with Janice and me. She looks young and happy in my dream.

Imagination takes over my journal writing. I write about my mother coming with me to the ranch. In one imaginary journal piece, I write about my mother overcoming her modesty and even shame about her body, because she thought she was flat-chested originally, and because she felt scarred from a mastectomy some years ago.

From my journal:

You looked on all the women's bodies, young, aging, scarred. You calmly step naked into a hot tub, finally unconcerned that your one breast and your scar show clearly. You sink into the warm water and talk with the other women. You dance the salsa with me, laughing at our mistakes. You used to love to dance when you were a teenager, but you gave up dancing because your husband did not dance. Today you dress in a turquoise blouse while your liquid silver necklace dances with you. You receive a massage from Conchita, relishing her deep, skillful strokes as she rubs lotion into your face, touching you tenderly. You eat too much guacamole and do not care. Tonight, you sleep in your own room and taste solitude instead of responsibility. On our morning hike, you tell me that you'd never slept so well. Writing about my mother's imagined experience makes her more present in my psyche. Who knows whether my joyful, healing images heal anything in my mother's spirit; they heal some of the ache I feel for my mother in me.

I extend my stay at the ranch. Here I am nurtured and calm; I can write, exercise, meditate, and sleep. I need this respite, and I feel grateful for the place and the time. I write in response to writing prompts from teachers and also back in my casita in my journal, siting under the ancient oak tree in my patio. The oak helps ground me when I feel in danger of floating away on the river of grief. On my father's birthday, I spend hours in the round stone building, Oak Tree Pavilion, looking out at Mt. Kuchuma, sacred to the native people of this area of Mexico. I weep, then sit in silence, contained by glass, stone, and sunlight, with the mountain outside. Later our meditation teacher suggests we make a life list of a few important wishes before our deaths. I cannot do this yet. She gives us Mary Oliver's poem, which I know well, challenging us to think about what we will do with our one wild and precious life. Will I be able to love my life without my sister? I want to live a brave and courageous life for Janice, but I am not yet able to claim my own life. Right now, all I want is rest and a quiet filling of the well of grief.

May, 2005: Returning to Tincup

Ed, Tom, and I return to Shalom on Memorial Day weekend, 2005. This time last year, Gary and I learned of Mom's diagnosis. She died on July 4. Dad never returned to Shalom after one visit with Ed last summer. We three gather to transform the cabin. On this day, we feel the weight of what we are doing. This was our parents' primary home in the summer months for thirty-three years. We set ourselves two tasks: to go through the cabin, determining what to keep, donate, and throw away; and to prepare our site at the Tincup cemetery. We want to make room in the cabin for us and our friends and family. Ed and I are grateful to be able to store our family artifacts here; we leave the historical furniture in place. Great-Grandmother Lightfoot's red oak china cabinet sits against one log wall; it holds Mom's gold-banded wedding china. Grandmother Hocker's hand-painted china pitcher, sugar, and creamer rest on top of the china cabinet. Dad said the china, with its soft green and apricot pattern of peaches and leaves, stayed on his mother's oak sideboard through his childhood. The cedar music stand Grandfather Lightfoot made for Grandmother, who played piano, along with a small cedar chest, remain in their places where Mom and Dad used them. Several pieces of turn-of-the-nineteenth-century oak furniture hold a kerosene lamp and the chiming clock that Dad bought to remind him of home in Lampasas.

Reflecting back in time affords me relief from feeling stuck in my current situation of the most recent absence of family. Looking around the cabin helps ground me with my ancestors, as our parents carefully preserved a few pieces of furniture and many documents from both sides of their family. The two Indian chairs, bartered back from the Comanche, who kidnapped our Great-Grandmother Standifer, sit in the two upstairs bedrooms. From oral family history, we have determined that a young girl was taken from a wagon train, rolling into Central Texas from Missouri, in about 1845, when Texas gained statehood, and many settlers swarmed into Texas, feeling safer than they actually were. The great, far-ranging Comanche nation, not yet exterminated or put on reservations, controlled much of West and Central Texas. Comanches burned the wagon train and killed all of the adults. In this time, during the Comanche's desperate fight to maintain their families through the ravages of smallpox and war, both brought by intruding whites, they kidnapped many white captives. Settlers recaptured some captives; others were sold to white people. Comanches sold our great-grandmother, by then about seven, to white settlers in Central Texas in the town of Lampasas in about 1852. She became known as Anne Elizabeth, adopted by the LaGrone family. No one knew her birth name or who her birth family had been. Later in her life, the woman we knew as Nonnie, who married Grandmother Arenda Belle's father, lived with our dad and his parents in their home in Lampasas. Dad told us that his grandmother taught him rock games she had learned with the Comanche. She told him they treated her well, but she was not supposed to talk about those years. She did, though, to Dad. Nonnie brought the chairs with her when she moved in with Dad's family; they had been sold or traded with the little girl when she was returned to the white community. Mom replaced the old rawhide seats years ago. Originally they were probably cane. Gary thinks they are hickory wood from the Atlantic South. My cousin has the other two of the original four chairs. Ed and I hope to find a captive narrative housed in one of the Texas libraries, so we can document this family story. As I look at the Indian chairs, my mind and imagination expand back into history; ancestors accompany me.

We hang one of Mom's Flying Geese pattern quilts—turquoise, cream, tan, and red—high on the living room wall behind the stone freestanding fireplace that Ed built. Delighted to uncover more of Mom's quilted pieces, we find a place for every one—on tables, walls, and the bed.

The three of us work together with ease. We agree that we will not dispose of anything without checking with each other. Once Tom holds up a rusted Dutch oven he unearthed among camping equipment in Dad's storage space in the basement. Ed looks threateningly at Tom. "That's the Dutch oven Mom used to fill with stew makings at our camps," he declares. "We're keeping it." Tom learned that Mom would line a hole with rocks, build a fire in the bottom, burn it down to coals, and cover the oven with more coals and then dirt. The stew cooked all day; once when guests from the Rocky Mountain Biological Station in Gothic came for dinner, she jauntily put a shovel over her shoulder, announcing, "Let's go see what we can dig up for dinner." Last summer we cleared Mom's personal items out in too much of a hurry. In our exhaustion and grief, we moved too quickly; this time we sort deliberately. We make room for our generation and the next generations, and for past generations.

Even though bookshelves fill the cabin, we still have more books than can be housed well. I inherit the book-sorting task. I stack boxes of books I want to donate below the deck. A family friend who loved my mother pesters me, coming over to look through the boxes, knocking on the door many times during the time we are at Shalom.

"Hi, Edith," I say neutrally. Edith is a Rainbow (the name of our summer home group) resident who presents a conversational challenge. She chains her stories together with little chance for me to participate. She relies on a lot of conventional phrases of reassurance. I've made it clear that she is welcome to anything I place under the deck, because those are books I'm giving away; her agenda seems to include instructing me in how to be a respectful daughter.

"You can't possibly let go of that," Edith proclaims as we make stacks of donations on the deck. After Mom died last summer, Edith came over when we were quickly packing up, giving advice, offering to help, and chiding us about what these things meant to our mother. After the triple cemetery service she caught me in a bear hug, crying, patting my face, and gushing, "You poor, poor thing, you can come to me any time, any time." She caught me on the walking trail a couple of times, repeating stories that mostly featured her as the one who knew the right thing to do. Today she looks determined to coach me on how to sort these materials. Mom and Dad lifted their eyebrows about Edith, but they would want me to be polite.

"This was your father's study text for the Bible study that he led at the Tincup Town Hall in 1985." She holds it out after retrieving it from under the deck. "You cannot be thinking of giving it away."

"Well, Edith, I don't have room for everything, so I have to make choices," I reply. "I'm taking some of his books to the church in Colorado Springs," I add. Maybe this will placate her.

"Well, can I have what I *know* is valuable that you don't want?" she demands. I find my exasperation creeping into this conversation.

"Of course. Help yourself." I'm losing the politeness Mom and Dad would have wanted. "All the books I'm donating I'm putting under the deck, and you are welcome to anything there." I hope this pacifies her. I don't like her guilt-tripping.

But instead of taking what she wants, Edith leaves sticky notes on pamphlets and books, explaining why they are important and that I should not give them away. She knocks on the door, holding various books, informing me, "You must not know the history of these, or you could *never* part with them." She proceeds to tell me, "Your mother once loaned me this book. She treasured it, and wanted me to read it." *Mom was not that sentimental*, I say to myself. "We all gained so much from your wonderful mother. She . . ."

"Edith, we're going to the cemetery right now. I can't talk." Smiling grimly, I add, "I know you understand," and I close the door. I wonder if she is afraid her children will not honor her possessions.

Ed grins at me; I want to murder him. I notice *he* doesn't answer the door. We move books and pamphlets to the basement.

We rearrange furniture, create order, and make three or four trips into town to donate items to the Goodwill store in Gunnison. I hang Dad's red robe in the downstairs bathroom close to my room and hang Mom's upstairs; I will wear them when I visit Shalom. I've sewn Dad's "LH" monogram back on the red robe, and even though I never wear brown, I'm happy to have Mom's brown robe when I'm here. Mom was red-haired; our hair color is another way we seemed to come from different tribes. My hair is dark brown.

As we clear and sort items in the cabin, I enjoy making potato soup, meatloaf, oatmeal cookies, and other family favorites. "If we don't make a different plan, we're going to turn Joyce into Mom, and she'll never get a vacation here," Ed says at lunch one day. We decide that in the future, each adult who visits will shop for and prepare evening meals, and we'll fend for ourselves at the other meals. We still maintain this tradition.

Our second task is much more physically arduous. We clear many pickup loads of brush from our part of the Tincup cemetery, four miles from the cabin. One sign directs us to TINCUP CEMETERY, while another points out, CEMETARY. I don't know whether an unresolved spelling dispute remains alive, or if one sign-maker made a mistake. We pass the Catholic, Protestant, and Jewish knolls, along with Boot Hill. Again I remember Janice as an eight-year-old who sat so confidently on the fence a few feet from where her ashes now lie buried.

We laid the red granite markers for Janice and Dianne last summer, but they are directly on the ground. This year, Ed brings a large family marker, etched with a silhouette of the cabin, the Sawatch Range behind it. On the granite stone is our family name. Underneath is a line from Paul Tillich, "From Thee we come and to Thee we return, Ground and Source of our Being . . . Shalom." He brings, as well, a marker for Mom and one for Dad. On pieces of a cardboard box, Ed draws a schematic for measuring distances and placing the stones precisely in a semi-circle, with a space beside Janice's stone for Tom. We ground our grief in labor. We build forms for concrete out of scrap lumber, then mix it by hand in Ed's wheelbarrow. To do this, we carry sacks of cement from the truck and haul five-gallon buckets of water up the hill from Willow Creek in the meadow below. I've been lifting weights, and show off a bit as I carry two buckets at a time up from the creek. The guys seem impressed. We pour and shovel the concrete into the forms. Tom pats it smooth with his bare hands. We wait for it to set up, before placing the markers on the concrete. It takes all three of us to drag and lift the big central marker in position. Ed measures; if we are off a quarter of an inch, we have to reset the stone to satisfy his precise expectations.

Through the spring, the four of us have collaborated on the wording on the markers. On Dad's marker is "Light of faith, followed through," one of the lines from the TCU *alma mater* that I sang to Mom and then Dad as they were dying. Janice and I graduated from TCU as well; these words carry memories of football games, formal convocations, and campfire circles. Dad followed his light of faith all the way through his life. On his marker a chalice design of our denomination is etched. On our mom's is "She wove us together in love," with a spray of lupine, one of the mountain flowers she loved. On Janice's, we engraved "Born of Love, Bearer of the light of kindness," with an opened-up heart, one of the ends forming a dove. I am especially pleased with these words. Everyone who knew Janice remembers her exceptional kindness as well as her strong intelligence. Dianne's reads, "Not all who wander are lost," with a feather, reflecting her Native American heritage. Ed tells us that these words from Tolkien resonated for Dianne, with all her wandering.

For four days we sweat and work hard. I had no idea so much physical work is required to clear brush, haul buckets of water, make forms and pour concrete. Tom, Ed, and I labor cooperatively, continuing the home death tradition by performing needed tasks to lay our family to rest. We loved our people as they died, and now we love them as we create a memorial place. Back in Missoula, Gary crafts a hexagonal wooden box, reflecting the shape of the cabin, to hold Dad's ashes. Even though the box will be buried, he crafts it out of ponderosa pine and finishes it beautifully. I miss Gary and wish he had come with me to be part of this meaningful set of tasks, and our friendship. We plan a memorial service for

Dad in July at the Community Hall, a day and a year later than the service in the cemetery last summer. On our last day at the cemetery, we build a rock garden in the center of the semicircle. We transplant wildflowers among the circle of rocks. "They may not make it," Ed advises, "but the seeds will scatter over the site in ways we can't predict." As we leave for the last time, I realize we have recreated a symbolic fire circle, as we always did in our summer campsites. As our human forebears have done for tens of thousands of years, we plant flowers and scatter seeds, our archetypal gesture toward life in the wake of death.

In July, Tom flies to Missoula, and Gary, Tom and I drive to Colorado. We hold one more service in the Tincup Town Hall, where Dad preached so many times. The sign at the edge of the almost-ghost town still proclaims, "This is God's country. Don't drive through it like Hell." Family friends come, hugging us tenderly. They were not able to say goodbye to Lamar in person as they did to Jean last year. Gary prays, and Ed reads the eulogy and a poem he wrote. Ed remembers the times Dad comforted people who died from fires, adding a story I did not know. When Ed was in high school, a boy scout dived back into his burning tent, pulling out his friend, but he was burned himself. Dad visited him every day in the hospital until he died. Dad recognized nobility. I speak of Dad as a father, playing two excerpts from his taped sermons in which he speaks of his love for his family and his hopes for us. I do not give my own personal statement at this time, as I want to represent the whole family. Later, I regret that I did not speak of his influence on me. We sing two hymns he suggested, "Oh God, Our Help in Ages Past," and "Thine is the Glory." Dad had requested the Micah passage about doing justice, loving kindness, and walking humbly with God. We end with a recorded version of the "Hallelujah Chorus," also his choice. At the cemetery, Newton, the minister, gives a heartfelt sigh after speaking, and adds, "I hope the Hockers don't have to come back here for a very long time."

We do go back, every summer, to communicate with our people, grounding ourselves at this place. The historic cemetery functions as an old-style churchyard, where in the past, people walked past the graves of their ancestors every Sunday. We know where we'll memorialize Chris, our upstream neighbor, later this summer. We know that Molly and Morris will be buried right next to our plot. When I sit with my memories, I feel comfort in knowing where my own final remains will rest.

For me, the site serves as one place to voice my ongoing inner dialogues with my family members. I know now that death ends a life, but it does not end relationships. A few summers ago, I took my laptop to the stone semicircle, wanting to write a dialogue with Janice. I felt angry, troubled, and upset about my marriage. We were faltering due to too much grief, simmering resentment from both of us, too many differing needs, and lack of trust that we would regain our closeness.

I wanted to experience an internal, written dialogue with Janice, to carry on one of our deep conversations. I wrote my concerns and waited for an inner sense of what she would say. I do not think that her voice is in any literal sense more available to me there than anywhere else, but this pilgrimage felt right for that day. I did not think *she* was there, more than anywhere else, but the ground holds spirit for me in its sacred enclosure. I am able to meditate there. I wrote for a while. Silence. I asked open-ended questions. More silence. Then I imagined my father's voice behind me. Inside myself, I distinctly heard his low, resonant voice that would fill the sanctuary, the sound Janice and I used to call "the voice of God."

I have something to say, Joycie, I hear inside. And he did; I moved over to sit cross-legged on the pine duff with my laptop, in front of his marker. I typed for a couple of hours, barely getting in my own written voice because he had a lot to say. In my imagination, his voice sounded just like him, and the counsel sounded like his counsel. His words were firm, loving, definite, and wise.

I'm not saying you have to forgive or move closer to Gary, Joycie, but I think you'd better try. No one is perfect. You will be happier if you let these resentments go. I could hear his voice and his advice very clearly. I had sought Janice's kindly inquiring style; instead I received Dad's definite opinion. But he seemed to speak with a voice of love and wisdom. The ancestors speak when they want to, apparently, even in my own psyche. I'm not in charge of that experience.

Now I know what I would have said in that personal eulogy I did not give for my father. It's not too late for me to write it.

Dad, your strong voice lives on inside me. You are closer than breathing. Thank you for saying you loved me so often. Thank you for taking me to the libraries in Dallas. Thank you for talking with me about ideas during all of our life together. Thank you for treating me as an intelligent girl. Thank you for explaining your ideas on social justice, theology, and politics. Thank you for handing me your books to read when I was a teenager. I am grateful that you left me so many recorded sermons and manuscripts. Thank you for saying that you trusted me to figure things out my own way. You gave me my passion for an ethical life, and for social justice. You taught me to make myself present when people are suffering. You told me that nothing I could ever do would change your love for me, and I tested your statement several times. You taught me to speak up with courage. Not everyone remembers her father as a heroic, ethical man. I am so fortunate. You gave me the gift of your vulnerable, heartfelt speech. You asked my opinion and listened to me. Back in 1976, when I was sick with pneumonia, depressed, out of a job, and going through a divorce, you said, "Joyce, you are strong. I have known you since the day you were born. You will get through this." And then you touched my small girl heart when you asked if I wanted you to send Mommie up to Colorado from Texas to take care of me. How I wish I had said yes, and how I love you for asking. I go through my life with this, your benediction to me.

I will continue my interior dialogues with those I love. I am able to keep writing to them. I write about their unlived lives, about their special qualities, about my gratitude, my regrets, and my memories. We grow along together.

chapter seven

It's All Come Down to Me

When the memory keeper dies,
what happens to the memories?

August, 2009: Shalom

Here in the high country of western Colorado, I am alone at Shalom after visitors and Gary have left. The sun burns brightly during the day. Thanks to monsoon rains, the meadows remain green; asters have replaced flax, lupine, and paintbrush. At night, stars spill across the dark sky; Willow Creek provides a just-audible murmur. Some nights I hear an owl calling, even over Emmylou's singing, as I cook. Outside on the deck, we carry on a human-owl conversation. I don't know what we are communicating, but I feel honored to be part of the conversation. I remember the owl outside of Janice's window, a portent, a symbol—or just an owl in an unusual place? *Hoo-hoo, hooo.* One night we hoot back and forth for half an hour. On chilly mornings, a little wood smoke flavors the cabin air, and my walk leaves the scent of sage on my pant legs. Ice Mountain and the Sawatch Range focus my outward view from the dining table.

My view turns inward. With ten days of solitude, I anticipate time to reflect and do exactly what I want. The internet, cell phone, or mail won't distract me, since only a land line and snail mail three times a week gain me access to the world outside. I hope for the fertile peace that the name of our cabin promises. I still feel hollowed out by my own family deaths and the deaths of Gary's mother in 2005 and his father, whom I loved, in 2006.

On my first full day alone, I write a homemade book of hours. I adapt the idea from various religious orders that gave direction to their monks so their days unfolded in an orderly way. My journal rests open on the oak dining table Gary made for my parents' sixtieth anniversary. I've spent time alone here each year since they died, and find a gentle guide helpful for those times when the mid-day demon, acedia, comes around to spoil solitude, as the desert monks wrote. What luxury to throw on whatever T-shirt and shorts I find first, slather on sunscreen, and skip the makeup. I always plop on Dad's fraying straw Stetson with his name on the hatband. Weathered logs set on end serve as footstool and coffee table on the deck we enlarged after Mom and Dad died. I feed the birds and creatures for Mom before I mix granola into yogurt for my breakfast. Black flaxseed for the pine siskins, mixed seeds for the bigger birds, and dog food for the gray squirrels, camp robbers, and, sometimes, pine martens.

My daily plan reads:

1. *Feed the birds*
2. *Coffee and journal on the deck*
3. *Breakfast and spiritual reading*
4. *Work tasks: split kindling, stack wood, haul brush to trailer, clean part of the house, wash windows, do laundry*
5. *Continue sorting and clearing out*
6. *Hike for an hour*
7. *Visit neighbors, especially Molly and Morris*
8. *Snack lunch*
9. *Read fiction or memoir. Maybe nap*
10. *Fishing or photography*
11. *Prep for cooking*
12. *Deck for sunset; call Gary*
13. *Cook, music, freeze food, eat*
14. *Fire, read, sleep*

When I'm at Shalom by myself in the summers, I cook for Ed. When he comes to the cabin to hunt or spends time in the winter, which requires a snowmobile and skis, he defrosts food I've put in the freezer—chicken noodle soup, venison enchiladas, meatloaf, my summer bounty pasta sauce, spicy beans and rice, or Dad's favorite oatmeal cookies, made from his mother's recipe.

Ed is still single, despite my best efforts. I talk about how he might meet compatible women on our drives over Cottonwood Pass: "Ed, I was thinking that you could join an environmental organization, join a hiking club, check out a larger liberal church where there might be more unmarried women, tell your friends you're interested in dating again, maybe even go online." Ed doesn't go to bars to meet women. At least I don't make all these sisterly suggestions at once.

Long silence. Ed smiles slightly, "You have a lot of good ideas."

Ed met a few women after Dianne died, but none of the relationships worked out. He and I are now dear friends; without Janice in the middle we rely on each other. If we lived in the same town, I would round up my women friends and ask for networking and ideas. I don't want Ed to feel lonely, but he's an adult and has to work out relationships for himself. I remember how happy we were when Ed met Dianne.

Ed and I talk about our new friendship. "Of course, I loved you from the moment you were born," I tell Ed. I recount that after he was born in Dallas, Mom and Dad placed his crib in a screened sun porch, just on the other side of two windows opening into Janice's and my bedroom. "I felt sorry that you had to sleep in your own place, when Janice and I had each other in our room," I tell him, "so I would hold your hand through the window at night so you wouldn't be lonely."

"I never knew that," Ed ponders. "I had a sense that *something* friendly was on the other side of the window, but I didn't know you held my hand." He pauses for a while. "Thank you," Ed says softly. We round the hairpin curves toward the top of the pass, bouncing over the wash-boarded gravel road as it winds to the 12,100 foot summit.

Our parents left the cabin to us; we transferred Janice's part to Tom. We all work out our plans and have no conflict over what to do to the place.

I plan not to sort documents and photographs in this time of solitude. I've been sorting too much in the last few years.

I write in my journal:

I can either make sense of the past for unknown future read-ers or story-keepers, or I can live my own life while being a steward of the past for the future. I cannot make meaning for people who are gone, for people who are unknown. The buck stops here, with me, as Harry Truman said. Now it's about my life, not theirs. When I am gone, the stories will be gone as well; the web of connection will be torn away. I have no children, and I have no feeling that there is anyone else in my family except my brother who cares about all these pictures and letters. When the memory keeper dies, what happens to the memories? How do I live my life now? I'm not going to spend this vacation sorting through all this stuff. I have had enough of death in life and I want to get on with mine.

Making Meaning

Is it true that I cannot create meaning for people who are dead? Their lives as individuals are done. I now see that it is hard for me to distinguish the line of separation: is the work of memory for *me*, as it helps me clarify my identity, or is it for the *ancestors* whose nar-rative lines have broken into death? I may not, after all, be doing this work *for* the children and grandchildren and great-grandchil-dren I do not and will not have, or even for my nieces. My current psychological work will be to clarify my identity. We, the recent and long-past ancestors, seem to be participating in an ongoing dialogue. In making meaning about deceased family members, through my writing and archiving, I simultaneously make mean-ing for myself. These questions fill me as I come again to Shalom, seven years after the first family death. This year's visit promises a time of quiet retreat for me. I set no writing deadlines for various conferences, only a time to *be*.

My writing strikes me as defensive when I reread my journal entry about *not sorting stuff* the next morning.

While I want a quiet retreat, I don't feel peaceful. I feel haunted. In the seven years since my sister-in-law, sister, mother, father, mother-in law, and father-in-law died, I have taken a major or minor role in cleaning out or sorting through the possessions of six people, sometimes more than once. The unsorted objects here at the cabin pull at me. In addition to what is here at Shalom, at home in Montana there are many more family letters, my sister's journals, and more photos jamming my guest room drawers. An astonishing volume of papers and pictures reflect our strong family bonds. I treasure these artifacts; I know I will continue my labor of love as I someday organize and annotate them. This will be part of the work of grief for me. The hospice chaplain explained that grief is love. My mother's oak jewelry box is here on her dresser, with key pieces of her jewelry that I enjoy wearing while I'm at Shalom, but my sister's recipe box and most of their jewelry found places in Missoula. I've had enough organizing for now.

The tasks that love demands often bring me tears of sorrow, occasional humor, and puzzlement over what to do with all the *stuff* left behind. Janice wrote about Psyche's tasks; one was to sort out a mix of seeds and sand dumped in her room or die by Aphrodite's jealous hand. Ants came to her rescue. Where is my army of discriminating ants? I volunteered for the task of clearing out my mother-in-law's study after she died in Seattle. The sons wanted no part of it. I felt more detached; it was easier for me. On the front page of Marcia's address book she wrote, "Do *not* destroy. God is watching you!" I took the chance that God was busy and tossed it, while at the same time I registered her poignant wish that many far-flung friends would gather for her memorial. My mother-in-law left about five thousand pieces of paper with notes, "Save! Important!" And they were, to her, but this experience has taught me to cast a steely eye at my own possessions and give away everything I can. As of this writing, our home in Missoula now contains empty cabinets and drawers as I continue to donate and recycle. But, like my father before me, I keep items of value. My father left a small lock box in the basement of this cabin affixed with a stern note: *"Nothing of value to anyone but family. Do not take."* Cassette tapes from the seventies and eighties we used to send back and forth to each other make up this family treasure; they served as round-robin communication sent from one to the next, to the next. Dad kept them all when they ended up at the cabin. They are full of everyday happenings, just staying in touch. We left them in the now unlocked box in the basement.

Soon after Mom and Dad died, Gale visited the cabin with me and helped rearrange Mom and Dad's room so Ed or I could sleep there with more emotional comfort. We kept the 1940s oak dressers they bought when they married. The framed calligraphy, "They shall beat their swords into plowshares . . .," hangs in their bedroom. We replaced what we thought was a too-frilly, brown-and-white-checked, flounced cotton bedspread and end-table set with a patchwork quilt made by my mother. Grandfather Lightfoot's cedar chest still holds the linens, and the oak, glass-front bookshelves from Dad's home in Lampasas, Texas, hold the essential family volumes—the Hocker/Standifer family Bible with names back to the early 1700s, early books on the environmental movement, books about the mining towns and ghost towns of our immediate area, and some of Dad's favorite theology books—Buber's *I and Thou*, Jung's *Modern Man in Search of a Soul*, Bonhoeffer's *The Cost of Discipleship*, and collections of Fosdick's sermons. Many more fill the bookshelves in the living room. Space remains in the glass-front shelves for books we bring to read in the summer.

We gave Mom's sewing machine to Ed's daughter, Katie. We offered her fabric scraps to women in Mom's sewing circle. The dresser drawers are empty—except for all the photographs and artifacts. Over the years, we've rearranged Shalom for us. Tom, Ed, and I have cleared out pickup loads of possessions to donate, relocate, throw out, and recycle.

The summer before Mom died, I wanted to help her reorganize the kitchen so she wouldn't have to get on her hands and knees to dig out essential pots from under the counter. She was resistant until I assured her, "You don't have to give away anything. I only want to make the kitchen work better for you." She looked dubiously at all the stuff packed neatly into the cabinets and drawers of the small kitchen and explained why she needed it all, including seven sets of markers to fill in scratches in furniture, balls of string, and dozens of colored pencils for Katie. She wanted to keep the commemorative plates on the wall from almost every church they'd served. They still line the log walls of the kitchen.

On that visit I proposed we clean out the kitchen drawers. We came to that one that every family has, the junk drawer. Mom looked at it and said, "Nightmare." She shut it firmly. I got to it a few years later.

We cleared and emptied out—but not the pictures, letters, and documents. They've all come down to me; they seem to beg for my attention. Rather than settling down into my longed-for retreat time and space, I feel pulled at by insistent ghosts, specters from a distant past. My ancestors feel close now, like a companionable but persistent presence. They seem to follow me into my bedroom at night. Do they require something of me?

Emotionally blocked from doing creative work that feels more current, irritated that these ancestral presences call to me, resistant and resentful that I have to clean up all their messes, I am, myself, a mess. These pictures represent family history whose meanings depend on someone to impose narrative coherence upon these shards and linguistic scraps of life. Family stories live inside me. I know secrets and absent memories; ones that I can never know will remain unknown and untold. I am, incomplete as they are, the memory-keeper.

My family's narrative inheritance permeated our childhood. This stuff is not just reflective of *their* lives. I am involved. I planned a carefree time of reading, writing, and hiking. I'm feeling torn.

My brother offers a solution to my obvious ambivalence about the artifacts: "Just leave them where they are for now."

As I talk over my quandary with Gary, telling him I do not want to keep sorting, he says, "Good for you. You sound clear."

When I call Tom, he remarks, "You probably can't help making sense out of all that stuff. It's who you are."

I'm a psychologist; I know that all this resistance surely stems from wanting two incompatible things—to feel free, current and creative, and to continue sorting and making meaning of my family history. And so I ask myself, *Will going through all those boxes plunge me into a compulsive reduction of clutter? Can this process be meaningful for me? Do the ancestors need something from me? Whose remains are these?* Through the night these questions recycle through my dreams. As is always the case, the dreams do their work. I dream that a group of unknown relatives waits in the living room, patiently drinking coffee until I emerge from the bedroom. I awaken to claim the remains, the paper remnants of their lives. My current life intertwines with theirs. We are in this together, my family and I.

The next morning, I drag seven large cardboard boxes out of the haunted closet in Mom and Dad's bedroom and put them on Mom's rust-colored, patterned, shag carpet that we'll replace one day. I feed the birds and critters, cast a longing look at my deck chair, and go back inside. Skipping breakfast, I begin a process that turns into days of sorting, throwing away, saving, and writing notes on my laptop. Now, I am a woman possessed; the ghosts seem pleased.

They seem to be speaking to me: *Well, finally. Let's help the poor child all we can.*

Archive Partners

Over coffee, I tell Molly what I am doing. Molly is my touchstone at Shalom now. She watches how late the lights in the cabin burn at night. "I see you were up clearing those boxes," she says approvingly. "Your mother would be proud of you. I'm writing my memoirs too," she discloses, "and I'd better get on it if I want to ever finish." We talk every day about our progress. Molly's memory is sharp except for where she has put things, so sometimes I help her rummage through her piles. She thanks me, and observes about her own artifacts, "No one else will do this." I feel grateful. Molly is now in her late eighties. Morris is quite frail, although he still asks me to fix him, teasing me about being a shrink. I tell him I'll fix him in exchange for stories about the POW camp. Molly has to leave the room because she has heard them too many times. I ask him if he would write his stories.

"Nah. I lived 'em. I figure that's enough." He smiles. "It wasn't so bad." He must be forgetting the near-starvation rations he's told me about before. Three years later, I will officiate at Morris's memorial service at the Tincup cemetery, next to our site. I will say that he never needed fixing.

More questions arise as I clear, discern, puzzle, remember, and sort. Who will know or care that I peeled off stuck-together clots of small black-and-white photographs from the 1930s, or that I tried to identify and note where the trip might have been, who the people were, and what was happening? My brain functions as a time-kaleidoscope. Soon, stacks of pictures and documents, loosely connected, cover much of the rust-colored shag carpet. I leave one placemat at the table clear for meals; the rest of the table holds boxes, labels, markers, Ziploc bags, and documents.

That night, I light the first of many fires in the fireplace. With some trepidation, I place unidentifiable photographs and duplicate newspaper clippings in the wood stove. I reluctantly discard pictures from both sides of the family. Who is that young man pictured in 1898? He looks like a Lightfoot, but he is not my mother's father. An unsmiling woman with her hair parted severely in the middle might be my great-grandmother on my mother's side. I don't know who they are, but they look and feel familiar, bone of my bone, flesh of my flesh. For a few moments, as I blow on the embers in the wood stove, the images of people and places flare up again, and then die down. Goodbye to all these places I cannot identify; I know they were meaningful to these people whose images I burn. I feel the archeologist's reluctance to disturb a site.

Ashes to ashes, dust to dust.

Dad's Side—Hockers and Standifers

Coming upon a sepia picture, I see Grandfather Ed Hocker Sr. as a young man, then in his engagement picture, then standing around the Peoples National Bank with other middle-aged bankers in Lampasas, Texas, later as a father taking his son camping on the Colorado River, and finally as an older man posing in a studio portrait with my grandmother Arenda Belle. I read his obituary, headlined, "One of Lampasas's finest men is called home." He's identified as a pillar of the church for which his grandfather gave land. I treasure the picture of Ed and his staff posing at the bank, three-piece suits and hats identifying the time as the 1920s. I open a Peoples National Bank envelope to find a ten-dollar bill that he signed, in the days when banks issued U.S. currency; I give this to my brother Ed, his namesake, to frame. More pictures of Grandfather Ed's ancestors are scattered through the boxes. Most of them are unidentified, except for the Texas Rangers. I imagine that Grandfather Ed cares.

As the hours and days pass, the boxes of pictures and documents take on a numinous quality for me; they draw me in. I no longer have a choice; I can't leave them alone. I wake at night and sense the objects in the next room. I vacillate between irritation at my mother, of all people, for not organizing this stuff, and gratitude toward those unknown ancestors, probably women, who marked all these pieces with an invisible sticky note saying "Important!! Save!!" Still, I wonder what this process means.

I think back to my previous attempts to bring meaning to these physical scraps of life. I once asked my mother to bring a lot of these artifacts to Janice and Tom's house in Fayetteville during our last Christmas when we were all together in 2000. I proposed to help her organize them. After I spread them out on the sunroom table in Fayetteville, my mother, with a helpless look on her face, confessed, "I don't *want* to do this." And so we just packed them back up in the old blue Samsonite suitcase. Now they have all come down to me. I'm embarrassed at this point to have imposed *my* need for story and order on my eighty-year-old mother. They had all come down to her, as they now have to me, and she'd refused the task. My dad's mother, Arenda Belle, made a few notes on pictures, identifying formal studio portraits as "Mom," or "Dad," or one of her sisters, only occasionally writing down a name or date. I think my Grandmother Arenda Belle could not imagine that someone who did not know these people would, well over a hundred years later, puzzle over who they were and want more detail.

I protest, to myself, *Why were these saved but not cared for properly?* My feeling rests on gender assumptions that the women of the family should have cared for all these pieces of reflected memory. I bear the accumulated weight all those female ancestors must have felt. Did they remind themselves to someday get to those boxes?

Here is an envelope labeled in Dad's handwriting from 1968 labeled "Kids," with pictures of us three. I imagine him proudly showing us off to various parishioners and friends. Until this moment, I've never had the thought of why my *grandfather, father, or uncles* did not organize all these artifacts. In fact, my Uncle Fred later provided much-needed family history, the product of assiduous research using microfilm documents. My gender assumption must be revised. Women were the designated kin-keepers of the documents at that time, however. I reject this sexist assumption now. The admonition, "Let the dead bury their own dead," brings me no relief.

Now, they've all come down to me.

Dad's Sermons

My sentimental father saved everything in file folders; his penchant was for letters, essays, and clippings. He didn't organize chronologically, but thematically. He edited and saved some of his sermons on tape. Dating remained erratic.

As I sort through taped sermons in 2009, I remember one summer, in the late 1990s, when I visit the folks at the cabin. I see my dad in their bedroom, with headphones on, listening to tapes. I assume he is listening to lectures that he brings back from church conventions. He's in there for a long time, sitting in a black rocking chair that came from his house in Lampasas, a cassette tape player on the small bookshelf beside him. When I see him take off his headphones and stretch, I go to the door of the room. He's been at whatever he is doing for a long time. He says, "Come on in, Joycie."

I sit in one of the Indian chairs and ask, "What are you doing, Dad?"

"I'm going through these sermons," he replies, "throwing away the clinkers." I know he means the sermons he thinks didn't work out well. In his post-retirement interim churches, he has begun taping most of his sermons.

"But I am very glad to have *all* your sermons," I assure him.

"No, I don't want to leave clinkers," he says firmly. "I think you will listen to these. I want to leave my best work." He was right. I do listen, and I haven't found any clinkers. He understood me well. I fill a drawer at home with the cassettes. I heard many of them as a child or young adult, in earlier forms. Listening to these weekly messages gives me an even deeper understanding into Dad's theology. I love listening to his resonant voice. His typed sermons fill three large binders, revised and delivered at various churches over the years. He noted the dates and places in the upper right-hand corners. I found them in the filing cabinet downstairs in the cabin, early ones typed with his college-era Underwood portable typewriter, edited with a blue pencil.

I especially treasure one dated August, 1945, just after the United States dropped the second atomic bomb on Nagasaki. Dad led a prayer service for the young people in the Atlanta church. I was not yet a month old. In it, he gives thanks for the fact that the forces of evil are quelled, for now, but gives voice to his regret and deep doubt that war ever solves anything. He balanced the fervent gratitude of Americans that we won the war with his sorrow for all the chaos and the lives lost. His anti-war beliefs grew through the years. I prize a manuscript from 1954, the Sunday after the Supreme Court issued its desegregation ruling, *Brown v. Board of Education*. This is one of the sermons that led to later trouble in

Dallas. Again, I can read his convictions about race and justice. I probably don't have all his sermons, but as I put them in chronological order, I can tell that most remain.

What do people who aren't involved in family history—or memoirists, historians, analysts, or anthropologists—do with all this residue of former lives? Do they just chuck it out? How do they do that? I call my brother at work three hours away and check with him about whether it's all right with him to throw away outdated unrecognizable pictures and documents. He cares about our family history. After a long pause, he says, "You're the oldest, so you're the likely one of the two of us to remember the stories." Ed is taking my question seriously: "If anyone can make sense out of all this material, you're the one to do it. I trust you. No, don't save the discards for me to see."

I sort through bundles of pictures of my father and his father, with Dad's childhood friend, Royal, camping each summer on the Colorado River out of Lampasas. These trips form the genesis of my dad's passion for taking us camping. Gathered around a table with a Model T Ford in the background, photographs record a visit the older men's wives made. They wear formal dresses; possibly it's after church. Each summer they drove out once during the two-week vacation to have dinner and enjoy a picnic. I wonder if *they* had a vacation.

Here is a picture of sad-faced Grandmother Arenda Belle Standifer Hocker, waving from a train window as she traveled from Lampasas to St. Louis for medical aid for what we always heard was "female trouble." Later my aunt told me she suffered greatly from a prolapsed uterus and never really recovered, which might explain why I retain few memories of her smiling. Only sad, wan looks partly brighten her face in formal studio pictures with my father when he was three, her engagement picture with Ed, and what must be an anniversary picture, hand tinted, which makes her face look even more pale, a few years later. Always formally dressed in the pictures, she looks unhappy. I don't know her story. My father told a happy childhood story, but I weave a story that says that Belle was lonely, dutiful, and worried about her daughter, my aunt Edwina, who was difficult for her parents in high school.

Belle taught piano and played at the church for fifty-nine years. While she died shortly after moving to live with us, I cannot recall hearing her ever playing the piano in her late life. Where did her music go? I say goodbye again to Grandmother Belle, whose wedding ring I wore for many years during my second marriage. Her initials and mine are engraved inside the wide gold band.

I wish I had known you. You loved us. You are beautiful. Goodbye.

Education Matters

One picture reveals notes I have written, although I don't remember quizzing my father about the people. My handwriting from the 1960s reminds me that these two people are my great-grandfather Thomas Jefferson (T.J.) Hocker and his wife, Elizabeth Tankersley. I am surprised to see in my own writing that I have been working on this family history project for at least forty years. T.J. was known as Professor Hocker, from Missouri, who emigrated to Lampasas, Texas.

Janice and I often visited our Grandmother Hocker in Lampasas; she's Captain Standifer's daughter. He was one of the ubiquitous Texas Rangers pressed into service by anxious settlers for the then-dwindling Indian wars. Her Grandfather Standifer, also a Texas Ranger, led several battles with Comanche close to Austin. He married Anne Elizabeth, his third wife, when his first two wives died. She was the Comanche captive, sold with the Indian chairs to Lampasas settlers. Once, with directions from a relative, I found a commemorative brass plaque flat on the ground in the field by the Austin airport that explains, "On this site, Captain Standifer surprised a band of Indians on the creek nearby, and carried the day." I have not been able to locate the plaque since the sixties, but I suspect it's still there, buried under concrete or weeds.

By the time of my Lampasas memory, in the 1950s, Grandmother Hocker, now widowed, has moved from the large house on the hill that Grandfather Ed Hocker built for her in 1904, in which my dad was born in 1917. She lives in a small house close to the church, where she still plays the organ and piano. She rents her second bedroom to Mrs. Tankersley, who sometimes will vacate the room to visit a relative so my parents can sleep in her room. Writing these memories, I think Mrs. Tankersley must have been a relative, but we didn't know that at the time. This time, Janice and I share a fold-down, uncomfortable, black horsehair couch in the living room. It's sticky. The water in the faucet tastes like sulfur, which we can't stand, but it's a little better when we pour it from the cold glass water jug in the refrigerator. We've been out back with a saltshaker, picking cherry tomatoes off the bushes in the garden. But now we're bored, so we decide to take a walk around the downtown square, which we're allowed to do as long as we don't go anywhere else, and Janice holds my hand when we cross the streets. I am eight, and Janice is five. In the hot Texas summer, we walk barefoot around the town square, noting the Peoples National Bank and the First National Bank where our grandfather, Professor Hocker's son, worked until he died at seventy-one. We go barefoot all summer, so our feet have toughened up. A dignified gentleman, Mr. Hosea Bailey, stops us.

"Whose children are you?" Mr. Bailey inquires. Everyone knows everyone in Lampasas. I tell him.

"So you are Professor Hocker's great-granddaughters," he proclaims. "My father went to his Greek and Latin school." He looked Greek or Latin to me, with his silver hair and antique elegance. "I will call on your grandmother."

Thinking about the role of Greek and Latin mythology in our educational history, I smile, as I have just discarded a list of email jokes Janice sent around about Greek mythology—the incorrect and hilarious answers that children gave in classes to explain who various gods and goddesses were. My sister wrote a book using Greek myths as an explanatory schema; we both studied Jung and mythology. We would not have been allowed to study in our great-grandfather's "Boys' Greek and Latin School," but maybe some germ of identity was ratified by Mr. Bailey that hot Texas day. I fill in the blanks—T.J. Hocker emigrated in 1845, when Texas became a state. The family story, for which I find no tangible evidence, is that he left Missouri fast, at night, after being charged with a murder that no one in our family believed he committed. But those frontier families must have been hungry for education, and he must have studied somewhere, so Professor Hocker taught his Greek and Latin school in his home.

A Doubled, Troubled Life

Many pictures of darkly beautiful Aunt Edwina, my father's older sister, emerge from the box. Disoriented when I find one that looks just like me at four years old, I try to remember if I was ever photographed in old-fashioned dress before I realize that this is my aunt, born in 1904. I find no pictures of Edwina in high school. Her daughter told me that one of her mother's high school friends said, in a visit decades later to my cousin, that Edwina was "promiscuous." I wonder what that term meant in 1920. Maybe it meant that she liked boys, liked to make out, and resented being denied the fun of dancing. Maybe she was sexually promiscuous, but that seems doubtful in a time before reliable birth control. She must have developed a reputation. In order to treat her depression, her doctor arranged for her to ride in a wagon every Saturday to immerse herself in the sulfur springs of the local swimming pool, in a section reserved for "treatments."

I now treat depression as a specialty in my practice. I find a thread of my identity in this depressed, sexually alive teenager. I terrified my parents with my early sexual development and experienced my first depression when I was fourteen. My aunt wanted a larger life than she could imagine in Lampasas. For a while she taught elocution, a precursor of speech communication, in which Janice and I earned PhDs. We both studied oral interpretation of literature before we found our way into other areas of communication. My aunt struggled with an overly constricted life, rebelled, and was judged for her rebellion.

Here is a 1920 newspaper clipping from the Lampasas paper that I have seen before; Aunt Edwina showed it to me when she was living in a nursing home in California. It's a simple announcement and farewell from the editor of the paper, letting the town know that Edwina was going to nursing school. During a visit with her, she said, "I want to show you something that will always be with me." She showed me the clipping, tearing up as she did.

"What makes this significant for you?" I asked.

"In those days, nurses were considered little better than prostitutes because they dealt with indelicate bodily matters," she replied in a flat tone. "My parents thought I would surely be ruining my reputation if I became a nurse, but it's what I wanted to do." She explained that having good wishes from a prominent citizen meant the world to her. She kept her copy of this clipping in her wallet.

Edwina defied her parents until they let her go to Baylor School of Nursing in Houston. Later she became the head nurse at Southern Methodist University; we became friends when I attended college in nearby Fort Worth. I loved it when she would put me up in an empty hospital room in her building, let me sleep in, and then invite me down for breakfast in her apartment. She relished administering a full-service health center.

One of Edwina's journals appears in a box I'm sorting. During the 1980s, I visited her every year when she was bedridden in a nursing home in California. She asked intelligent questions about my work and my plans, and would always give me one of her journals to read in my motel room at night. We talked about her memoirs on following days. Edwina was a fine writer with patience for handwritten detail. In this way I learned about her life during World War II and after.

One day we are talking about an episode she had written about her nursing school training in Houston. "I feel so guilty," she said. She looked unhappy.

"But you were following what you really wanted to do," I tried to reassure her. "What makes you feel guilty about that now?"

"I feel guilty about everything." I longed to comfort or understand, but I did not, until later. Right before she died, she told my father her secret.

While working at a hospital in 1941, she and a physician colleague fell in love. The doctor was killed right after Pearl Harbor. I read the alternate set of journals after her death; here is one in my box. She tells the true story of falling in love with the doctor, writing of her devastating feeling of loss, and how she knew she must reconcile with her emotionally abusive husband.

In perhaps the only way she could find to remain honest with herself, Edwina kept two sets of journals for much of her life. In one she wrote entries for others to read; in the other, she wrote the difficult truth. The one I unearth is one of the real ones. I must have put this journal here, hoping to eventually receive the others. No one knew that she had kept a double set of journals for much of her life. Before she died, she asked her older son to give the journals, the real ones this time, to me. Since we had discussed the journals over many visits, she must have thought I would understand her life better than her daughter, with whom she had a complicated, often critical, relationship.

This never happened. My cousin visited the cabin in 2012. On the deck one day she said, "Oh yes, I have Mom's journals out in the truck." My cousin lives in an Airstream most of the year.

"Could I read them again?" I asked, reminding her of her mother's request.

"Oh sure. I don't know why I keep them around; I guess I just don't know where to put them."

"Have you read them?" I inquire.

"No. They're just hurtful," she says with bitterness, "but I can't throw them away." I delicately ask if she might leave them at the cabin before she goes. She agrees. When my cousin leaves the next day, she leaves with the journals. In 2014, she visited me again at the cabin, and we talked more about her upbringing and her mother. Her mother, my aunt, treated my cousin harshly when it came to anything sexual. I asked my cousin again if she would consider giving me the journals, but she said they were locked away in a storage compartment. Once I thought I might write a brief biography of Aunt Edwina, but I would need access to her materials for a more complete story than the one that the single journal and my memory provide.

I myself keep journals—four decades of three-ring binders line my study shelf. My aunt's troubled, double life reaffirms something essential: write the truth, find someone to trust, or keep your own counsel, and try not to die with unresolved secrets. I teach Life Writing to people over fifty in our continuing education college, partly to help them liberate stories that are "crying to be told," as a seventy-five-year-old philosopher framed them for me. I acknowledge my aunt's influence. I wish she had been able to tell her stories and trust that we could have heard them and still love her. I keep the pictures that chronicle her life, with her warm, appreciative notes to me. *Thank you, you helped form me, I am sorry you experienced so much unhappiness in your life. I love you, you are beautiful, goodbye.*

Mom's Side: Lightfoots and Joneses

My mother, Jean Lightfoot Hocker, worked as diligently at being a minister's wife in the forties, fifties, sixties, seventies, and eighties as my father did at being a minister. I find black-and-white pictures of them around the time of their engagement in 1942. Dad stands proudly on the sand at the beach in Corpus Christi. My mother poses beneath a rose arbor belonging to one of the women in the Corpus Christi congregation where she, with her one year of seminary training, worked as a director of religious education. This must be the home of the woman who'd hosted her wedding reception, as Mom confided to me shortly before she died. While she worked at various jobs to supplement the meager minister's family salary my dad earned, she volunteered full-time at the church and raised children. Jean had little time or inclination for organizing what came down to her.

Pictures of my mother's high school friends from Thomas Jefferson High in San Antonio in the late 1930s emerge from another box. Faces dear to her, companions of her yearbook endeavors, her newspaper writing, her dances, trips to float the Guadalupe River on inner tubes—pretty young girls in home-made cotton dresses posing in front of a hedge, looking pleased with themselves—my mother's valedictorian picture, looking serious in her mortarboard. Here's the house in which she was born, the Ripley Street house. Coming across a picture of our mother editing the high school newspaper, I recognize her as a writer. My sister acknowledged her as her first writing teacher. My mother encouraged me to study hard and go to school, to be friendly so I would be popular in a way that she found difficult due to her shyness. I want to know the names of these girls, but I don't. I do know the name of her matron of honor, and find her picture that I remember from my childhood.

Thank you for encouraging me to study. You are beautiful, I love you, I miss you, goodbye.

I think of Mom's mother, Dr. Freddie Lightfoot, whom I also knew well. She was the ninth girl in a family of ten—Uncle John came along last. By that time, her parents, apparently tired of waiting for a boy, named her "Freda Jones," but she was always called Freddie. She also played the piano and organ at church, led the choir, sang, and gave private piano lessons on her baby grand piano in San Marcos, later in her life. She studied for her chiropractic license in 1928, in San Antonio. If I provide some meaning to Jean's mother's life—through her artifacts—maybe Jean, although no longer here, will understand why it's so important for me to do this archiving task. Or maybe all this sorting is simply part of my grief work.

Since Dr. Freddie worked every day as a chiropractor, either in downtown San Antonio or the small towns around the city, my mother's practicality and home orientation must have developed as she helped the housekeeper, Josephine, run the house on Ripley Street while her mother saw patients. Dr. Freddie's patients seemed devoted to her. I wonder if they had little access to more traditional, costly medical care due to the Depression and their small town locations

A later picture, from 1950, shows my grandparents' two-story white frame home in San Antonio, with a small lighted sign that I decipher with a magnifying glass, *Dr. Lightfoot, Chiropractic Medicine. Ring bell.* That house fell to freeway development. As children, we thought her *Science of Mind* magazines were weird. She made us drink warm lemon water in the mornings and often scared us, especially Janice, with her adjustments on our necks and backs. She usually showed an unsmiling face, and wore her regal long red hair wound on her head in a braid. She left us a tape of her singing, with a friend accompanying her on her baby grand. The tape's label reads, "For my grandchildren." She told me once, fiercely, that I could do *anything I wanted to do*. My early adolescent feelings were hurt once when she and Mom watched as I tried on Mom's wedding dress. I could barely fit into it, and the buttons wouldn't fasten over my breasts.

"Where did we get her?" my grandmother asked, as she and Mom laughed. I know now they were acknowledging my early sexual development and my body's difference from their slim, small-breasted physiques. But then, I thought they were making fun of me, and I was wrong, somehow, with my more full-breasted body.

I embodied Dr. Freddie's confidence as I went back to graduate school for a second career as a psychologist. Here is a picture of me in the 1980s in my psychotherapy practice waiting room. A framed picture of Dr. Freddie, standing in the doorway of her waiting room in the Majestic building in San Antonio, hangs close to the teapot in my own waiting room. My clients often comment on the stern-looking woman standing in the door of *her* waiting room in the 1930s, with women patients sitting in chairs and around the table where my mother came to do her homework after school. Dr. Freddie's mahogany love seat and chair accommodate some of my clients today. No, Dr. Freddie was too busy to organize pictures. My mother learned, as well, that current life tasks take precedence over history. I trace a thread of my own identity as I reflect on my grandmother and her life. Did my own pull toward healing and helping originate with my Grandmother Freddie, as well as my father? My identity may be more closely associated with my ancestors than I have thought.

Streams of Stories

I'm thinking now about the convergence of identity, the streams of genetic and storied inheritance coming down to me, creating me. Education figures heavily on Mom's side of the family as well as my dad's. Indeed, we are a family of writers. I find a folder of crumbling papers held together by a rubber band. In the folder I discover a program for the graduation ceremonies of the Greenville, Kentucky, Female Academy, in 1869. This early female institution later became Bethel College. I discover a collection of essays bundled with the program, including what must have been the required graduation essay, written by "Miss Sala Pate." I unfold an entire portfolio of elegant, handwritten essays, from 1868 and 1869, along with one letter from "Miss Sala Pate," a nickname for Sarah, from 1864. She grew up on a large plantation in Kentucky, in a privileged household. Kentucky was a border state during the Civil War. Her family was Union.

Consulting the family genealogy and my memory, I remember that this is my Grandfather Lightfoot's mother, my great-grandmother. She was the second wife of her sister's husband, whom she married after her older sister died in childbirth. He was a doctor in the Union army, Dr. Nathaniel Lightfoot. My Uncle Fred found his discharge papers from 1863. I don't know when his first wife died; I imagine the grief and consolation that may have come to these two people as they continued their lives and bore more children. My own grief for Janice transports me back in time to Sarah's grief. She may have loved her sister's husband; I'm certain she loved her dead sister. I have no way of knowing their truth, but I find solace in her love for her sister's children. I'm grateful they could shelter in each other. At home in Missoula, I keep a patchwork name-quilt, embroidered with initials and dated 1864. I realize now this quilt with names embroidered on the blocks must have belonged to Sarah's sister, made by her friends before her wedding. It remains unfinished. I find no pictures of my great-grandmother in her young life; in 1869 everyday photography remained uncommon.

One of her essays, handwritten in her fine copperplate script, is entitled, "The Role of Modern Woman." The 1869 graduation program indicates that Sarah read her graduation thesis aloud at the ceremony. She describes somewhat humorous attempts to learn to cook after the cooks left their household. I assume this happened just after the end of the war; she describes crying as she tells her lifelong friends and cook goodbye. I don't know whether these were slaves or free women whom her father could no longer afford to pay. Sarah makes a mess of cooking for the family, and doesn't appear to master any of the other domestic virtues, having come as she did from a wealthy family. She describes reading Homer and letting the pan of cornbread burn. She ends her essay thus:

> *I have not mentioned milking. Oh! That the men of Kentucky, like their Northern neighbors, could realize that part of their duty consisted in relieving their fair sisters of this labor. But no, they will sit by the blazing fire and quietly smoke their fine havanna's [sic] while we poor persecuted creatures must venture into the barnyard and risk our lives in the society of these horny monsters—cows. . . ."*

She then mentions washing and cooking as activities she wanted any suitors of hers to embrace.

> *So, my gentle sisters, let me prevail on you to come to the same resolution, that you must marry men whose mothers taught them cookery, and then a new era will dawn for the daughters of America.*

I laugh and shake my head at the tone of this essay. Sarah seems to be trying to be both funny and perky, while wanting a change in the division of labor. She must have come to this resolution after her earlier attempts to take on household tasks failed. I imagine her declaiming this essay at graduation, to the applause or disapproval of some of the audience.

Several clues to my own identity emerge with Sarah's feisty words. When I taught school in a small town in South Dakota in

1966, as the English teacher, the girls asked when we would start to "DEclam," with the emphasis on the first syllable.

"Umm, I don't know what that is," I responded to the high school girls.

"You know, DEclam, when we memorize speeches and go to speech and debate meets."

They had not heard of declamation, but they did know DEclam. Now I did, too.

I find another thread of my own identity, having taught and written on the topic of gender equality all my adult life. I lead women's retreats, form groups for women in my practice, teach about women's stories in my classes. My great-grandmother's bravery in writing about changing roles of women awes me. Those changing roles still provide difficulties for us today.

Another copy of Grandfather Roy Lightfoot's one published novel, *North of the Rio Grande*, with its worn red cloth cover, rests under his mother's graduation papers. I know the first page almost by heart since I reread it so many times in the San Marcos house that my mother's father built, stone foundation and all. Three quarters of the way through the novel, the characters, immersed in the Texas Revolution in 1836, against Mexico, come to life. Grandfather Lightfoot writes:

> *"What on earth has happened, Mrs. Todd?" replied Mrs. Alden and Molly in chorus, as the former opened the door to admit their good friend and neighbor.*
>
> *"Plenty has happened. Juan has returned. He has seen Tom, and he is with Sam Houston's army that is retreating ahead of Santa Anna's army. We will have to leave at once and go somewhere right this minute, as Santa Anna has threatened to kill every Anglo-American in Texas, male and female. . . . Most folks are headed in the direction of the Trinity River."*

In Granddad's book, the heroine marries the humble, good man instead of the aristocratic brother of Stephen Austin, and all is well.

Roy Lightfoot and his personality presented complications for some in the family. From my child's view, my grandmother Dr. Freddie seemed to barely tolerate him. I remember an unfinished conversation with my mother a few years before she died.

"I'll tell you something someday, but not right now," Mom said during the family reunion at the cabin.

"Would you tell me now?" I asked.

"No, it's hurtful, but someday," Mom replied. She looked tense.

During the time we were caring for Mom at the cabin, I returned to this conversation. "Mom, you said a few years ago that you would tell me something, I think about your family, that I did not know." I probe. "Do you remember?"

"No, I can't imagine what that might be," Mom replied.

Whether Mom did not remember our previous conversation, or did not want to discuss it now, I was left with an unanswered secret.

I conjecture that the secret is about her father, Roy Lightfoot, who worked as salesman/construction worker/stonemason/writer/real-estate developer. He sometimes sent a dollar home during the Depression, when he was on the road. Mom told me of running to the mailbox in their home in San Antonio and sometimes finding nothing. Grandmother's seeming dislike of her husband was palpable in the house in San Marcos. But *I* liked him because he let me read his library of Texas history and bragged about how fast I could read. My brother Ed adored him because Granddad doted on Ed. At our cabin now, I sit in front of a beautifully crafted stone fireplace built by my brother Ed, Roy's grandson. Ed dropped out of college during Vietnam, working as a stonemason before he returned to college to become a transportation planner. I wonder if love of stone runs in the genes.

My excitement rises as I search through all the remaining documents and pictures, sure that I will find a lost treasure I've been hoping to recover for over forty years. As I began this task of sorting archives, it seemed like just an arduous job that I needed to do. Now I am intrigued by my discoveries. I can hardly wait to see what I will find next. I follow clues about my identity and family stories planted by ancestors who did not know I would avidly follow the trail of their mysteries.

Dr. Freddie Jones Lightfoot also wrote a novel. I can see it now in my memory, pages roughly typed on her Royal manual typewriter, with cross-outs and corrections. The pages tightly filled a tattered, blue, cardboard typing paper box. She wrote *Mary of Blackgum*, a story of her family of nine sisters and one brother who lived in Indian Territory, trying to prove up some Cherokee land. They could have been granted land if they'd had proof of their part-Cherokee heritage; however, those papers had conveniently burned in a Georgia courthouse fire, so eventually their family had to move off the land they tried to gain by their labor. She wrote it through the eyes and experience of Mary, her favorite sister. We knew Aunt Mary. My mother volunteered me to type it when I went to college, but I never did. I finally gave it back to Mom, with apologies. Now, hoping for redemption, I promise myself to get it printed for the family if I find it. To my sorrow, I don't. We've been looking for years, but the box is missing. I read it when I was seventeen. My grandmother wondered if the voice was too colloquial and if she should make it less full of dialogue and more objective. I urged her to leave it the way it was. Now I realize her work is truly lost.

To my surprise, I find a book my mother wrote in junior high school, neatly typed and bound. I have never seen this book, full of poetry and essays that reflect a dreamy and intelligent thirteen-year-old girl. Janice presented just such a typed and bound book to our parents when she was in college, complete with a made-up copyright symbol. She knew she was a writer. This book is dedicated to "Mama, who taught me Beauty, and Daddy, who taught me Truth."

I grieve for Miss Sarah Pate, whose writing from 1869 I only just found well over a century later; for my mother, whose book was never mentioned; and for my Grandmother Freddie, whose story is lost. I find myself in the company of unknown female writers who long to tell their own stories.

We've also lost the notes Roy Lightfoot took on a yellow pad, verbatim, from survivors of the Alamo. These were the grown children of the Mexican women who served as cooks and nurses to the "Texians." A Lightfoot ancestor died defending the Alamo. I read those notes my grandfather wrote. He wanted to write another book; upon his death, however, Dr. Freddie had his cherry roll-top desk hauled to the dump and burned. Maybe the notes that I remember were in the right-hand drawer where I last saw them. The possibility of his Alamo book may have been lost in the angry fires of an unhappy marriage. Ed and I speculate on the source of that hostility. Did Roy support another family, maybe Mexican? Could that be how he gained access to these survivors? Is this the secret that my mother promised to tell me but did not? We'll never know.

Here are pictures of Grandmother Lightfoot, Grandmother Hocker, Janice, and me in 1949. The two grandmothers, Janice, and I sit on Roy's rock steps. Janice is a chubby baby; I am a big sister wearing black patent leather shoes and an adoring look for my sister. We wear sunbonnets, which must have been made for us by our grandmothers. I picture the Singer treadle sewing machine my Grandmother Hocker owned. Later, she gave it to my Grandmother Freddie, who in turn gave it to my mother, who finally gave it to me. I remember her telling me, "This runs beautifully, don't sell it." The machine, refinished by Gary, sits in our entryway at home. I haven't sold it, although I still can't sew. My feeling of pride in Janice, obvious in my gaze when I was four, only grew as we matured.

Pictures of Grandmother Lightfoot show her aging through the years. In one, she is bedridden in San Antonio, my mother sitting on the floor by her just before her death in 1983. I remember my last visit, when I thanked her for how she influenced me.

Holding her hand as she lay in bed in her son's home, I said, "Grandmother, you once told me I could do anything I wanted to." Recounting her modeling professional work for me, while volunteering at church and raising three well-educated children, I thanked her for her impact on me.

Sighing, she said, "Well, maybe I did some things right." I think she regretted a difficult marriage, and I wonder if she longed for a closer relationship with her family, from whom she had to be geographically distant in order to support them. I wonder if she, like my mother, regretted that she did not celebrate my mother's marriage with more generosity. I think that she knew she raised three children, who in turn raised their own children with her strong work ethic and sense of values. I don't know what that sigh meant, but I remember the kindness in her eyes when I thanked her for the many gifts she gave me.

I take a break from sorting, remembering, and reverie. Wandering through the meadow between the cabin and Willow Creek, I return with a handful of asters and wild grass to put in Mom's knobby white milk-glass vase. I remember how Molly kept the vase filled during Mom's dying and decide to take it over to her cabin.

"I worry about you staying up so late," Molly cautions. "I don't want you to ruin your eyes." I smile as I remember my mother saying that to me when I tried to sneak in one more hour of reading before bed.

What is Lost

In addition to lost stories, some ancestors remain absent in memory, as well as in pictures and documents. Ed and I talk about how we didn't know them. My twice-great-grandmother was a Cherokee woman. Along with her half-white daughter, she was forced out of her home in the South and made to trudge the cold and deadly Trail of Tears in 1838. Because Cherokee land went to the women who were forced to relocate to Indian Territory, many young girls immediately fell prey to ambitious white men, who then owned their land after marriage. Until recently we only knew this girl as Mrs. Mary Mershon Jones. Then my uncle Fred Lightfoot found her family name in county records in Wise County, Texas. She and her daughter shared their name, Mary Ann Duce. The second Mary Anne's daughter was Dr. Freddie's mother. The extended family holds reunions at Tahlequah, Oklahoma, although no one is enrolled in the tribe. Lake Tenkiller covered the original homestead, which the family ultimately had to leave because the records of heritage were burned. That Cherokee girl's grandchildren's children gave ninety acres of beautifully forested land to Northeast Oklahoma State College. Researchers conduct forestry projects there.

Here is a picture of the plaque listing all the family names; I visited the forest preserve during a reunion in Tahlequah. I served as a consultant for the Indian Health Service for many years, but I never talk about this distant connection because some Native people dislike the too-frequent white claim, "I'm part Cherokee." But I am a descendant, in my feeling and absent memory, and I honor that girl, whose story and name I barely know.

I experience more of the peace of Shalom, as I weave threads of stories and discover who I am. I maintain an internal dialogue with these ancestors; they are beginning to feel less restless, more at peace in my psyche. I've almost emptied the boxes. I find comfort in reflecting further back than my own recent losses. My tight box of grief releases as I feel a sense of companionship with those who came before Jean, Lamar, Janice, Dianne, and now Ed and me. Millions of people died before my own beloved family members did, and millions, billions more will. If someone had told me this in 2004, I would have felt no comfort. Going through the family artifacts does, however, bring me a sense of acceptance. This trail of life and death helps me put my own losses in perspective.

Pictures emerge from my own lifetime. One I have always loved: Janice, smiling, rests her hands on the shoulders of my brother's daughter, the only Hocker grandchild. Janice looks gently down at Katie as my brother and I sit close to my niece. We are sitting by Willow Creek in a place I locate in the distance outside the cabin window. Katie's daughter Keira was born on her great-grandfather's birthday. Katie and her daughters, Keira, Addison and Isabella will inherit Shalom, if Western Colorado wildfires allow the cabin to stand by the banks of Willow Creek. All these pictures, documents and letters that I'm sorting will remain here. Right now, the pictures are in Ziploc bags sorted by decade. Some decades require four or five Ziplocs. At the time I write about my archive mystery hunt, I can see all the finished scrapbooks on the living room shelf.

Sitting by the fire late one night after finishing more burning, I draw close to the stove, relishing the smell of pine smoke, even though it makes me hoarse and irritates my eyes. I don't mind; we all grew up loving the sound, sight, and smell of wood smoke. Tonight I am alone, but sit with a cloud of witnesses.

How did I know what to discard? I used my intuition to decide what was either mundane or so particular to a person that no one else would ever know or need to know the meaning of the photograph or document: paid tax bills, Dad's Nature Conservancy Card, legal documents and wills for people who have died, old driver's licenses, church bulletins from Dad's friends, expired life insurance policies, unknown photographs that sparked no resonance of memory in me, the silhouette picture of my first husband on a beach, group photographs of dozens of kids at summer camps in Texas, pictures of my mother's Sunday school classes without my mother, unknown scenes in Colorado and Texas, bad photos of Yellowstone and the Tetons taken by me with my Brownie Hawkeye camera in the fifties (although I kept the ones with the bears), countless church newsletters, and letters from parishioners thanking Mom and Dad for hospitality at the cabin. Knowing I could never reweave an intact web, I burn more documents in the wood stove.

In addition to pictures, now roughly sorted by decade, what did I keep? I again trusted my intuition. Birthday cards to and from me, including the one from my pediatrician on my first birthday. All the letters to and from the five of us, and our former and current spouses. Mom and Dad's love letters. All the drawings Janice made to illustrate her childhood stories. Postcards to my mother from a friend in England. Mom always wanted to go to England but wouldn't leave our dad, who would only go to the Holy Land. A picture of the living room of an elegant house in Corpus Christi. I think it must be the house where an older friend gave my mother's wedding reception. I treasure a picture now to go with the story of her wedding and reception that I will never fully know. The absent stories take their place in my psyche. I release secrets that went to the grave, grieve lost and unwritten books, and consign the unknown to the deep past.

What sense can it possibly make to weave, one last time, the web of memory, even as I know forgetting will set in more quickly than I can imagine? I continue to discover who I am in who they were. The double-headed Greek goddess, Mnemosyne-Lemosyne represented memory and forgetting. Years ago I drank from her spring in Greece, and now this goddess of memory and forgetting lives inside my body and brain. Mnemosyne may have enlivened those family ghosts who compel me to tell their stories and reclaim my own. Memory, along with language, is the force that makes us human. I give obedience to Memory, knowing her sister, Forgetting, lives just a turn of the head away.

Kierkegaard wrote that we live our lives forward but understand them backwards, as though we are standing on the platform of the last car of a train from which we are looking back. These pictures and documents help me reflect on the significance of my ancestors and the artifacts they left behind. Stories and memories are like rhizomes under the ground—they connect the living and dead in unseen ways.

Who cares about all these artifacts? I do. And maybe the ancestors care as well. I can't know that, but their lives rose to the surface while I was here at Shalom. Yes, forgetting will come; Lemosyne will have her turn, but so will Mnemosyne. The meaning I made in August flowed underground from the Trail of Tears and the Colorado, from Sulphur Creek in Central Texas and the Missouri River, from the San Antonio and Guadalupe Rivers. On the banks of Willow Creek, for now, it all comes down to me. One day I, too, will be swept away by the river of time. Until then, I'll drink from the water wherever it rises above ground.

chapter eight

Writing Remains

The dark Missoula winter sucks most of the light out of our valley. We're experiencing another inversion; layers of smog build up in the valley as the heavier cold air above us traps the warmer polluted air in our valley. My body mirrors the sky—heavy, leaden, and stagnant. It's February 18, 2011, one day away from the seventh anniversary of Janice's death. When Janice asked me to take her journals home with me, I knew that a time would come when I would have to decide what to do with them. That's why she asked me to be her journal personal representative. Today is the day.

We're not supposed to burn in our fireplaces because of the inversion; however, I recognize a greater desire today than being a good citizen and avoiding adding to our valley's pollution. Today I will feed into the friendly flames of our tall rock fireplace those parts of Janice's journals that I no longer want to keep. She entrusted me with this delicately demanding task of discernment. Sleepless the last few nights, I read some of her entries for the last time, marking with sticky notes the pages to tear out of her spiral notebooks and consign to the flames. Gary kindly builds me this fire, stacking plenty of logs on the hearth, ignoring the no-burn directive.

I drag my teal chair in front of the fireplace, surrounded by journals on the floor. A pot of Earl Gray tea steams on a nearby end table. I plan to give this process all the time it deserves.

"Do you want me in the room, or just around?" Gary inquires.

"You are welcome to come and go, but I'd like mostly to be by myself."

Behind me, the long, low walnut altar table Gary built from Tom and Janice's gift of a massive plank of walnut sits under east windows. Walnut does not grow in Montana. We came home from work to find a six-foot, bubble-wrapped package by our front door a few years ago. I hid it under the bed until Christmas morning; obviously the gift was a plank of wood from Arkansas, but I wanted to play Santa and prolong the surprise. Gary built a four-foot table, preserving the massive plank, gentling it with a subtle arc and a floating top—he crafted a gap between the supporting rails and the smooth surface. The table itself speaks to me of Janice. I imagine her helping to choose it in the off-the-beaten-track lumberyard, stacked with Southern hardwood and owned by an Arkansas man who seems to know everything about wood. We all visited this place once; I can clearly picture it.

My cut glass Waterford vase holds white roses and stargazer lilies; these flowers also remind me of Janice. One of the black-and-white photos taken a few months before she died rests on an open book support; in this one, she sits on a chair, legs crossed, hands folded in her lap. Her long blonde hair spills over her lacy black jacket, covering part of her low neckline. A black, beaded filigree choker necklace encircles her small neck. Janice looks out with a slight, knowing smile, brown eyes wide open. Appearing about thirty-five, not fifty-five, she looks composed, relaxed, and elegant. In Miami, the week before this event, Janice told me that she was so tired she could not imagine preparing meaningful comments to deliver at a friend's wedding; she wanted only to go home and sleep.

Pieces of her jewelry lie on a red silk square scarf. Tangible reminders of Janice's grace and beauty ground the opposite end of the room from the fire. Aunt Lillian's diamond-and-platinum dinner ring, made in the 1920s, anchors one corner of the red silk. With the ring are the black, beaded, dangly earrings I took to Costa Rica while Janice rapidly declined in Fayetteville. Years later in Belize I temporarily lost one. My friend Donna went with me to search everywhere in the sandy dark. We spotted it back in our hotel room. The lost-and-found theme continues. I set out the pink-and-silver earrings Gale and I searched for, along with Janice's antique amethyst pendant and earrings, the crystal pendant with a gold rose embossed on it I gave her one Christmas, and her thick gold hoop earrings I wear many times a week. By the red silk square, I arrange a gift from Janice, a paperweight and matching bud vase, made of heavy red, turquoise, and gold blown glass. For a little lightness on this heavy day, I fold her red T-shirt with white letters proclaiming, "I know what I know!" One of her research methods classes gave this to her when they apparently didn't understand the mysteries of inductive analysis that Janice taught. Long-lasting objects balance out the paper I will burn.

I ignore my allergies caused by the fire, just as I did at Shalom when I burned family artifacts. Today I live in a season of endings, ready to act on my personal responsibility to sort and let go of Janice's intimate writings. This task seems different from the sorting I completed at the cabin; Janice trusted me to know what to do with what remains of her writing, while the older ancestors lived their lives not knowing what would happen to their written and photographic remains.

Stacking Janice's journals in chronological order, I recall three years ago when I prepared a presentation on sibling loss. I consulted her journals then, to speak to themes in her life. At that time I wrote, "I flounder to a stop. I cannot contain her, I could not save her, and I cannot present her to you so she will live again."

Up until now, I could not fathom letting go of any of Janice's writing. Now time, my own writing, and analysis have loosened my death grip on objects. It's time to bless her life, all of it, and let go of carrying all she could not live out. I intend to make absolutely certain her privacy is protected in case I am not here to serve as guard.

Here they are—the journals from 1985 to 2003, with one scrap from 2004, which I have tucked into the last volume. Art, photos, and writing from her childhood and early adult years are stored at Shalom. I know the journals she wants me to go through—a collection of three-ring binders and spiral notebooks, some written neatly by hand, some scribbled quickly and messily, and some printed emails.

Janice kept her journals differently than I do. Mine are organized by year, with collages of pictures, quotes, and cards decorating the front and back covers and the dividing pages inside. I write serious material in my journals, but they also serve as a scrapbook for me, and include dreams, letters, emails, notes from others, speeches, and all the meaningful-to-me particulars of my life. I would not want anyone else to read my journals; nevertheless, I take pleasure in creating a sense of beauty along with my interior analysis. Janice created something starkly different. Hers contain no fluff—that is, no artwork and no diary-like passages about going to farmer's market, the weather, people she saw that day, or comments to give context. No, her journals are stripped to the basics—dreams, comments on dreams written in her careful handwriting during her sessions with Anne, and passages in which she is working out her interior and relational life. These are workbench-of-the-soul pages. Janice's journals record spiritual and psychological formation, guided by her inner voice. They are serious, intense, focused, brave, raw, and exploratory—deeply in relationship with herself in these pages.

What an honor that she wanted me to read them.

A few years ago, I talked with a writing colleague about my dilemma.

I told Carolyn, "I will need to destroy some of Janice's writing, in order to keep faith with what she asked me to do."

"Wow, that does bring up some issues," Carolyn replied. She teaches the ethics of personal writing. "Memoirists are usually obligated to show their work to others implicated in or by their writing, allowing them to respond and talk back about how they have been represented in the text, but you can't do that."

"No, it's because they have passed on that I'm writing about my family," I responded. "So I don't have the option of checking out what I'm writing with them, except against my own sense of ethical responsibility."

Carolyn asked, "Would someone, a student interested in the development of women's voices in academia, find material they could use in her journals?" She's a teacher, always considering the research options for her students.

I pondered. "They might, but I won't pass on these personal documents to anyone. I know Janice wanted me to learn how she felt, even more deeply than I knew, and then protect her privacy."

I wrote Tom, who ratifies my choice to destroy some of the journals. "She gave them to you," he writes back. "Do what you want to."

I follow Janice's request.

Seven years along, the river of separation from Janice has carried me to a new shore. My own mortality looms more clearly. Janice has lived her life, mined these documents for her own writing, leaving tailings of deep-rock excavation. She wanted me to know how she felt. I do.

Will some descendent read sections of Janice's writing, and my own, as I have recently done with my ancestors at Shalom? I also imagine Colorado wildfires sweeping away Shalom, along with all the documents and pictures. Many scenarios could easily unfold, including all of this family history being tossed out in a change of ownership. I have no ultimate control over what remains.

I tear out most of the pages from 1992 through 1996, her midlife crisis years. She wrote about painful struggles to realign with Tom twenty-plus years into their marriage, while they explored their inherent differences, as every conscious couple does. I watch those pages curl up and catch fire, thinking of the fire of passion, the necessary cooling of those fires in a long marriage, and the challenges of remaining intimately connected when a couple finds that their differences might destroy their union, or must resolve into compassionate acceptance. Gary and I have come to compassionate acceptance after six years of intense struggle. Janice and Tom also reached that marital plateau, but not without conflict, loneliness, and anger, along with reconciliation and love. In 1995, when Janice accompanied me to Belize for one of my women's retreats, she wrote, in response to my invitation to produce twelve-word poems, *Somewhere,/ along the way,/ my angels have died./ Maybe they are composting.* She looked heartbroken when she read those words. She found new sources of inspiration from the women she interviewed and from her own life stories, as she wrote her last book on the relationship of women and men in academic life.

I burn all the entries Janice wrote about her anger, disappointment, boredom, and incredulity at various episodes of faculty politics. These entries would be perfectly all right for others to read; I am joining with her in rejecting much that is stultifying in academic life. She repeatedly counted down the days until she had to go back to work. Janice wanted more free time, without the annoying faculty meetings, editorial duties, or student advising challenges. She detailed these challenges in her book. I learn again from her—"Take the time you have for precious life projects and for enjoyment." I remember how she cried when a colleague would not accept her refusal, in December of 2003, to be on yet another doctoral dissertation committee. I burn her reflection on how angry and exhausted she was, and how she knew the male colleague would have accepted the negative response from another male colleague with less manipulation and more grace. I retain the warning to keep my boundaries firm and clear, while I let go of Janice's struggle with this endemic issue.

For seven years I carried in my heart some of the painful episodes in my sister's life. She lived her life. I cannot fix it, heal the wounds, or salve the disappointments. And she would not want me to try. I let go of what I could not and cannot change. With the papers I consign to the fires, I let go, as well, of anger at others who contributed to the problems in Janice's life. All that big-sister rage pales next to my warm admiration of Janice's well-lived life. My heart grows lighter as the smoke rises up my chimney.

Her Belize journal of poetry and reflection remains precious to me. That journal belongs back on my shelf. Janice wrote in her book about going to Belize in 1995, having kept careful notes describing her time there. We met with a Mayan healer, Rosita Arvigo, who wrote a book called *Sastun*, an account of her apprenticeship with Don Elijio, an herbal and spiritual healer in Belize. Rosita organized the women and men who knew the secrets of jungle plants in a country-wide effort to conserve and transmit their physical and spiritual healing properties.

Janice's last writing appeared on a small sheet of paper titled, "Notes to Janice from the last few weeks," tucked in her desk blotter. She must have written this list in late January of 2004, when I was in Costa Rica. I picked it up after she died.

First on her list: "Let my students write about what they want to." While Janice did not elaborate, I imagine she meant that she wanted to encourage her students to find their deepest topics, and explore them, even in the structured academic world.

Second: "When I love my students, I am helping them the most."

Her number seven on the scrap of paper reads, in unrecognizable handwriting: "Rosita. Sastun. Write about this with Joyce." As I led the conversation with Rosita, Janice discreetly pulled out her notebook, looking at me with a sly grin as though to communicate nonverbally, *I'll take notes, you talk*. Ever the ethnographer, she detailed the Mayan system of dream analysis, compared to the Western system about which I was teaching. She thought about our partnership during her last days. I take her words as encouragement today—I am writing about what I want to. She loved me, and that helps me most of all.

One big surprise does emerge during the nights I review her journals, even though Janice told me there weren't any surprises. At the end of her book, Janice recounts a dream in which she flies above an academic conference, swooping down to pick up a little girl who is following her. She decides to name her Joy. We have marveled that Janice experienced this dream, not consciously knowing she was dying, speculating that it came to her in late November or very early in December of 2003, as she was finishing her book. I have cherished this as Janice's last dream, taking great comfort in its transcendence and wholeness. Anne and I have concluded that Janice's soul work was over, and that she left her life carrying Joy and rising above any limitations.

As I review her journals, I find the dream, written almost

exactly the way it's printed in her book. Janice finished the book in December of 2003. Disoriented as I read the dream in one of her journals, I double-check the date. This dream, titled "Above the Crowd," came to Janice on April 26, 1993, more than ten years *before* she finished the book. It was *not* her last dream; instead it is the dream she chose to complete her book, and her active life.

The dream came a decade before her illness. This one dream made her death almost bearable to me—that she soared above the conventions, holding fast to her own child, Joy. In the book she adds, "In my family, all the girls were 'J' names. My mother is Jean, my sister is Joyce, and I am Janice. This little one will fit right in." Her transcendent dream has been a comforting talisman for me.

I must change my thinking about time and chronology. If I cling to my former belief that what made this dream meaningful for me as Janice was dying is that it happened just before she died, I am in trouble. Time must be more like a series of folds, or like a wrinkle in time, as Madeleine L'Engle famously observed in her book of the same name. Janice chose this dream to represent the life issues she worked through for at least ten years. She names joy, compassion, and hope as attributes that lifted her life. I continue to learn how to integrate grief and sorrow into my life, this time, from Janice.

I've kept all the rest of Janice's journals, with her sticky notes, from which she chose dreams of hers for her last book. I ponder her writing, reflecting our life together, and nuances of her interior life that I could not have known otherwise.

In the period immediately after Janice's death, I looked for proof that she loved me, even though I had never doubted her love before. Having lost her, my need for reassurance shoved aside my sure sense of our shared love. Rereading all her journals, I come to appreciate that we forged a complex, layered relationship with periods of irritation, some disappointments, great affection, and understanding. While I certainly did not understand Janice completely, nor did she thoroughly understand me, love pervaded this faithful, long, layered relationship.

As part of the Belize retreat, I asked the women to draw their circle of heroines and heroes—who is in the center of the circle, who and what activities are outside? On that day in 1995, Janice placed my name in the center point of her circle. In other places in her journal, she worries about me, about having the right gifts for me—an ongoing theme in her dreams placed her on Christmas Eve without a gift for me. Thankfully, this dream series ended as we talked through the meaning—about how much of her emotional energy she gave to me, sometimes resulting in her worry that she had not given enough.

For some years she felt sad for me that she had a close relationship with our mother and I did not; she tried to make up for that. Our relationship spanned fifty-six years. Of course I was not always first in her heart. When I was anxious or in love or depressed or overworked, she was not first in mine. But the silver sister-thread weaves through a bright fabric of our own design. I recognize my own colors in her words. I no longer wonder if she loved me, having given up the childish, grief-driven demand that she love me *best*. When I say that Janice was the love of my life, I mean that I experienced a deeper, more accepting love of her and from her than any other I have yet experienced in my life.

I am grateful that Janice wanted me to know how she felt.

My Mother's Secret

Unlike Janice and me, our mother did not keep journals. I recognize kinship with Terry Tempest Williams. In Terry's memoir *When Women Were Birds*, she tells the story of how her mother, a Mormon, told Terry, shortly before she died, that she had left her journals for Terry in a certain closet. Mormon women live under a requirement to keep journals; possibly this practice was useful to women who tracked weather, planting, harvest, the community's resilience after disaster, and family ancestry. Terry did not know, however, that her mother had followed this expectation. After her mother's death, Terry found the perfectly organized journals, filling three shelves. Some of the journals were elegant and fancy, some plain spiral notebooks, and some beautifully bound books. As Terry tells it, one night she felt ready to see what her mother

had written, but had never discussed. To her extreme mystifica-
tion, all the journals were empty; in the rest of the book, Terry
speculates on what this defiance or resistance might have meant.
She searches for her mother's voice, and the voices of other women
who leave no record of their interior lives.

No shelf of journals awaited me after my mother's death. I
imagine our practical mother must have thought that writing in
a journal would have pulled her away from more urgent matters.
She wrote letters faithfully but left no journals. I knew my mother
reasonably well, even though we were not intimate until a few
years before she died. After all, I collected all the letters from
my parents beginning in 1940. I am also the keeper of all the
rest of the family correspondence, even archiving emails printed
from my mother's computer after she died. I did not expect the
surprise—I will even call it a family secret—that I came across
during the summer of 2009 when I went through the family documents at our summer cabin.

In a file cryptically labeled, in my dad's handwriting, "Memories," I find non-chronological, assorted documents. Among
them, I am surprised to read a rejection letter to my mother from
Yale Divinity School, dated March of 1942. How can it be that
I never knew she'd applied to Yale? Why hadn't I ever heard the
story? The juxtaposition of the surprising document and the
lack of a story, in a family in which we siblings knew most of the
important stories about our parents, surprised me. This mysteri-
ous document propelled me on a course of imagining more about
my mother's life than I actually know, or will ever know.

In 2012, eight years after Mom died, I visit Texas Christian
University for a class reunion. I make an appointment with the
dean of continuing education at the seminary to see if I might fill
a part-time, intermittent teaching position back in Fort Worth.
I remember with poignant regret that I turned down a request to
apply for a job at Brite Divinity School in the 1990s. The roads
not taken in my life beckon me. I especially regret my turn away
from seminary teaching and ministry, solidified when one of my
college professors reminded me that girls did not need to take

Greek. He advised me to abandon the idea of attending seminary to follow a vocation that would be useful to my husband. Back at the same seminary, in a building constructed after my years as a secretary when I did my undergraduate work, the dean receives me kindly. However, she has no need and no budget for a former professor from Montana to fly to Texas to teach continuing education classes. A door closes.

Daughters often live out some of the unlived lives of their mothers, especially on the unconscious level. Janice and I often talked about not having children, and how we kept going to graduate school with fervent focus. We wondered together about what parts of Mom's unlived life we might be living forward. It's possible that my late-in-life desire to teach in a seminary is an unconscious echo of Mom's thwarted desire to attend Yale Divinity School.

After my trip to TCU, I sense a deep desire to fill in the absences in my mother's written record of her life. I reread all our letters to each other. After years of not noticing our similarities, I want to explore those threads of convergence. My mother's physical life is over, but her influence lives on in me. I am intrigued.

Here is what I do know for sure: Jean graduated as valedictorian of a 600-student class, but even with her academic scholarship, she could not afford to leave her home in San Antonio to attend college elsewhere. Instead, she lived at home and attended an excellent Catholic liberal arts women's college for three years. Jean benefitted from the help of a powerful mentor; her home church minister from San Antonio later was chosen to serve as dean of the seminary at Brite Divinity School, and then president of TCU. He secured a Religious Studies scholarship for her so she could go to TCU for her senior year, and then to seminary after that. When she arrived, she found that these scholarships were only for men, but Dr. Lindley fixed that problem, making Jean the first female Christian Service Student at the college in 1939. I, and then my sister, followed our parents to the same considerably expanded university. In 1963, I arrived, also with a Christian Service Student scholarship. Professors on campus talked about our parents. In one of Janice's letters to Mom in 1967, she relates:

Guess who I sat next to at the Mortarboard banquet? The chancellor! And he just wanted to talk about you. Everybody knows you on this campus.

Once, a professor of mine told me in an advising session, soon after I married a seminarian, "Your mother was the perfect minister's wife because she knew there could only be one boss." I suspect that he was not-so-gently telling me that he saw problems ahead for me and my new husband since I didn't know my place.

Jean and Lamar relished their lives at TCU. Soon after they met, they began to date. I love a photo of Jean perched on the steps of the divinity school, a happy redhead in this black-and-white picture, clearly sitting in the spot where she wanted to be. She majored in English and journalism, along with religious studies, knowing she wanted to go on to seminary, which she did, but only for a year. At that point, dating but not yet engaged, she left in 1941 to work as a director of religious education in Corpus Christi. This was just after the United States entered World War Two.

Apparently she applied to Yale during that year. Dad told me she rejected his first proposal; now I know more about that story. We all knew the story of the proposal she *did* accept. Now I know that her acceptance of his proposal occurred *after* she received this rejection letter from Yale.

For a young Texas woman—twenty-two years old, with no financial resources—to apply to Yale surprises me even today. She must have felt so bolstered by her mentoring and good experience thus far that she dared contemplate stepping outside her culture and family background.

Where did our mother's academic dreams go? They seem to have found a home in the unconscious lives of her daughters. We *almost* lived out the unlived life of our mother, becoming academics. We just didn't know that what she *really* had wanted, at least at one time, was a master's of divinity and seminary education.

In my effort to fill out my mother's interior life, the life I did not know about, I wrote a presentation for a convention in 2012, crafting imaginary journal entries to fill in my mother's voice. I noticed that my audience looked confused, as well they should have. Who was speaking? One day, I put aside my fantasy. I filed away the imaginary journal entries. Someday I will burn those pages as well since I don't want to risk confusing future generations. I could not let my mother go until I had filled out her inner life more. But I had written *my own* version of her inner life. The writing I completed brought me deeply into my mother's life with an empathic bridge, but I built the bridge, not my mother. I must let her unknown-to-me life remain hers, unknown and now unknowable. Writing my version of her voice helped me get to know her, backwards in time. Imagination, with love, can be part of the work of grief.

Correspondence with Mom: Looking Back

I kept actual words from Mom in her letters, ultimately more satisfying than my imagination. These are real archives, and they bring her unique personality alive for me again.

September 1963, Friday

(Letter from Mom to me. Mom and I had finished a phone call in which I explained that since I was working as a secretary at Brite Divinity School, I felt as though I were enrolled there instead of in college.)

> *I know your feeling of attending Brite instead of TCU. That is exactly what happened to me, since I went in as a senior and a religious education major at the same time. For me, though, it was a refuge, for I would have been real lost without those people. . . . With your experience, personality, and ability to think things through, I know you will be able to figure out some ways to make friends your own age.*

I notice how my mother is encouraging me, and understands me. In my sophomore year I wrote:

From 1964 and 1965 Letters
(Letter from me to Mom.)

> *It was so good to talk to you and Jannie—I really do miss*
> *you all. . . . Yesterday I had a conference with my advisor*
> *and . . . guess what we talked about—you! He said that he*
> *didn't think we were anything alike because you were so much*
> *more outgoing than I am when you were here. . . . I real-*
> *ized there was so much about you that I didn't know. . . .*
> *Recently I seem to hear so much about you—all the people*
> *who went to school with you think you are just wonderful.*
> *I've always thought of Daddy as being the one I'm most like.*
> *Maybe so, but now . . . many values and attitudes that you*
> *have are influencing me. . . . Sometimes I wonder if my*
> *temperament will ever fit into the role of wife and mother . . .*
> *I really wonder, sometimes, if I'll ever be able to marry.*

After the San Antonio firing in 1964, the rest of the family moved to a church in Colorado Springs in the fall of 1964. I met and married a young seminarian just before my junior year, surprising everyone, including myself, with such an early marriage, since even then I prized my career orientation. I now believe that I was unconsciously creating a zone of safety for myself. While I rested in the assurance of my family's love, the ground kept shifting under our feet, and I wanted my own ground. My parents were surprised but, as always, supportive. I know now that I projected my own fast-fading dreams of seminary education on my fiancé, falling in love with him *and* the dreams.

Mom lets me know that she still loves the activities of the career she did not follow, at least in a paid way. In a letter from September 29, 1965, she writes:

> *Tonight is going to be our first teachers' conference. . . . I've*
> *done a lot of reading in preparation . . . and have thought about*
> *you two in your new jobs.* (Co-ministers at a church in Fort
> Worth, which only lasted a short time—I retreated from

the difficulties of partnering.) *I almost feel like a director of religious education again!*

Mom seemed energized as she entered into unpaid but valuable work at the new church in Colorado Springs. In only four years, this congregation would fire Dad for his stand against the Vietnam War, but for now, she is enjoying putting her education to use.

The writing that my mother did leave helps me remain close to her in my heart and mind. This connection, after she is gone, sustains me as an unexpected bonus in my life. Rituals connect me to Mom, especially when I'm at Shalom. I don't set up altars the way I do for Janice; instead, I wash windows, knowing that her hands kept all the picture windows clean. With every swipe of the newspaper and window cleaner, I feel my mother scrubbing every speck and spot. I dust and clean, even the few silk ivy plants that I wanted to toss that first summer after she died. I shake them in a bag with salt to clean them, following Mom's directions pinned to the bulletin board. I have organized all the sheets and pillowcases—sets that belong in each bedroom now have their designated place. In the room Ed sleeps in, I put the linens in his old toy chest that Mom covered with tan printed fabric years ago. I can hear her delight in my mind, *Now, why didn't I think of that?* Sometimes I display the handkerchiefs she saved and show them to Keira and Addison, my grand-nieces. They don't know what handkerchiefs were used for, so I explain that every lady carried one in her purse. I remember playing with my Mom's handkerchief in church when I was bored; they smooth and fold the old-fashioned fabric. Ed and I cook meals to put away in the freezer for later; often we cook together, talking about our lives, and remembering Mom as we use her kitchen utensils.

From my mother, I learned adaptation, compromise, relationship focus, and how to work extremely hard. Learning from her unlived life, I create a new way for myself. I take trips with women friends and by myself, decline requests for visitors when I want solitude, only cook when I want to, long ago refusing the endless treadmill of meal preparation that punctuated almost every day for her. I don't know what she'd say about this, maybe something like, *Times have certainly changed.* She might add, *You have a lot of freedom, and I admire that.* She might also advise, *You need to be sure you're not neglecting Gary.*

When I imagine a different career path, a road I didn't take, I see that in many ways I did grow into my mother's unlived life while honoring her well-lived life. When I reflect on my own choices in marriage, I comfort myself with how hard it might have been for my mother to decide to marry when she did. When I feel concern and even rage at the continuing problems women face in the workplace, I know that these emotions also belong to my mother, tamped down. I live them out loud.

What I choose to be and do in this last chapter of my life will emerge from my own clarification and reflection. My generation, unlike hers, enjoys that privilege. As Iris Dement sings, "My life may be a grain of sand/ but I'm tellin' you man, this grain of sand is mine!"

I am not my mother; I am my mother.

chapter nine

Leaving What I Love

At one point, I decided that I would work into my eighties, or until they wheeled me out, hoping my mind would last about the same amount of time as my body, so I could go out gracefully. I envisioned myself as a grey-haired, wise old woman, welcoming third and fourth generations of clients into my lovely downtown office in a historic building. I fantasized about more silence than conversation from me as I listened to my clients' stories, my deep listening helping them find a new narrative in which they could thrive. In 2011, I am six years past my father's death, almost seven years past Janice's and Mom's, and twenty-six years into my clinical practice, my chosen second career. While I will always continue the work of braiding loss into my life, I often feel happiness, and even the kind of joy made richer because I no longer take life for granted.

My work life unfolds in a downtown neighborhood. I could draw my work world the way Janice drew her idealized vision of our Colorado campsite. At art shows in the gallery at the end of the block, I keep trying to find a painting of the stretch of Higgins I call my downtown home.

Deborah, who orders coffee, tea, and herbs, knows what blend of coffee I want as I walk through Butterfly Herbs through their back door from the parking lot. Often I greet four or five people by name in the short walk to my office. I run down three flights of stairs to the bank anchoring our office building, where everyone greets me by name; sometimes one of the tellers takes the stairs to the third floor for exercise and slides my deposit slip under my door.

Hide and Sole provides most of my shoes; I buy all my books at Fact and Fiction. Years ago, when the independent bookstore was struggling to survive in another location, Barbara, the owner, exclaimed on one snowy day when I took a break for books, "Great! Here's Joyce. Now we can pay the rent."

"From my checkbook to your account," I say.

"Maybe we should set up an automatic deposit, to make it all simple," Barbara suggests.

The bookstore moved two doors from my building, making book runs easy. The sandwich shop staffers begin to make my favorite egg salad sandwich when I walk in. The art gallery and the department store a block away provide pleasant spots for a break. We've built these relationships over many years of proximity, kindness, and routine.

My place in the neighborhood is about to change.

I'm thinking of leaving what I love, this time choosing my loss instead of death severing the connections.

Early February, 2011: Shooting the Rapids

Gary and I plan to travel to a family wedding in California in May. I look forward to vacations this summer, both at home and at Shalom, and to a conference in the fall. Counting up my planned weeks away, I clearly see that my desired vacations exceed the number that someone in private practice should take. I can't fit in everything I want to do. I become angry, which I hope I manage to hide, when a long-term client asks if I am going to take my usual August vacation (she means August *only*). She knows that my vacations have lasted longer in the past few years, after re-establishing a coherent routine in my practice following the family deaths. With a sly smile, Amy, one of my clients, asks if I am even planning to come *back* from vacation. My clients pick up on my ambivalence about how long I will work. They deserve better.

Now I face the challenge of protecting my clients' trust in me while planning enough time to restore and renew my spirit. I consult with therapist friends about the crossroads choice to work a few more years or to close my practice.

One friend who is younger than I am has carefully worked out her downsizing plan. At lunch she says, "Joyce, your life kayak seems to have begun its plunge through the rapids. You can't turn back." She's known me a long time, and she sounds clear.

"Like when our group headed down the Dearborn River at flood stage?" I reminisce, referring to a women's group reunion when we unwisely disregarded the high water and embarked on our planned raft trip.

"Oh, please, don't remind me." My friend broke her arm on our ill-advised raft trip. We laugh about the metaphor of floating down a river at flood stage.

My friend has worked out a step-by-step retirement for the past few years. Over the weekend, I feel exhilarated as I imagine braving that unexplored chute down the river to retirement. As my relief and excitement rise over the weekend, I register that my decision has already been made, and now is a time for action. It's too late for me to plan my work life around the wedding in California or my desire for a long time at Shalom, and it's way too late in my work life for a self-granted sabbatical. I feel buoyant as a great sense of ease washes over me and I rest in an eddy in this river of decision.

"Hon, I want to set my retirement date," I tell Gary.

"You've been saying that you need to stop for a long time, hon." He sounds relieved. "You're ready."

Equivocating, not ready to declare my decision, I reply, "But I love this work, and we haven't planned our finances yet." I hesitate, suddenly less sure than I'd thought. "Maybe I should keep working another year or so." Maybe Gary will take the devil's advocate position, and I can gain more clarity.

"I know you love it," Gary agrees. "I also know you are too

exhausted to plan fun things for yourself, and you need to rest," he reminds me.

Gary has listened to me countless times as I explain my desire for time to myself. The time has come. This is new, for me, to choose to let go instead of simply enduring loss. And I know I will experience loss, even grief, on many levels, along with more freedom. I haven't completely explored this new idea—I might, indeed will, choose to leave work that I still love.

When my people died, I had no choice, except the choice to love and be present or not. I've spent years integrating these losses. How do I choose to leave what I love? Am I making a big mistake? I have never longed for retirement, not even liking the word.

The draft of my desultory, distant letter informing clients that I will close my practice in four months needs major rewriting. Gary reads my vague letter, saying that he can tell I am far away by my distant language. He's right. I want this leaving part to be over. I'm not letting myself feel much right now, after emotionally connecting deeply with my clients—and with myself—through the years. Am I telling myself that if I open myself to all my love and respect for them, retirement won't be an option? I remind myself that through the loss of Dianne, Janice, Mom, and Dad, I endured wrenching emotion, and I am still alive. I write the authentic letter my clients deserve.

Why Do I Need to Stop?

Compelled by my sense of responsibility to rush back to work after every time I was away, crazily arriving on the late flight back to Missoula, I would arrive at my office the next morning, short of sleep and not having fully landed yet. I never considered taking a personal sabbatical. Even though I had pleaded with Janice to take medical leave when she was tired, not knowing yet that she had cancer, I did not think of taking family leave for myself. Like me, Janice decided to postpone needed rest until later. I need to close my practice because grief colonized my psyche for so long. While death made me a braver therapist, I don't feel the vitality

I used to feel and want to experience. I denied myself significant time away to begin to recover from death's impacts on my life. I sometimes say to my friends, "I have a bad boss."

I need to close my practice because my persona defines too much of who I am. The persona describes a solidifying of personality, half-consciously sculpted for everyday life in the workplace and the street. Jung wrote about the persona making up the first layer of the psyche. The word comes from the Greek word for mask, but it does not mean a fraudulent Self. The persona, constructed of the ego and the conscious and unconscious parts of the whole psyche, is the way we move through the world. The persona is what others see and perceive, one's own fallback personality. My persona usually shows up with a calm demeanor, fairly formal clothes, since in Texas we dressed up for work, a neatly composed and made up exterior, and friendliness. One of my friends calls me fancy, and I'm pretty sure that's not a compliment. In exhaustion, once I cried that I dress myself up as Joyce Hocker and send her off to work. This cry reflected an unfortunate split in my personality. My closet holds mainly career clothes, workout clothes, and hang-around-at home clothes. I'd have to scramble for something attractive to wear to a casual gathering of friends. I live in a small city; I go nowhere without seeing my clients. While I love the coziness of my downtown block while I'm working, I also crave the anonymity of a big city and travel. My introverted self loves moving through a place where I am completely unknown. Some of my most restorative vacations are taken alone, like my time at Rancho la Puerta in Mexico.

I long for my private life, which diminished when I started studying psychology and lost my previous more-or-less-free academic summers. My clients receive the privacy they deserve; I feel exposed to public scrutiny as I go about my non-work life. I can't afford to keep my desire to slow way down hidden much longer. I'd rather make a conscious choice to end my practice instead of letting stress or serious illness make me too sick to work.

I need to close my practice because I have already cut my hours, accepting no one new for two years. The people remaining are all dear to me—hard-working clients, they use their time in sessions well. Many are other therapists and health-care professionals who bring their own patient burdens into our work. Still, I am too tired at the end of a week. My clients are not the problem; I seldom feel off-duty. I need relief from carrying and remembering others' stories, to care from more of a distance. I want time and energy for new stories in my personal life, and time to drift. These on-all-the-time symptoms describe a kind of post-traumatic stress.

Termination Doesn't Mean Death

I reread everything I can find on the termination phase of therapy. As Rogers and the humanistic psychologists taught more than fifty years ago, warmth and positive regard characterize all good therapy, including termination. I, too, desire warm regard from my clients, as I easily give this gift to them. I want to know I've done a good job. Trained long ago not to expect thanks, when gratitude does come my way from clients, that warmth feels like a balm to my raw feelings. I am leaving what I love, and I've chosen this termination. Each client ending brings new grief. I will not be part of my clients' joys, celebrations, sorrows, and healing except in memory, theirs and mine. My death experiences have prepared me for loss, but I don't yet know how I will say goodbye to the privilege of deep conversational intimacy during psychotherapy. The act of going to work has brought me, for decades, the expectation of knowing others' private sorrow, struggles, rage, betrayal, recovery, healing, and joy. Memory and mutual influence remain, but not a shared, ongoing future.

At the same time, I sense a tingle of excitement about my new life, as well as apprehension. I wonder if I will feel disoriented, bored, and empty. Anne reminds me that if I won't tolerate any boredom, I won't learn anything new.

I wonder how my clients may feel. I love these people, and each goodbye brings poignancy for them and for me. One example is Marie, two years after her mother and two sisters died. Marie relates to the loss of her mother and sisters with a sense of weighty guilt and responsibility. She is heartbroken and sad, wishing she had done more to help at the end of their lives. She did everything any loving person could have, in her position, but that comment would not be a helpful comment. As we talk, I can hear her guilty responsibility turning to sorrow. I feel my own guilty sorrow; six-plus years after my father's death, what else might I have done—move him to Missoula, spent more time with him at the end, or taken a sabbatical and cared for him while in Colorado? Marie's story advances my healing, as my story moves her forward in our delicate dance of growth and understanding.

My head and heart feel full. These might be the best months of therapy in my life. I seem to be getting it right, following my intuition with a sure internal compass, speaking easily, listening well. The saying, "Hanging does tend to focus the mind," applies to me. Leaving what I love, and those whom I love, focuses my heart as well. At every choice point, I go for broke, allowing myself to experience the good-byes. I've learned more about loving and letting go.

Mac comes in for his last session. I really don't want to say goodbye to him. Our work has been intense, no holds barred. Today he tells me he's received a clean bill of health from his cardiologist. "No more meds and just that two hundred minutes of exercise per week you've been nagging me about," he announces gleefully. Last summer Mac looked gray when I opened my waiting room door. Leaning back in my teal wingback chair, he said weakly, "I just need to go home. I'm sick. But I knew if I could get here I'd be all right."

This kind of confusing double message makes any therapist ask more questions. After calling his doctor, we determined that he was having a heart attack.

"Get him here as quickly as you can, and I will meet you in the ER," she ordered. Stumbling down the back stairs, we walked in tandem to my car and drove the five blocks to the hospital.

He received expert care and lived. Mac had come in to tell me that his sister was dying of cancer. Almost a year later, we decide that *heartbroken* was a true diagnosis since part of his main aorta had collapsed and died. Today we celebrate that he did not die.

He's fallen in love but wonders if he should give it more time since he's still grieving his sister's death.

I don't have time for us to thoroughly analyze this quandary over several sessions, so I say, "You really aren't in charge of your heart. You learned that last July." I remember his gray face in the waiting room. "Choose life," I urge, using a favorite phrase from the Old Testament. As we say goodbye, he unconsciously puts his hand on his heart. I do, too. We smile and don't mind the tears.

I remember a dream from decades ago, going home to find it in my journal. The dream fits my situation right now:

> *I am floating down a huge river, maybe the Columbia. I realize a concrete spillway looms immediately downstream, and I'm moving fast. If I can't make it over to the side, I will fall over and die. I can't make it. At the last minute I decide to jump, preferring to choose my death rather than being swept over, out of control. I land gently in a pool of deep, calm water. Quickly, I climb out, run up the river and tell everyone that when they reach the precipice they must jump, that they will not die.*

Just as Janice chose a dream from years earlier to close her book, I find meaning for right now in my long-ago dream.

Of course they and I will die, but not right now. I have chosen to ride the river of my psychotherapy work to the end, and I am alive. I hope I have the chance to make a lot more jumps into the unknown.

Moving Out

In March, I ask around on the floor of my building to see if anyone would like to lease my waiting room. I'm keeping my consultation room for now. My last clinical day is May 6; maybe someone will want to rent my room on June 1. Right away, a young attorney around the corner says she wants the room, but she wants it April 8. My fantasy of an exit planned out perfectly by me evaporates as I sign the lease over to her. Endings usually can't be perfectly planned. That's part of what causes distress. I'm not in charge of timing.

My friendly banker downstairs helps list furniture on eBay (this *is* a small town), and I tack up a sign over the water fountain detailing the furniture I'm selling. Immediately a young woman in the building sees my sign. A young couple comes in wanting everything I listed—the teal wingback chairs, stained glass lamps, and Queen Anne tables that I used to have in my home, back in a more formal phase. I donate about twelve boxes of books to the library and move the rest home to my study. Someone else in the building buys my framed prints of Japanese art. I keep the cream-and-green Persian rug and the iris-themed, lavender-and-green stained-glass lamp, along with my collection of iris art. Irises carry a meaning of renewal, originally from a goddess named Iris. I wanted the symbol of new life surrounding the people who came to work with me, and now I want this art at home to remind me of the cycle of life.

As people buy my possessions and I donate books and old lecture tapes, this phase of letting go feels joyful. I am alive to see who receives my former things; I retain the privilege of deciding what to give away. No one has died; selling and donating brings me joy and not sorrow. Choosing to let go creates healing for me.

In early April, Gary helps me move the few items that remain. Very little remains. We stand in the empty room where together we conducted couples therapy for fifteen years. Gary and I have cleaned out homes and belongings of our people many times now. Together we finish cleaning out one of the rooms of my life. Closing the door, we bid goodbye to all that the room contained for twenty-six years, both tangible and emotional. I no longer harbor any illusions about owning anything material—I've put too many of my family members' belongings in plastic bags for donation to think that mine will ultimately be any different. I feel peaceful as I imagine my former belongings taking their new place in others' lives.

On Monday morning, I learn more about letting go. The young attorney and her partner excitedly show me the new colors they are considering. Modernist aqua, lime, and brown patches smear my soft peach walls. The leaf-pattern wallpaper border three quarters of the way up the extra-tall ceiling is ripped off. Enthusiastically they say, "We want to brighten up the room. What do you think?" I'm speechless for a few beats. "And we're going to take out the carpet and have maple flooring laid down, and paint the ceiling white. Do you like it? Which color do you like?"

I think, but don't say, *Well, I liked it quite a lot the way it was, and I think the colors are ghastly,* but I find a way to encourage the young entrepreneurs. They are happy. I feel like the senior citizen who's been moved to assisted living.

I honor myself for knowing when it is time to jump.

chapter ten

A Penultimate Fall

February, 2014: Sisters Writing

Our guest room also serves as my writing room. I look out on the morning sun, to a filtered view of the mountains to the east and south through the bare willows of winter. Hungry deer nibble at the red berries on the mountain ash. I expected Janice and Tom would stay here every summer, as they did for years. My east-facing room links me emotionally to my downstairs room in Tom and Janice's house, the house Tom shares now with his new life partner. In my memory, the house I knew remains unchanged. A psychic meridian connects the spaces over the two thousand miles. In this room, echoes of the glee Janice and I expressed when I would sit on the side of the bed as she unpacked her summer clothes gently resound.

"Four whole weeks," Janice would say, with a smile.

"I'm *so* glad you're here," I would reply.

We four would relax on the deck the first night, then go out to eat at Shadow's Keep, overlooking the Missoula valley, the second. We followed the same vacation rituals, including discussing our clothes.

"Is this too casual?" Janice would ask, holding up a short navy blue dress with a flirty skirt.

"Just right," I would reply. We'd compare our jewelry to see if we wanted to borrow anything for the night. Gary snapped a picture of the two of us putting on our makeup, Janice leaning over the counter that was too high for her, to reach the mirror. We became again the teenage girls who consulted each other on our appearance.

This cold February, I know that once again Janice won't be coming for the mid-summer vacation. I position a picture of Janice on my writing desk, planning to call on her encouragement as I write. To the left of my writing desk hangs a gallery of family pictures. I indulge my love for visual artifacts in this room, keeping it filled with family treasures. I smile at the toddler and infant pictures of Janice and me with our grandmothers, and Mom looking beautiful in a 1940s-style, cream-colored suit, nipped in at the waist. She would have sewed this suit herself.

On the bay window, for memory and inspiration, I lay a shard of a small crystal and gold bud vase bought by Janice; she saved up for it with the dollar an hour she earned at her secretarial job at the seminary. It was her Christmas gift to me her freshman year in college. I add a round, rose-colored oil lamp. Every night in January and part of February, I light the lamp. Before I go to bed, I sit for a while before blowing it out.

"Night, Jannie," I whisper. "I love you."

I don't light the lamp again after February 19, the night she died.

Psyche's Sister

I prepare to write a paper to present in New Orleans at the Southern States Communication Association. Most years I attend this conference so I can see Tom, present papers, and talk with Janice's former students and colleagues. An award in her name will again be given at a luncheon, where I will meet another early career award recipient. Often professors will look at my nametag and introduce themselves as "Janice scholars."

Year by year, when I talk with the award winner, asking if they knew Janice, they are likely to respond that they never had the pleasure of meeting her but knew her work well.

Last year, a young man called out my name as I crossed a street. Turning around, I realized I didn't know him.

"I'm one of Janice's MA advisees," he said as he hurried up to me. "She made all the difference in my life," this man tells me. "I was at her memorial service in Fayetteville."

"It's very meaningful to me to meet people who remember Janice," I say, as he fills me in on where he teaches and what he is writing. I realize that Janice's former students talk to me because they can't talk to her, as when they said goodbye to Janice *in absentia* when I cleaned out her office at the University of Arkansas.

"Oh, I don't *remember* Janice. I *love* her," he sets me straight. I smile. "So do I."

Talks and presentations have greatly helped me loosen my grief. The auto-ethnography division, which I call "memoir with an academic twist," welcomes personal narratives. Janice and I talked about how the emergence of this group in communication studies might have been enough to keep me working as a professor. I am at home with these people. Tom and I schedule dinners with Janice and Tom's friends, now also my friends.

I appreciate presenting papers to this Southern group, as I continue narrative writing projects that Janice helped me begin back in 2003. Writing—and teaching life writing—has become a welcome avocation since I closed my practice. Everyone incubates stories that want to be told. Writing about my most important life events, even those not imbued with mourning, has helped me release the tangled knots of grief and reclaim my life.

I plan a presentation about my last ten years of mourning, finding a resonance in my experiences and the tasks that Psyche, the ancient Greek goddess, had to undergo before she was reunited with her husband, Eros, the god of love. Janice devoted three chapters at the conclusion of her book to exploring the Psyche myth in depth. Tom chose a photo of a sculpture of Eros and Psyche from the Louvre for the front cover. I familiarize myself again with Psyche's labors after she married Eros, barely escaping marrying Death. The Psyche myth can be read as one of a woman's individuation, or coming to Self, without remaining subservient to a man, or the patriarchy. Janice delved deeply into this myth to frame stories of contemporary women, including her own stories. After falling in love with Love, Janice's interviewees, as well as Psyche, find a way to love themselves. In Janice's dream with which she ends the book, picking up her child "Joy," she celebrates her own wholeness. My ordeal of loss, grief, and restoration over the past ten years is a story I want to tell. I plan to explore my identification with Psyche as I tell my own tale of individuation.

In the tale told by Apuleius, Psyche grew so beautiful that she began to be compared to Aphrodite, the Great Goddess. This proved to be dangerous. To get this young challenger out of the way, Aphrodite arranges for her to marry Death. Eros, Aphrodite's son, sees her great beauty and marries her himself. Psyche's jealous sisters urge her to look upon the face of Eros, whom she is not supposed to see. Psyche lights a lamp, sees Eros, and falls in love with Love himself. But since she has broken the Great Goddess's rule, Eros flies away home to Mother. This myth gained its form when humanity was emerging from the worship of the One Mother and into a much more diversified Olympian system of religion.

Aphrodite sets out four tasks for Psyche to perform if she wants to save her life. She must sort a giant pile of seeds before nightfall or die, then cross a river and gather some golden fleece from deadly rams living across the river. She must fill a crystal jar with water from the River Styx, the heavily guarded river of death. Finally, she must, most dangerous of all, descend into Hades to steal a box of Persephone's beauty ointment. Persephone, the goddess of the underworld, must live in Hades half the year, emerging only in the spring when she is released to her mother, Demeter, a bargain brokered by Zeus. The earth cannot ripen and flower while Persephone lives in the underworld.

Psyche, which means "feminine soul," guided me for years in my work with clients. Her knowledge of the underworld, the unconscious, illuminates my dreams and analysis; to prepare, I read several variations of the Psyche myth again. The myth, true on the psychological level, sheds light on my current situation.

April, 2014: New Orleans

Delighted to visit New Orleans again, I settle into the convention hotel, close to the French Quarter. I haven't been here for many years. Tom and I find a great restaurant across the street from the hotel. We enjoy this first night as we catch up with each other and talk about our current lives. We toast Janice, knowing how much she would enjoy our Creole food and the prospect of a rich convention filled with friends and colleagues. Tom and I check our schedules—we will share dinners and evenings with good friends. I know that Janice's friends miss her and take some comfort in seeing me. Through the years, we have developed our own relationships, enriched by our love for Janice.

Michael, the editor who, years ago, first recognized Janice's writing as brilliant, always says to me, "I miss Miz Myth."

We hug. "I do too," I say.

"She'd be glad we're all together," Michael says.

I enjoy a full afternoon of wandering through museums on my own, taking in the complex history of this most diverse American city. Far from feeling lonely, I'm enjoying the intellectual and cultural stimulation.

For the purpose of presenting my own ordeal, the work of grief, I identify first with Psyche's descent into the underworld. In one version of the meta-myth, Persephone gets stuck for half the year in Hades as she looks for her dark sister Eriskiga, queen of the underworld. I have spent ten years looking for my sister, lost to me in the other world. Like Psyche, often I was lost in the dark and in emotional danger.

"I looked for her everywhere," I tell the audience. "I read her journals and wrote interior dialogues and studied every glimpse of Janice in my dreams." I wandered in the vast underworld, seeking my sister, just out of reach. I recount a dream in which I see Janice at the edge of an ocean, floating above the beach. She wears a long crimson dress. She floats over and kisses me. We look into each other's eyes, and I realize that she is using great psychic energy to hold this form so I can recognize her. Then she flies back to the other end of the beach to resume her task. She is blessing the humpback whales. They rise and fall with her arms. This dream teaches me that Janice, at least in my own unconscious, follows her own creative work, and I must follow mine.

I awaken reassured from this dream. The Janice in my deep psyche continues to perform creative work, sacred work, about which I know nothing. More life will arise in me, I feel confident. Some of my energy is busy constellating, forming, in my unconscious. I recognize Janice/Joyce in my symbolic world by our color crimson, and by the strength of the love. Life that might have been lost to death will be awakened by love—love for others, and love for myself.

"My husband thought he had lost me to Death, like Psyche," I relate. He was partly right. The world of death often seemed more real than the upper world as I wandered in the narcissistic land of grief. Only my losses and longing felt real in the early years. I neglected our marriage, and our bond frayed, as I struggled to make myself at home in my dark world. Gary's stories of work and frustrations—even his descriptions of ideas that excited and energized him—fell on my grief-deaf ears. I don't like remembering my self-absorbed, preoccupied way of listening, but it's the truth. I gave everything I could muster to my clients, and often, at home, I just wanted to be left alone. Gary stopped sharing much with me, since I was preoccupied. In the way these communication spirals work, I can't tell which came first—my not listening well or Gary's not sharing very much. Perhaps both came first.

Psyche had to sort out a huge mound of valuable seeds, impossibly mixed with sand. All these tasks assigned by the Great Goddess were life-and-death tasks. In her exhaustion, Psyche fell asleep one night, and the ants, representing instinct, came to her aid and sorted the valuable seeds of the Self from the detritus of sand. I let myself wander for some years sorting artifacts, discarding no-longer-needed objects, and preserving what felt most valuable. The years spent performing tasks of love and memory helped save the seeds of future life for me. Writing and discerning clarified what still shimmered with life and what I could let go. Writing stories about the people now lost to me helped me find out what is not lost.

"I even wrote imaginary journals about my mother's life," I admitted to my audience, and only then could I release more of my own unmet wishes for her life. "I wrote my father's life through the lens of civil rights and his activism," I continued. "How wonderful to find that, with careful sorting of documents, memory, and history, my father emerged from my sorting as a contemporary hero, a man I could and do honor."

Psyche was also required to dip water from the River Styx with a crystal goblet, then to carry the water of life to Aphrodite, her stern mother-in-law. She had to descend prepared into the underworld, ready like a mythic girl scout, to feed the dogs of Hades and scoop up the water from exactly the place in the River Styx where both death and regeneration flow together. At one point, Psyche stands on a tower, thinking maybe she will jump into the river and let herself be swept away. I can relate to her despair, from many lonely times when I could not find the tower's far-seeking perspective, and only wanted to let myself be swept away into my emotions of grief and surrender. I did not know how I would accomplish the life-giving work I needed to complete.

On Janice's birthday in January, 2014, I drop the delicate gold-and-crystal vase she gave me long ago, the one that I set out to inspire me as I write. On the same day I break the vase, I smash a curved Aynsley china hostess plate, with its painting of pink and red flowers and bluebirds, as I put it away in the china cabinet. I've already replaced that plate once. I won't replace it this time. Gary, seeing how upset I am, gives me a hug. On my annual trip to the dermatologist, I hear a sickening crunch in the parking garage under the hospital. I've put a big dent into the side of my car. This seems like a good day to stay home, a broken-heart day. I write a note to Janice in my journal:

> *Janice, I broke your gold-and-crystal vase today. I wept as I remembered opening the Christmas present your freshman year. I put it on my altar, the broken pieces. Like my heart is broken for you, so is this fragile treasure. I no longer tell myself that I can lose nothing more of yours. I will ultimately*

give up everything I value. Except love, I believe. For now the
morning sun catches the broken gold-and-crystal, connecting
me in memory to you. I took a picture. Thank you.

"I am learning to live in the broken places," I tell my audience. "Shards from a broken vase will do for gathering up the water from the River of Death. I use what I have at hand."

I am learning to patch my Self together, perhaps with analytic duct tape. Sometimes my vessel looks like a kindergartner's clay pot, but it holds water. I am alive, and I can share some of the water of life with others.

"As for the beauty ointment?" I tell my audience. "My dermatologist suggested that I might want to skip that task." She enjoyed hearing the Psyche story. Psyche must learn to see herself as beautiful without modern-day miracles of reconstruction or ancient beauty secrets.

Ten years later, I emerge into the sunlight to see that my friends are still with me, and my marriage has survived the descent into death. Sometimes lightness and humor lift what Janice called the "little psychic descents."

Soon enough, I will descend again, I confide to my audience, but for now, I choose life. I took a class on happiness twice, apparently failing it the first time, learning from research on happiness that in successful love relationships, the ratio of positive actions to negative actions needs to be about five-to-one to sustain the relationship. My remembered happiness ratio with Janice seems to be about a thousand-to-one; our relationship will sustain me and remain alive for the rest of my life. Gary and I have reengaged with each other. We're improving our ratio of positive to negative experiences; we even joke about it.

As I conclude my presentation in New Orleans, I am gratified. I have lived into the rhythm of descending, sorting, containing the water of life, discovering the deep source of beauty, and ascending. With the singer/songwriter Christine Kane, I feel comfort as she sings, "Fear not the trials of love, the heart is made well / When your world comes undone,/ I'll be your angel."

I deeply appreciate Janice for telling my story, along with so many others, in her last book finding encouragement in her respectful retelling of our stories. In the book, Janice reported me as saying to her, "Any woman with a voice makes a difference." As I sit down, it seems to me that Janice and I wrote this presentation together. We will continue our dialogues. But now, I'm going to get ready for dinner with Tom and friends, and enjoy New Orleans.

A Penultimate Descent

On the way to dinner, Carolyn and I run through the rain, clumsily sharing one umbrella, to arrive at a noisy restaurant to join Art and Tom. She is the friend who talked with me about the ethical issues I pondered before I burned selected portions of Janice's journals. We eat family style, enjoying the white wine and huge platter of grouper. It's hard to talk over the noise, though. At the end of the dinner, Art asks Tom, "Are you coming to Tampa next year? If so, you both can stay with us."

"Yes, and I'm bringing my new partner this time," Tom announces, looking happy.

I didn't know this.

"I haven't decided whether I am coming," I say, "but thanks a lot." I actually have just decided. I won't be there. I am not fully aware of what I realize later, that Tom's inclusion of his new love into what had been our conference means that the ritual will change. I don't want it to change. I am now happy for Tom in his new life, although my acceptance of his new partner has taken me a while. I did not know that the ritual of remembrance, that first night for Janice, would turn out to be a phase, not an ongoing certainty. I begin to feel lonely as Carolyn and I dash back through the rain, still sharing an umbrella, bemoaning the fate of our fancy shoes. Forget the stockings—they're a wreck. Arriving in the hotel lobby, everyone scatters to their rooms to dry. I feel numb. I wander through the lobby for a while, looking for someone I know, but I only run across casual acquaintances.

Janice used to help me feel included at conferences, and I am surprised at how alone I now feel.

In my room, I glance at the clock. I had better pack in a hurry for an early flight to Missoula. I've already called a taxi to pick me up at 5:30 a.m. I kick off my wet shoes and begin to toss clothes into my suitcase. I need to get some sleep—maybe five hours, before I get up again. I'm not going to take my prepaid shuttle to the airport— I want the convenience of a taxi and a few more minutes to grab some coffee. When I've finished packing, I lift my suitcase in an awkward diagonal position. Forgetting my soggy high heels under-foot, I trip over them and lurch hard, with my suitcase, against a ninety-degree wall. Ouch!—big ouch. I might have broken a rib, but I know there's nothing to do about that. Exhausted, I swallow ibuprofen, drink a big glass of water, and fall into bed.

Kind travelers assist me on my three long flights home, since I cannot lift my carry-on overhead. We fly to Charlotte, Denver, and finally home to Missoula. I sleep a long time in my own bed, and in the morning notice a nasty bruise forming on my left side.

I hope a good workout might get the blood flowing, so I spend time on the elliptical at my gym, but I'm too sore to lift weights. After another night's sleep, I drive to my office to see one of the younger therapists with whom I've begun working. Jessica called me about four months ago. She knew I had retired, but was interested in receiving some Jungian consultation for her work with clients.

Jessica and I met for lunch. It didn't take me long to know that we shared a passion for clients, a feeling orientation, and wrenching grief experiences. Our collaboration promised to be rewarding. I like her; after three years of retirement, I'm glad to say yes occasionally to requests like hers. I don't feel well, noticing the effects of the bruising fall in New Orleans.

Not long into our session, I feel very dizzy and odd.

"I need to close my eyes a few minutes," I tell Jessica. "Something is really off, and I don't know what is wrong."

When I open my eyes, Jessica looks alarmed, her phone in her hands.

"I feel awful," I say.

"I can see that," she replies.

"I'm going to take a nap, and then call my husband and ask him to come get me." Jessica raises her eyebrows as I continue, "Why don't you go back to your office." I'm eager to lie down. "Please don't check on me, because I may be asleep."

Jessica looks appalled, but trying to respect my wishes, she says goodbye. I stay seated in my chair as she leaves for her office on our shared floor. Just at that moment, the worst pain I have ever experienced grabs my abdomen. I never endured childbirth, but this feels like my nightmare of a bad labor contraction. I gasp. When I stand up, I am in serious trouble. Blood runs down my legs. I barely make it to Jessica's office, holding on to the wall as I walk. Thankfully she has not closed her door.

"I need help," I gasp, at Jessica's door.

"I *know* you do. You were out for five minutes." Jessica talks rapidly. "Lie down on my couch and I will call 911 again. I went to my office and got my phone while you were unconscious." I had no idea. "I called them to be on alert because I might need them."

I collapse on her leather couch. Jessica calls 911 again, clarifying where we are. She retrieves my purse from my office, locks my door, puts a note on my door to cancel my next appointment, and finds my cell phone so I can call Gary. I'm worried about getting blood all over her leather couch. Jessica brings paper towels to mop up the mess at my request. "Don't worry about this," she assures me, "We're going to get you help." I try to apologize, but she's not listening; she doesn't need my apologies. I hear her calling the ambulance again. She knows just what to do. This call is to make sure the medical personnel know where her office is.

Soon the ambulance crew arrives at her office. As they pack me gently onto the rolling gurney, I struggle to hold on to consciousness and answer their questions. I used to joke about the time when they would wheel me out, because I liked my practice so much; now the fantasy is horribly coming true. Jessica situates my purse on my belly, and I thank her repeatedly. I assure her I will ask Gary to call her and tell her what's happening. Five or six people assist me. I manage to call Gary from the ambulance and leave a message. The ambulance crew asks me what happened and I tell them about my fall. I also tell them I thought I was all right, and worked out at the gym.

"You might have died there," one woman flatly informs me. "Also on the plane."

I don't find this information helpful at the moment.

"Are you usually very pale?" a man asks.

"Yes, pretty much," I try to remember if this is true.

"She's not that pale—her B. P. is forty!" someone else snaps.

In the ambulance I am aware that I may be dying. I feel strangely calm, thinking that Janice went through this—death—and I can, too. I wonder if I will make it to the hospital; I wonder if I will see Gary again.

In the ER, I answer their questions. "You are one tough chick," one nurse says. "Weren't you in terrible pain?"

"No, not really," I reply. I remember massage therapists telling me my pain tolerance is too high. "Only these last few minutes did I feel anything awful." I describe the pain. Apparently my blood pressure is going up and down fast.

"Call the surgeon," I hear someone say. *That call's for me,* I realize. I have never had surgery before.

A nurse wheels me down the hall, very fast, for a CT scan, then returns me to the ER.

Gary arrives at the same time the surgeon does.

Gary holds my hand and verifies insurance and doctor's information. I ask him to let Judy, my primary care doctor, know what is happening. Everything happens fast.

The surgeon asks more questions about the location of the pain; at the same time the nurses determine what my medications are, who my doctor is, and what I'm allergic to. I can answer. Gary holds my hand tightly.

"What's the plan, Brad?" I ask the surgeon, whom I know peripherally.

"You and I are going to get much better acquainted in the OR, right now. Your spleen is ruptured. The sac around it filled with blood. I will try to save it, but I don't think I can."

He looks at Gary, "I have to check the other organs as well. We're doing this *right now*." He continues, "If you had come in two days ago, I would have been able to watch you, but I think it was already gone."

He asks if I have any questions.

"Can I live without a spleen?" I ask.

"Yes, you can," Brad replies. "I need to check everything else out to see if we have more problems than I can see in the scan."

"You're the expert," I say, when he asks if I have more questions. I want to ask if I will live, but I don't. I don't want to die, but I don't feel panicked.

A nurse enters the room and begins to ask more questions. "Didn't you notice all the fluid building up in your abdomen? Did your husband say anything?" No, he didn't.

"I guess I thought I'd just eaten too much Creole food," I respond. I hadn't noticed. There's a brief silence.

"Hmm, you're tough."

As I'm rolled to the OR, the anesthesiologist explains that he is inserting an epidural for pain control after the surgery. I thought they just did epidurals for deliveries, but I'm not questioning anyone. I sink into anesthetized oblivion.

I awaken, scared and agitated, in the Intensive Care Unit. I watch my arms flail around my head. The ICU nurse takes care of every need. I understand why people call them angels. Gary tries to see me, but the nurse refuses. "We have to stabilize her. You will have to wait." I am surprised at the urgency in her voice.

Now I experience, as did Janice and my mother and Dianne, the mercy of expert pain relief. I wake and sleep. Gary is there, then not.

I am disoriented and even frightened, when two nights later I am moved to a regular medical room. During a shift change, no one comes to help me for a long time, or so it seems. I am scared now, and alone. All the noisy machines keep me awake, and I can find no peace. While I am hooked up to many machines, as the days pass, I am able to walk, pushing my tree of medicines along with me. I can move my legs to the side of the bed, surprising the nurses. All that weight lifting is paying off.

Gary takes care of his class, driving back and forth from the hospital to bring me needed items from home. One night I send him away, tell him to go to our favorite café, and get someone to bring him a good dinner. Two friends, Sally and Jean, come to visit. Hearing me worry about what's on my calendar, they remind me, "You are not responsible for everything, Joyce." They back each other up. "Ask for help. Repeat this after me." They actually make me repeat the mantra aloud.

"Um, I'm not responsible for everything I said I would do," I manage to say. I don't believe it, though. "But I need to check with you, Jean, about the plan for the consultant's visit at the church—"

Jean firmly interrupts me. "It's covered."

When I am released from the hospital, I have a good reason to completely stop, to rest, for the first time in more than eleven years. I don't think much, and I can't read. Cyndy comes to offer Reiki—her gentle hands helping the healing process along. More friends, the same women who brought me flowers for a year after Janice died, bring food and flowers. I nap, eat little, and sleep long.

I am alive.

chapter eleven

Stepping Out of the Absence

Love of my life, I am crying,
I am not dying, I am dancing.
—Cris Williamson, "Song of the Soul"

January, 2015: Her Birthday Brings Sorrow

It's Janice birthday; she would have been sixty-six today. I write in my journal that I feel sorrow in my bones. While leaden grief predictably arrives on schedule, more and more I am able to choose life, to feel hope, and to use my new strengths and skills such as active imagination and relying on friends. Memory and forgetting both help me live well. Writing both deepens my life and lifts my spirits. Today, however, I dream a dream that I call, *"I Can't Get off the Ground."* In it I feel the familiar sense of sodden heaviness. In the dream, a neurologist friend patiently helps me get on a plane, checking my bags and orienting me. On the plane, I find I have brought nothing to read; I don't know how I will cope during a long flight without a good book. Sometimes I should rely on friends to lift my spirits, the dream reminds me.

With the unrelenting, accurate timing of yearly grief cycles, I remember that this day was the day Janice's neurologist gave her the first of a series of diagnoses that only became more hopeless. "There were bad days," Tom said, "and then there were worse days." I wonder if my bookless flight in my dream is teaching me that all my beloveds made their final flight with nothing to distract them. Reading always serves as my solace, except in the deepest times of grief in the past when I could not read. I will take this flight, as well. But not yet.

February, 2015: Falling With Friends

I'm in Sayulita, Mexico, on a beach holiday with women friends. Tired from an early flight, the five of us finally reach our destination, settle in, and walk the uneven cobblestones to find a café close to our rental house. Suddenly I find myself smacked hard on the ground, having tripped over a paving stone. My poor eyesight, fatigue, and lack of depth perception have landed me on my left hip. One of the women says, "You will be holding on to my arm at night from now on." I'm grateful for her sure steps, and her friendly arm, when we venture out. One morning, I get up early to make breakfast for the group. I prepare a Mexican frittata with *queso fresco*, salsa, onions, and potatoes, setting out fresh yogurt, ripe mangoes, and grapefruit, all bursting with sweetness inside our mouths. Extra strong coffee offers us an invitation to pour fresh half and half with every cup. My friend, whom I've known for forty years, looks at the hematoma on my left thigh, visible in beach wear. She kisses me on the cheek.

"You've got to stop falling, honey," she says. She knows about my fall last year.

I agree. Walking on the cobblestones at night, taking an arm feels safer than making my way alone. When I go back to Montana, Gary soothes yet another wound, this time on my leg, as he gently rubs the orange-size hematoma down, night after night. As happened last summer, more than an abdominal scar or a nasty bruise heals with his loving touch. I enjoy the love and support that I need.

Gary and I developed a tradition some years back of reading aloud to each other during the winter nights. This year, Gary suggests James Hollis's *Hauntings*. I resist for a while, thinking this wise Jungian might be helpful, but that I'd rather dive into a mystery or a great novel like *All the Light We Cannot See*. Gary persists, and *Hauntings* turns out to be just the book we both need. The book helps us let go of ghosts of sorrow, despair, alienation, and distance. We feel close to each other as we read in the winter nights, lighting beeswax candles to form pools of warm light in our living room. We integrate ideas at the speed of thoughtful reading aloud. We pass the book back and forth as our voices tire, talking about the ideas. While I often select our books, especially fiction and psychology, this time, Gary has chosen just the right book for us. When I return from Sayulita, we pick up where we left off. As William Faulkner reminds me, "The past is not dead; it is not even past."[1] Hollis adds that what we resist will persist— as haunting.[2] I don't want my past to be dead, because then I would lose the memory and presence of love that rearranged and transformed my life. I dove deeply into the love and grief I felt. I would be sick or dead myself if I had resisted the wretched grief that I did feel. Grief and joy wheel around the year, an orbit in my psyche, as they appear in my memories and dreams.

On the night before another anniversary of Janice's death, I dream that I find a beautiful bell in the earth. It belongs to me. I don't have the right tool to make it ring, but I know the bell has potential for a beautiful sound. For now, I'm simply glad I've found it.

May, 2015

Gary and I attend a retirement party for our friend whose husband died of pancreatic cancer last year. She will move back to the town where most of her friends remain. Her husband occasionally stopped by our house on his way home. He and Gary shared a passion for woodworking. Bruce asked me questions that I found hard to answer, with no intervening chatter, such as "How do you know that what you are doing with your clients helps them?"

Bruce looked at me, waiting for an answer. Another was, "Do you see yourself as a healer?" He wanted to know.

Internally squirming, I said, "Sometimes, but I can't bring healing into anyone's life without their desire to change, and I am not in charge of the process."

Bruce served in Vietnam, later working as an educator and craftsman; he and Gary shared project design, physical work, fishing, and a love for cookies. I always had the sense that Bruce knew time could be foreshortened, even before he became ill. Gary officiated at Bruce's memorial service last summer, at a glorious Montana ranch on the upper Blackfoot River. The July day shone.

I am reluctant to go to this retirement party. Most of the people are from the English department, and I've been long gone from the University environment. Instead, I'd like to plant my pots of flowers on the deck—purple, rose, and yellow pansies, deep blue, deer-proof salvia out front, yellow dwarf dahlias and Egyptian papyrus, geraniums—this year in pinks, crimson, and lavender. Planting my deck pots ushers me back into growth and life each summer. I smile at my memory of Janice out back, in her denim shorts and navy embroidered top, bossing me to deadhead the plants, annoyed that I was neglecting them.

I would dutifully go out, mostly to be with her, and to clean up the plants. She seemed to feel responsible to teach me how to tend to them.

"Do I really have to do this?" I teased her. "Won't they just fall off?" She was precise. I am more of the "plant and see if they make it" kind of a summer gardener; she tended and nurtured the deck plants when she visited our home. Today, I come home from the nursery and place the flowers on top of the dirt in the pots, planning my planting strategies.

Resigned to the party, I arrive with Gary at a house in the University area, much like the house I lived in for many years when I first moved to Montana. My former husband and I bought a lovely bungalow on University Avenue for a now ridiculously small amount of money, adding a second floor later. Gary and I lived there for a few years before we moved. I dream about this house, maybe one hundred or more dreams in the years since we moved, the nostalgic house of my heart, although the place we live now suits Gary and me well. Walking into the house for the party, I feel right at home.

Right away I introduce myself to Debra, a woman I don't know, who, as it turns out, is a well-known Salish author, originally from the Flathead Indian Reservation north of us, who teaches in the MFA program. She and I talk about writing; I tell her about my stories about grief and resilience, she tells me of losses she endured in 2008. I tell her how writing helped me move through and analyze my grief. We talk about the Greek etymology of analysis, which refers to the loosening and unweaving of stories. She thinks in different symbol systems. She reveals that she often lies on her couch and feels some spirit sitting on her head, and she cannot move for a while. We talk about how grief brings fatigue. She says she might try hypnosis to help her. I pass on what I learned in my hospice group, that along with fatigue, grief brings dehydration. She thanks me for that tip. Debra tells me that she has written a book on the imaginary lost journals of Sacajawea, and I tell her one of my projects a few years ago included imaginary journals of my mother. We seem to have a lot in common, and I like her warm, unpretentious conversation.

After an appropriate amount of time, after weaving the connections that abound in a small university town, Gary and I prepare to go, gathering up our potluck dish of red beans and rice, and our belongings. I want to go home and plant flowers.

Just before we leave, Debra and I converge again for more talk. Gary joins me for this conversation. She tells us about a Salish ritual in which grieving people have their wrists and ankles bound with deer hide because they believe that the physical dissolution of the body of the departed pulls on the body of the grieving person; they must tie themselves to their physical body so they won't fly apart. All of a sudden, Debra physically moves toward me.

"I just sensed something," she says, as she moves toward me. "You are bound up, encased. I can see it." She is firm and clear. "May I do something?" Her eyes focus not on me but on something around me.

"Yes, of course," I reply. I trust this woman.

"Things are stuck to you," she says as she sweeps her hands downward around my body. "Our souls really are porous, and when we don't remember that, we block the energy, and it doesn't move through like the wind." Debra plucks at my clothing. She moves fast; I am willing.

"We see ghosts and step into that *absence*," she continues. "We can get stuck there in the absence. We see an outline of the absence, and think it's a *presence* and step into it. But then we have to step out. Our medicine people would say, 'Push it away, push, *push.*'"

Her hands make a sharp pushing motion away from my body. Fast, strong.

Debra offers no explanations; I don't need any. I resonate with the deep truth of what she is saying. I have indeed stepped into the absences these past years. The slight breeze of her hands around my body stays with me.

"You're a good couple. You moved right into her when you felt what was happening," Debra states. "You're a good couple."

"We've been together only twenty-one years," I explain. "We met by accident. Both of us were thinking, 'I'm done with marriage.'"

"You're a good couple," she reaffirms. I don't think she buys the accident theory.

As we leave, I take her hands and look at her; she looks at me.

I step out of the absence into the present.

At home, the lavender twilight lingers as I plant the flowers. Spring has finally arrived in our cold Montana world.

June, 2015

Gina asks me a question. She's the stylist who gently chided me in 2004 when I couldn't decide when to get on the plane to go see Janice.

"What have you planned for your birthday?" she inquires. I don't know how she keeps up with all her clients' birthdays.

"I thought maybe I'd just skip it this year." I recently said the same thing to my best friend.

"Are you kidding me?" She stops clipping and waves her scissors around as she continues. "You nearly died last year. You have to celebrate being alive," Gina declares. As usual, her sense of priorities sets me straight.

The year since my fall and emergency surgery seems full of jewel-like images of capital-L *Life*. During the long, gentle summer of 2014, after I resigned from tasks, stopped all work, and gave myself the summer to heal, I learned to rest. I wonder if this late-in-life learning came to me for the first time since our family camping trips in Colorado. Plus, as a child, camping in Colorado or playing with my friends in Dallas, I don't remember *needing* to rest, instead reveling in the bursting energy of a healthy girl. Some of my happiest moments occurred after lights out when I read library books by flashlight in the double sleeping bag I shared with Janice.

Days of deep rest have happened in my life. I still recall arriving at a *pension* in Italy, decades ago, after an arduous Eurail Pass vacation in Europe, stretching out gratefully on a bed overlooking the ocean in our ten-dollar-a-day room. My body deepened into the rhythm of the waves as I slept the whole afternoon. Midweek naps restored me at my favorite health resort in Mexico, when my overworked mind and body finally reached the deep peace that I included as a theme song in most of my women's retreats. On a sabbatical trip to California that Gary and I took a few years after we married, before any of the family deaths, I rested deeply. After some years in my clinical practice, I took seven months off, napping through most of Northern California, especially at a wonderful seaside inn in Mendocino. Gary pretty much entertained himself during the afternoons, something he is good at, as I slept. The summer after my fall brings a new way of resting into my life—resting at home.

I require rest—rest to heal from surgery, to lie down after more than a decade of grief and loss, to experiment with the present phase of retirement, and to ponder the inescapable truth that no one can give me a permission slip to rest and heal except myself. Throughout the healing summer, I nap when I need to—every day, sometimes twice a day—read when I feel enough energy to hold a thought, and relish my delicious surrender to sleep every night. Gary strokes, massages, and gently touches my breast-bone-to-navel scar; almost every night he rubs in emu oil to reduce the scarring. To my great benefit, Cyndy taught him Reiki, inspiring him to practice on me. He didn't know what I was also feeling until later—his stroking soothed the invisible scars from all the nights when I felt too alone to let go, too sad to sleep, and too agitated to settle down. Friends bring meals to me, reminding me of all the meals people provided when Janice was dying. Friends support me like sisters; they hold me up in a web of connection.

I don't kayak down the Blackfoot River when our book group takes its annual adventure in the outdoors. I show up, rested and relaxed, at their camp on the river, feeling grateful that I had not been swept down the rapids of the Blackfoot, as I had been on the Clark Fork River a few years ago. On the Clark Fork the river roared at a higher level than we had expected. Paddling with as much strength as I could muster, I missed the takeout point. Major rapids loomed just beyond.

"Paddle left as hard as you can," Gary and Robin yelled, as they waded in the river to try to catch my kayak.

"I'm trying," I yelled as I dug the paddle into the river with all my strength. Gary and Robin coaxed me within reach of their life-saving grab on the edge of my kayak. The river was too swift and strong for my skills. For this trip, my surgery would not allow me to even try to make it down the Blackfoot. I relish rest in the company of my book-group friends.

My psyche rests and digests as well. I dream that I return to an earlier house, where my mother scrubs the threshold and my father speaks from within. Janice is with me, young, terribly sick, and needing their care. In the dream, I know that I need their help to take care of her. I leave her at the house with my parents. Releasing my long sense of responsibility for my departed family, I hold fast to the love and release my guilt.

Close to my birthday, I dream that colleagues organize a panel of people to write a long book. Janice appears in the room, sparking in me a great idea. I request that the organizers put me on the panel with Janice. We will write the book together. In my dream, I know that Janice is dead, but this appeals to me as a brilliant solution to the problem of writing the book. This summer, I read *The Snow Child*, a modern retelling of a Russian folktale. In the book, a longed-for child disappears after living a mortal life for a while. She is deeply loved by her adoptive parents and her husband, but, as is true in so many folk tales, eventually she leaves to return to her true realm of "faery." Both these dreams assure me that Janice lives in my psyche, in an ongoing, creative way. Like Psyche in her myth, I have returned to the upper world of psychological spring and summer, with the winter gifts of an underworld journey indelibly embedded in my own inner life.

Ed reads the book as well. I save used books for Ed that I think he will like to read. He looks forward to opening his box of used books each Christmas. I wasn't sure about *The Snow Child*, but Ed loves it. We email each other about the story.

Ed writes to me:

> *What a fascinating read. What is it that makes a child "ours?" Where did Faina* [the child in the book] *go, and why? Why did she leave behind the blue mittens and scarf? Were the people in the story living their own fairy tale, or were they actors in someone else's story? What about our own lives?*

Ed is participating via email in an imaginary book group discussion with our group in Missoula.

He continues:

> *This story brought up a lot of my own grief, particularly for Janice and Dianne, who couldn't stay, for their own reasons.*

Replying to Ed, I write:

> *I felt grief reading the book, as you did. That sense of having, but then losing, a beloved other feels overwhelmingly sad. In*

the story, I sense mortals stepping into a larger story, one
that precedes them and goes on after them. My take, now
that you ask, is that Janice was enchanted by the divine child
archetype, and she was seen in that light by so many.

I feel fortunate that Ed and I now participate in these kinds
of discussions, the way Janice and I used to. He and I trade tales
of our Texas ancestors and plan a trip to Texas to chase down
more family history when he retires; we also talk about the big
questions in life.

Stace, the former graduate student who told me that Janice
was ill all those years ago in Miami, has returned to Fayetteville
for the next chapter of his life. He taught Janice's "Mythology and
Criticism" class when she became ill. I see him at conventions,
and we reminisce about Janice, sharing a special bond since he
transported our family members so many times. I look at the three
t-shirts I kept from Janice's stash, the "Big Hawk Seven" one, a
small, stretchy, blue denim shirt with sparkles on it, and the one
her Colorado class gave her after she taught her first qualitative
methodology class, proclaiming, "I know what I know." I ponder
sending one of these to Stace's mother for the quilt she is making
for him; these are pieces the mortal Janice left behind, like the girl
in *The Snow Child*. Maybe I will let one more object go.

During this summer of healing, on my mother's birthday,
when she would have been ninety-four, I feel gratitude for the
last years of her life when we were closely allied. Mom helped the
family function well, and I honored her for that work of love. I can
now remember and enjoy more personal memories, just between
the two of us. I think about the only trip my mother and I ever
took together, without others. We went to a family reunion in
Tahlequah, Oklahoma, close to where my great-great-grand-
mother was granted land after her Cherokee family was forced
to relocate on one of the Trail of Tears marches. Mom never felt
comfortable taking trips without Dad, no matter how many times
Janice and I asked her to accompany us to England, France, or
somewhere closer.

"What would Lamar do while I'm gone?" she would ponder each time, before kindly saying no to our invitations. But this invitation to the Tahlequah reunion was one she could justify. Taken during my thirties, this was the only time Mom and I were ever alone together overnight. She turned to me at the banquet, realizing that all her mother's siblings were in attendance with their children and spouses.

"We're the only ones representing Mother," she remarked, looking surprised. She was not used to mothers and children traveling without the father/husband, as many did at this reunion.

More memories return to keep me company as I think of Janice, Mom, and Dad. I wish I had more memories of Dianne, since she was so important to Ed. I dip into a well of almost forgotten memories, a gift of recall that now seems greatly expanded.

On my midsummer birthday, I blow out a candle at a favorite restaurant overlooking the Clark Fork River. I feel joyful. Pictures show me looking more peaceful and relaxed than I have felt for a long time.

That night, I write in my journal, "For my birthday wish, I claim happiness."

The other quality that matters in my life is compassion. I know that love conquers death because my love for those I lost is as fresh as always. I know this for sure, through my body, psyche, dreams, and memories. When one of my family members shows up in a dream, often they accompany me, without drama, as I go about the everyday activities of my life, reliable and friendly presences.

In the fall, Janice appears in a dream, in an unknown bedroom with me. I show her personal possessions that she might like—a pair of gold-and-turquoise earrings, a soft ivory silk scarf, and a brooch that she rejects as not right for her. I want her to choose something of mine for her own. We relate very warmly, as equals, the scene reminiscent of the happy times when Janice unpacked her things for her summer visit in Missoula. She accepts the gold-and-turquoise earrings, but I can tell she does this for me; the objects are not important to her.

Smiling fully, looking healthy and happy, Janice states, "I am full of wisdom."

This is not something Janice would have said in her life. In the dream, her assertion seems simply true, not a boast. I may be learning that objects that used to belong to Janice are not important now. Gaining wisdom *is* important.

June, 2015: Tincup

Gary and I spend a few days alone at Shalom. At the cemetery, we gaze again at the open circle of stones in the middle that reminds me of campfires. For the first time, I am not crying. We sit quietly on the log that serves as our rustic bench, dragged to our site when we finished setting all the marker stones, so we would have a place to rest, to look out at Napoleon Pass and observe which wildflowers might be blooming this season. I don't take pictures this time; we have enough grim pictures of Ed, Tom, and me kneeling by the central family marker. After a while, we head back across the wooden bridge, able to leave some of the weight of all the years in the ground. We have outlasted and out-loved the tumbling down of these lives.

July 15, 2015: Wisdom Sisters' Birthday

Sally and Blossom offer to give me a birthday party. At first, we plan it for the deck behind our house; Blossom, not knowing our street address, spontaneously decides to hold it at her bed and breakfast. I inform my friends that this year I would like no gifts, but something that might help me with my wisdom project, an idea Janice ignited when she declared that she was full of wisdom, in my dream. As soon as I arrive at the party, I am comfortable, at ease with a circle of eighteen women plus Gary. All of these women play a part in my life in Missoula, from back in the seventies to more recent friendships. We have shared book discussions, feminist theology, dreams in groups, classes, writing, and many birthdays, weddings, graduations, and celebrations. Some of these women offered a listening afternoon in 2004 for me to show pictures of Janice and tell them more about the person she was. They gave me an elegant, tall, slender, glass vase with a promise to keep the vase filled with flowers once a month for a year.

We gather in a circle, and everyone shares an object or a story they have brought. Gladys brings a little book of wise and funny sayings about aging. She used to work for a Washington, DC, lobbying concern for seniors; she's been collecting these sayings for a while. Cyndy brings a beautifully handmade pink-and-red card, in which she thanks me for helping get her started with finding her words in a writing class. Sally creates a soul card, an intuitive craft she and I learned at a workshop together, on which she creates a collage of meaningful symbols from my life, with a heart grown around with flowers in the middle of the card. Gary reads a list of pithy attributes Ed sent:

- *Not afraid of the dark*
- *Carries Janice with her every day,*
- *Worthy reflection of Dad's complexities and Mom's generosity of spirit.*
- *Keeper of family stories*
- *Wants to know why you thought that*
- *Sometimes sleeps outside to watch the stars fall*
- *Best big sister*

Gary reads a poem he has revised, which ends:

You are the ear of our hearing,
the one to remember a revealing phrase,
a line from a song,
the sound of the voice that says,
"This way, my love. Let's keep going."

We sing, "Love of my life I am crying, I am not dying, I am dancing."

As I look at my friends, soaking up the stories and their love, I have been granted my birthday wish. I have gained Wisdom: she is sitting in a circle with me. She gazes at me with compassion through the eyes of all my friends.

In addition to their stories, they give me a tangible present, a vase, shaped like a swan, a black swan, recalling the black-and-white swans of forgetting and memory that swam in the Castilian spring. The vase spills over with flowers from my friends' yards, and one handmade pink flower.

When I fill the vase, in the future, with water for another bunch of flowers, I will bask in the love in this wide sister-circle. Yes, forgetting will come. But not yet. The flowers remind me that for now, I am alive, and I am dancing the long buried song of my soul.

Acknowledgments

Many people accompanied me on this trail. My brother, Ed Hocker, not only was present at all the family deaths, he read parts of this book to help add his perspective. He is my friend as well as my brother in all these events. My husband Gary Hawk lived through these events and helped me heal through the losses with his love, writing, and reflections. As many writers' spouses do, he supported me from original inspiration, to writing and revising, and the publication process. Thank you, Gary. I give love and thanks to Dr. Anne DeVore, Jungian analyst extraordinaire, who has walked this life path ahead of me since 1976. She offered me analysis of dreams, guidance in active imagination, encouragement in writing the stories that became this book, wisdom, and loving acceptance. The fact that Anne also worked with my sister, Janice, knowing her deeply and well, provides a double blessing in my life.

Members of an early writing group gave me encouragement and helpful comments—thanks to Leslie Burgess, Nancy Hile, Chris Fiore, and Candace Crosby. A later group of writers, brilliantly led by novelist and writing coach Richard Fifield, read and commented on every word in this book, several times. Great thanks go to Sally Thompson, Cyndy Aten, Gladys Considine and Richard Fifield. Donna Mendelson graciously offered to help with final proofreading, contributing her expertise as an editor. Sally Thompson encouraged me throughout all phases of this project, offering sage counsel and editing final chapters one last time.

Janice's husband, Tom Frentz, read and commented on the writing connected to Janice. I appreciate his invitation to contribute to the *Southern Journal of Communication*. Some of the chapters appeared in earlier forms in *Qualitative Inquiry*. Thank you to editor Norm Denzin, who creates a place for personal narrative in the academic world.

Art Bochner and Carolyn Ellis read early drafts and helped me discern the writing path I would ultimately choose. I am grateful for their invitations to present at conferences, and for their encouragement to keep writing the stories. I am grateful to my students at the Montana Osher Lifelong Learning Institute at the University of Montana and the Red Willow Learning Center, who responded to short sections of this writing in my Life Writing classes.

I am grateful to Brooke Warner at She Writes Press; my superb copyeditor, Jennifer Caven; and Elisabeth Kavanaugh, who proofread the book. I am very grateful to Crystal Patriarche, my superb publicist.

Notes

Chapter Three

1. Rushing, Janice Hocker. *Erotic Mentoring: Women's Transformations in the University.* Walnut Creek, CA: Left Coast Press, Inc. 2006

Chapter Eleven

1. Faulkner, William. *Requiem for a Nun.* New York: Vintage Press. 1975.

2. Hollis, James. *Hauntings: Dispelling the Ghosts Who Run Our Lives.* Asheville, NC: Chiron Publications. 2013.

About the Author

Joyce Lynnette Hocker grew up in Texas, returning to her parents' home state after being born in Atlanta, Georgia, and living in Charlotte, North Carolina. She is a descendent of four generations of Texans on both sides. She obtained a PhD in communication from the University of Texas–Austin, and later received a PhD in clinical psychology from the University of Montana. Her academic career as a communication studies professor brought her to Missoula, Montana in 1976, where she began her private practice in 1985. Hocker is the author of *Interpersonal Conflict*, a best-selling text used in more than 250 colleges and universities, now in its 10th edition. Now in semi-retirement, Joyce teaches in the Lifelong Learning Institute at the University of Montana, and Red Willow Learning Center, a nonprofit in Missoula, which supports resilience in people who suffer difficult life experiences. She lives with her husband, Gary Hawk, and their tuxedo cat, Lonestar.

Selected Titles from She Writes Press

She Writes Press is an independent publishing company founded to serve women writers everywhere. Visit us at www.shewritespress.com.

Four Funerals and a Wedding: Resilience in a Time of Grief by Jill Smolowe. $16.95, 978-1-938314-72-8. When journalist Jill Smolowe lost four family members in less than two years, she turned to modern bereavement research for answers—and made some surprising discoveries.

Filling Her Shoes: Memoir of an Inherited Family by Betsy Graziani Fasbinder. $16.95, 978-1-63152-198-0. A "sweet-bitter" story of how, with tenderness as their guide, a family formed in the wake of loss and learned that joy and grief can be entwined cohabitants in our lives.

The Beauty of What Remains: Family Lost, Family Found by Susan Johnson Hadler. $16.95, 978-1-63152-007-5. Susan Johnson Hadler goes on a quest to find out who the missing people in her family were—and what happened to them—and succeeds in reuniting a family shattered for four generations.

Don't Call Me Mother: A Daughter's Journey from Abandonment to Forgiveness by Linda Joy Myers. $16.95, 978-1-938314-02 -5. Linda Joy Myers's story of how she transcended the prisons of her childhood by seeking—and offering—forgiveness for her family's sins.

Where Have I Been All My Life? A Journey Toward Love and Wholeness by Cheryl Rice. $16.95, 978-1-63152-917-7. Rice's universally relatable story of how her mother's sudden death launched her on a journey into the deepest parts of grief—and, ultimately, toward love and wholeness.

From Sun to Sun: A Hospice Nurse's Reflection on the Art of Dying by Nina Angela McKissock. $16.95, 978-1-63152-808-8. Weary from the fear people have of talking about the process of dying and death, a highly experienced registered nurse takes the reader into the world of twenty-one of her beloved patients as they prepare to leave this earth.